Drieu La Rochelle and the fiction of testimony

DRIEU LA ROCHELLE

and the fiction of testimony

by Frédéric J. Grover

University of California Press
Berkeley and Los Angeles   1958

University of California Press. Berkeley and Los Angeles, California
Cambridge University Press. London, England
© *1958 by The Regents of the University of California*
Library of Congress Catalog Card Number: 58–8656
Designed by Ward Ritchie

To My Wife

preface

       This study was written primarily with the aim of reassessing the literary importance of Drieu La Rochelle, leaving aside as much as possible moral and political judgments. However, Drieu's own conception of literature made it impossible for me to disassociate entirely the artist and the man. Since I started with Drieu the artist, the man that emerged is almost entirely the result of my interpretation of his fiction. This fiction is full of subtleties and contradiction that are in rather strong contrast to the usual picture that one gets of Drieu in which political considerations often weigh heavily.
    Perhaps the nuances of Drieu the artist led me to overemphasize qualifications to his totalitarian political position. Politically-minded critics may object to my portrait of a "reluctant" fascist citing the fact that Drieu was a collaborator who went to the lengths of rejoining Doriot's party during the occupation and whose attitude toward antisemitism was, to say the least, ambiguous.
    Judging Drieu as I do from his literary works, I would answer that Drieu was reluctant about every human commitment, including the political one. He was a reluctant husband (twice divorced), a reluctant lover (the Don Juan type), a reluctant man of letters (condemning literature and yet wanting a claim on posterity), and a reluctant soldier (condemning

preface

modern war and yet behaving well in action). Is it any wonder that he was also a reluctant fascist?

Far from having any personal reasons to sympathize with Drieu's political position, I was actually on the other side. Because I was on the other side, I felt free to be as dispassionate and understanding as possible.

I am greatly indebted to many people who have helped me in the preparation and the writing of this book. I want to thank Michel Mohrt whose contagious enthusiasm aroused and maintained my interest in Drieu La Rochelle. It would be difficult to exaggerate my debt to Warren Ramsey who read and criticized the manuscript at every stage. Most of his valuable suggestions have been incorporated in it. Marianne Bonwit took a warm and active interest and helped me considerably with her encouragement and suggestions. My colleagues at Swarthmore College, Harold March, Jeanne Whitaker, and more especially Edith Philips, gave much time and many valuable criticisms and suggestions. Jean Hytier whose seminar in aesthetics had awakened in me a lasting interest in the novel as a genre helped me throughout by his sympathetic interest. My wife, Gloria Waldron Grover, was my editor; the importance of her contribution can be measured by the fact that English is not my mother tongue. Acknowledgment is also due the editorial staff of the University of California Press for excellent advice and assistance. I am very grateful to the Research Committee of Swarthmore College who helped me with a generous grant and to my indefatigable secretaries, Muriel Bishop and Karlene Madison. So many people gave me helpful advice at some stage of development of this book that I must end with a collective acknowledgment of my gratitude.

F. J. G.

Swarthmore College
Swarthmore, Pa.
August, 1957

acknowledgments

Permission to excerpt freely from Drieu La Rochelle's works was granted by Gallimard which holds the copyright for most of his works. I should like to express my gratitude to Gallimard and to Drieu La Rochelle's heirs for their generosity.

Acknowledgment is also due the following publishers for permission to quote from copyrighted material for which full reference is given in footnotes and in the bibliography: Bernard Grasset, Paris; Editions du Seuil, Paris; *La Table Ronde*, Paris; Editions du Sagittaire, Paris; Alfred A. Knopf, Inc.; The New York *Times*, New York.

contents

one	WHAT IS LITERATURE?	1
two	THE NARROW, INERADICABLE SELF	31
three	WAR AND REVOLUTION	55
four	THE EMPTY SUITCASE	81
five	THE VOYAGE	113
six	THE THIRST FOR THE ABSOLUTE	134
seven	THE WORLD OF PRETENSE AND ILLUSIONS	162
eight	THE REAL WORLD	178
nine	THE MAN ON HORSEBACK	213
ten	THE TRAITOR	229
eleven	THE FICTION OF TESTIMONY	247
	BIBLIOGRAPHY	259
	INDEX	269

one

WHAT IS LITERATURE?

> "I am one of those in a generation
> who make the liaison, at their own risk,
> between politics and literature."
> —Genève ou Moscou, p. 208

Although Drieu La Rochelle is a minor figure in contemporary French letters, he is a remarkably interesting one. A study of his career helps to illuminate the literature of the three decades 1914–1944 and to understand the new element in what Gaëton Picon called the "new" French literature.[1] Drieu represents in himself various experiences critical to recent French literature—the ineradicable trauma of World War I, the romantic revolt of surrealism, the political commitment to extremist parties, and, finally, a desperate preoccupation with decadence in general and the fate of France in particular.

How then can one explain the fact that Drieu is usually ignored by critics or treated with a contempt that often con-

---
[1] Gaëtan Picon, *Panorama de la nouvelle littérature française*. (Complete bibliographical information for materials cited in footnotes appears in the Bibliography, below, pp. 259–268.

ceals ignorance or personal dislike? Why have none of his works been translated into English? Why is even his name almost unknown to the English-speaking world? To attempt to answer these questions may seem futile and presumptuous: futile because Drieu's relative obscurity is undeniable and literary "rehabilitations" are usually highly artificial; presumptuous, because the author has little justification for swimming against so strong a current. Nonetheless, it is worth while to introduce this controversial figure to the English-speaking public, because he has his place in French letters—a place which was acknowledged recently by François Mauriac. In an essay[2] which does Mauriac honor because Drieu in his lifetime had showered scathing criticism on him and on occasion had violently opposed his ideological views, Mauriac tries to look without prejudice at Drieu's "light and tragic shadow." "Drieu is here," he says, "it is not necessary for us to restore his place to him: he occupies it as you can see. It is certainly not, at first sight, a very large one ... Perhaps not a very large one but his own: that of a man, of a novelist, of a political writer whom one always talked of as a failure, who was wont to use this same word himself about every one of his books." And Mauriac goes on to remind us that some of those who are considered "failures" by their contemporaries are judged differently by posterity. Literature is crowded with those "immortal failures" whose frail shadows emerge above the dust and ashes of reputations which once seemed solidly established.

Without losing oneself in speculation about Drieu's growing importance to posterity, one can define this present place that Mauriac speaks of by considering his work as a whole. Is it necessary to add that this study was undertaken with the conviction that Drieu's place, when objectively assessed, would turn out to be greater than it looked at first sight?

The chief difficulty in considering Drieu's work as a whole is that it is constituted by two apparently heterogeneous main groupings: his fiction and his political writings (books, essays, and journalism). The two bodies of works are not judged

---

[2] "Drieu," *La Table Ronde*, No. 18 (June, 1949), 912–917. (All translations from the French are my own, except when otherwise indicated.)

usually by the same persons. The literary critics have had a tendency to overlook Drieu as an artist because he was too much involved in politics, and the "specialized" political writers generally dismiss his political writings as the hasty generalizations of an artist meddling in politics. Finally, the unpopular political position taken by Drieu has unfavorably influenced everyone in his judgment both of the man and of his work.

Since Drieu's conception of life commanded his idea of literature and since it was in the logic of his philosophy that he would become more and more committed in politics, it seems essential before examining his life and his work to analyze the interrelationship of life, literature, and politics in his thought. That is the purpose of this chapter.

As a young writer Drieu faced very early a problem which has troubled many writers of our own decade: what is literature? It is hardly a new problem. Every generation has to answer it implicitly or explicitly. New conditions demand new solutions, however, and the upheaval caused by two world wars as well as by the communist and fascist revolutions seem to justify the reëxamination of the validity and the purpose of literature. Drieu's origin, the circumstances of his life, his intellectual formation, the idiosyncrasies of his personality all forced him to examine the question from an angle peculiar to himself and the answer that he evolved was, of course, personal. But if, separating form from content, one considers his reactions in broad outline, a pattern emerges which appears to be that adopted by many intellectuals in our time.

Drieu considered the problem of literature from several points of view successively. He began by considering it from the point of view of the writer. What justifies his taking a pen and addressing his fellow men? How does he enter the vocation of literature? Is it a matter of belonging to a special caste: the caste of the writers with its subtle hierarchy similar to the nine ranks of the mandarins, the public officials of the Chinese Empire? Who decides that he belongs to this privileged order? Other writers? Is literature then a self-perpetuating order recruited by coöptation?

what is literature?

As a writer Drieu did not go through the usual torturous efforts to achieve prominence. With the publication of his first war poems at twenty-four, he found himself famous overnight. He was praised by the critics and hailed with real enthusiasm by both critics and writers, as a soldier-poet. *Interrogation,* published in 1917 by Gallimard, had broken the profound silence in which the front-line soldiers were immersed. Its author wore the halo of an authentic combatant whose bravery was underlined by official decorations and citations. He benefited from the general inflation of literature which immediately followed World War I and he was the object of the expectant attention devoted to the first literary efforts of the "sacrificed generation." He was one of the very few surviving writers of the generation which was twenty-one in 1914. Literary reviews, like *La Nouvelle Revue Française,* (then really new and young), *La Grande Revue, Les Ecrits Nouveaux,* were eager to publish his poems, stories, and articles. Capitalizing on this welcome, he published in 1920 what French authors call *fonds de tiroir* (bottom of the drawer) under a title which is in itself a characteristic mixture of witty irony, sincerity, and flippancy: *Fond de cantine* (bottom of the footlocker), a reference to the fact that some of the poems were still war inspired. He published then in quick succession *Etat-Civil* (1921) labeled as a "novel," a political essay, *Mesure de la France* (1922), and a collection of short stories which had first appeared separately, *Plainte contre inconnu* (1924).

Perhaps because of this easy entrance into letters, the young Drieu was self-conscious about his new role as a "writer" and he asked more than the usual number of questions regarding this role and the aim of literature itself. The gratuitousness of his fame caused certain doubts:

I wrote a book [*Interrogation*].... And here were the people of Paris, telling me that I was a writer, winking at me admiringly. Yet God knows what a sloppy job it was.
No. I was not a writer.[3]

[3] *Le Jeune Européen* (1927), pp. 50–51.

The nature of this first book of poems, born of action or meditation linked to the life of the trenches, gave Drieu a feeling of difference from other French writers. He had written because he had participated in a great collective experience. How many among the men of letters of his day could have said: "We have made history; it is something else than to read it."[4] " 'Make history,' leave a scar on the face of the earth!" The intellectuals of Drieu's generation will have other ambitions than to polish sentences which analyze the complications of the human heart. How valid, anyway, could a literature be that is based on the exploitation of a very limited experience of life? ". . . lyric poets with your narrow days, analysts satisfied with such a thin slice of heart, on your stale bread of aged children, you did not venture very far in the dangerous country of your ego: not farther than the dog at the end of his chain. Your lives were not exemplary. I do not forgive you that your lives can be separated from your writings."[5]

"The legend of a man of action" as the author of a recent study on Malraux entitled his biographical chapter[6] will haunt the imagination of many a writer from then on.

Back from World War I, Drieu did not want to continue in the footsteps of authors whose lives had been so uninteresting, who diluted so little "blood" in so much "ink." Is not their "literature" (exercised in a vacuum) almost synonymous with insincerity? he asked. What constitutes then the authenticity of literature: the fact that it is based on a lived experience rather than on imagination or on other books, according to Drieu.

Drieu spent the formative years of young manhood, from twenty to twenty-five, in the army and at war. This may explain his emphasis on the necessity of coupling dream with action. The over-intellectualized young bourgeois, after a year of unrealistic military preparation in a Paris barrack was

[4] *Interrogation* (1917), p. 78.
[5] *Le Jeune Européen*, p. 53.
[6] W. M. Frohock, *André Malraux and the Tragic Imagination* (Stanford, Stanford University Press, 1952).

thrown into the realm of death, violence, and the absurd. The young solider "whose legs had been painted in red," as he said of himself referring to the antiquated French uniform of 1914, had the revelation of a world very different from what his books, his professors, and his family had led him to expect. Few books stood the test of this harsh reality. Even Pascal's *Pensées* or Rimbaud's *Une Saison en Enfer*, or Nietzsche's *Zarathustra*, read differently in a second-line shelter under the constant threat of impending death than within the peaceful walls of one's study.

The shock of surprise first made Drieu blame his elders for not having prepared him for the new experience, then led him to the extreme consequence of condemning everything in his education, and especially the rationalistic philosophy underlying it. Until the end of his life Drieu was to reproach the philosophy of bourgeois France for entirely lacking "the sense of the tragic."

The bookish formation was of little avail, if not actually a handicap, in a true struggle for survival. The intellect was humiliated. Before the war, Drieu's suspicion about books and pure reason had already been aroused. There was a rumor in books to the effect that books were futile. One of his most admired authors, Nietzsche, had taught him contempt for thoughts that are the mere echo of other people's thoughts. The author of the *Will to Power* had praised above all the lived experience, had claimed that he wrote his books with his whole body and with his whole life and that he could not conceive of purely intellectual problems. The war experience confirmed in Drieu the antirationalism which was a powerful trend of thought in the decade 1903–1913 corresponding to Drieu's years as a student: "For us, young men educated by the proud message of Nietzsche and of Barrès, Paul Adam, Maurras, d'Annunzio, Kipling, agitators of the Western World, war offered a fresh temptation."[7]

Drieu, being a student of political science, had also read Vilfredo Pareto's *Socialist Systems* (1902–1903) and Georges

---
[7] *Interrogation*, p. 86.

Sorel's *Réflexions sur la violence* (1908). In philosophy, Bergson's influence pervaded the whole intellectual atmosphere. (His *L'Evolution créatrice* was published in 1907.)

The "despisers of the body," already denounced by Zarathustra[8] had been poor prophets. Contact with the elements—thirst, hunger, sickness, wounds—revealed the importance of the body, forgotten by the dwellers of the big cities who, cut off from elemental life, entertain the deceitful notion that humanity has eradicated its traditional scourges and put an end to the unending fight with nature. Drieu, in his war poems, sings the "Restoration of the Body." He even foresees a revolt against the exaggerated importance of the intellect. He prophesies that when peace returns, the disturbed times will not be over: "because life, tired of so much thought will perhaps seek rejuvenation in a bath of sweat and blood, in an age-long relaxation of Sport and War."[9]

Beneath the bombastic rhetoric of those first poems, one senses a pragmatic, antirationalistic, Nietzschean view of life: thought cannot build its foundations on other thoughts for it becomes then the shadow of a shadow; action and thought must support each other and, life being composed of contradictions, only the test of action at each step permits a progression of thought. A courageous soul requires a strong and well-balanced body at its disposal. If the intellectual lets his body degenerate he will also lack moral courage because it is impossible to separate body and mind. Drieu concludes that physical courage at the risk of death is necessary to preserve a sense of the tragic and of true commitment.

Such a philosophy is hard to reconcile with the concept of the writer as a contemplator, the high priest of pure thought, the "cleric" using the term with the special meaning it has retained since Julien Benda's *Trahison des clercs*. If the readers of the *Will to Power*, most of them part of a refined élite, had continued to read Nietzsche in the stifling atmosphere of bougeois society, in which he had evolved his philos-

---

[8] See *Thus Spake Zarathustra*, Part I, § 4, in *The Philosophy of Nietzsche* (New York, The Modern Library, 1927), pp. 32–34.
[9] *Interrogation*, p. 53.

ophy, in all likelihood the concept of the writer and therefore of literature would not have been modified by Nietzschean ideas. The war experience, at least in certain privileged moments, gave to some intellectuals like Drieu, the thrill of direct action, the reaction of instinctive leadership, and the feeling that they had achieved in action a previously unknown self-fulfillment. Thus Nietzsche, who had seen so little of action, whose life could be so easily condemned in terms of Nietzschean standards, became for Drieu, and many other intellectuals of his generation, a prophet. These young writers tended to make a mythical hero of the Basel philology professor, a recluse who was a madman for the last ten years of his life. Paradoxically, Nietzsche much more than the great men of history, became for them the ideal of the "great personality," and they tended to mold their lives (and their writings as expressions of their lives) on Zarathustra rather than on Nietzsche himself. Malraux, writing about T. E. Lawrence, has analyzed this process of mythification. Malraux observes that the idea of "great personality" corresponds to two human figures: "The first one is that of the man who has accomplished great things: it is less and less convincing. . . . History seems to us less and less a guarantee of greatness . . ." As for the other figure "it comes entirely from the domain to which Lawrence owed his formation and his dreams: literature. For his imagination, as for ours, Nietzsche was not a professor called Fritz by his mother, who, in addition, was writing great but misunderstood books; Dostoievsky was not a Russian man of letters, a sick person and a gambler; each of them was first of all the mythical character born of all the writings he had signed . . ."[10]

This more or less mythical figure of Nietzsche, coupled with the lessons he had derived from his war experience, made Drieu critical about the previous generation of writers (Barrès, France, Bourget) and the idea of literature that they represented. He was very much interested in the surrealist movement which was intent both on destroying the past and

---

[10] André Malraux, "Le Démon de l'absolu," unpublished text quoted by Picon, *op. cit.*, p. 299.

reviving completely the concept of literature. Here again the emphasis was on the irrational aspect of man and on the preeminence of living over writing. Drieu was then Louis Aragon's close friend; he knew intimately André Breton, Paul Eluard, and their friends. He collaborated in 1924 with Soupault, Eluard, Delteil, Breton, and Aragon in the pamphlet directed against Anatole France: *Un Cadavre*. He was a "witness" at the "trial" of Barrès organized by Dada and the surrealists in 1922. Even though he was never himself a surrealist, Drieu shared with these friends the conviction that it was necessary to liquidate the past, "kill the dead," and start afresh on a *tabula rasa*. He had a keen sense of the novelty of his century and he felt that none of the past solutions could apply to new conditions. In the eternal *querelle des Anciens et des Modernes* raging periodically in French letters, he was aggressively on the side of the moderns. To him, the surrealists and their revolt against the established order were in line with the revolutionary movements inspired by a dynamic philosophy of action which had Nietzsche as its source.

In an interesting essay in which he opposed Nietzsche to Marx, Drieu delineates a connection between activist philosophy and the arts which throws some light on what surrealism represented: "Is not the genius of Lenin, so tactical, so much at ease in his writings as a polemicist, impregnated with something resembling this philosophy of mobility and action propagated at the same time by both Vilfredo Pareto and Georges Sorel in philosophy, by Poincaré in science, a philosophy later to appear in the arts under the forms of futurism, cubism, surrealism—all doctrines founded on the negation of reason and being, on an idealistic phenomenalism commanding pragmatism in ethics?"[11]

When the surrealist movement became more definite in its political affinities and many surrealists became communists, Drieu felt that his friends were betraying their higher aims—the quest, for an Ideal, an Absolute, the sense of which was so lacking in Europe. He knew them too well to believe that they

---

[11] "Nietzsche contre Marx," in *Socialisme fasciste* (1934), p. 66.

could give up their freedom to obey party discipline. A trip to the "real" could only be disappointing to those pilgrims of the surreal. "La Véritable erreur des surréalistes," published in the *Nouvelle Revue Française,* in August, 1925, is a sad farewell to the dream and the companions of his youth, especially to Louis Aragon with whom Drieu broke at that time: "I was hoping that you were more than men of letters, that you were men for whom writing is action and all action the quest for salvation."

Drieu tried a little longer to maintain the freedom of thought of the intellectual and his right to judge politicians and parties. He saw in communism a purely Russian phenomenon, a cloak for Russian imperialism when practiced outside the U. S. S. R. A French Communist was for him a Russian agent—the contemporary equivalent of what some Jesuit fathers had been in the politics of other centuries.

Rather than the party man of the type of Aragon, Drieu admired André Malraux. The latter's communist orthodoxy was more questionable and his political commitments—whatever they were—seemed not to have affected the integrity of the man nor the authenticity of the artist. As early as 1930, Drieu described Malraux as the embodiment of *l'homme nouveau.* For Drieu Malraux embodied the ideal combination for the modern writer of action and contemplation; he felt that Malraux's work reflected the happy proportion of literary transposition and of faithfulness to a lived experience. In a long article, published in the *Nouvelle Revue Française* he praised the then little-known author of *Les Conquérants* and of the more recently published *La Voie royale.* He insisted prophetically on what was to constitute the major novelty of André Malraux:

"Malraux seeks and finds his equilibrium in the fact that he is a man and the fact that he is a writer. He has sought and found his place between this external activity called action and this inner activity called thought...." Drieu then pointed out the originality of Malraux's fate as an artist: "He has wandered through philosophical and historical speculation,

Asia, Revolution. He will always roam in those diverse provinces to renew his booty but he will not settle in any single one. Politican? Archaeologist? Businessman? It is too much or too little for a man. Writer? Again too much or too little."[12]

Here at last was a man and a writer whose example provided a solution to the problem which Drieu had analyzed in the first part of *Le Jeune Européen*, strikingly entitled "Blood and Ink." "Should one live for one's writing, or should one write merely as a part of living?" In 1927 he had refused "literature" because he refused to sacrifice in himself the man to the man of letters: "After all, I am not uniquely a writer, I am a man besieged by the problems of all mankind."[13] Beauty had to be in one's life before being in one's writing. Already the ideal "honnête homme" of French literature had refused to give up any of the human activities and had shown a certain amount of scorn for the professional writer. Malraux seemed to be the modern embodiment of the ideal of traditional French humanism. The list of men faithful to that tradition in French letters was long. Drieu, in *Le Jeune Européen*, had named a few: "Montaigne, La Rochefoucauld, Racine, Fénelon, Saint-Simon, Chateaubriand, Constant, Beyle, Barrès, even Rousseau, and even Gide. None of them refused to cut a figure in his century. Was it not an act of courage for each of them to try to live according to the standards of his century? They are more natural than Flaubert."[14]

What was the lesson of those humanists who tried to live as fully as possible in their century and at the same time to leave an imperishable name in letters, asked Drieu: "You shall write, they tell me, only after having lived and acted. Then you shall give an account of what you have done and felt." Drieu distinguished three possible objectives for such an account: "You shall write only to become aware of your springs of action and of your motivations, to prepare new

[12] "Malraux, l'homme nouveau," *Nouvelle Revue Française*, No. 207 (December, 1930), 881. (The *Nouvelle Revue Française* is hereafter cited as NRF.)
[13] *Le Jeune Européen*, p. 92.
[14] *Ibid.*, p. 84.

acts, to elucidate your will through your intelligence." Or, "if you do not write to facilitate your own life, it will be to facilitate the lives of other men." Or still, "you shall write, after having lived fully, to remember, to reassemble your past days, to leave a more efficient version than the rough draft of your life, to recapture yourself before disappearing."[15]

In his article on Malraux (and we must bear in mind that it is written in 1930 before Malraux's full development as a writer and as a man of action) Drieu places him in a slightly different tradition: that of the writers who have accepted only rather late the idea of devoting themselves entirely to the discipline of a single attitude, of a single métier, whose curiosity has remained awake and who have remained open to diverse solicitations: these include Diderot, Constant, Stendhal, Conrad. These writers may have spent the greatest part of their lives in their study, like other writers, but they maintained themselves in a state of alertness, of availability to the outside world; their reward is that their work—at least in that part of it which is "direct confession" or "confessional fiction" as Drieu describes it—has a virtue of directness and immediacy not to be found elsewhere, a virtue of "practical humanity which is irreplaceable."[16]

It is true that they have fulfilled entirely only one of their potentialities and that they have passed to posterity only as writers. From this, Drieu draws a general conclusion showing that he was reconciled, in 1930, to the limitations imposed on the writer but that he still considered the lived experience essential for himself. "If one takes literally a writer in his attempts at action [*ses ébauches d'action*] one will find reason to rail at him and to scorn him but one will misunderstand him. The writer's undertakings in the realm of action never

---

[15] *Ibid.*

[16] "Malraux, l'homme nouveau," *op. cit.*, p. 882. It is interesting to note that Malraux himself twenty-three years later, asked: "How many masterpieces of the novel are the works of authors for whom the novel was only an 'entr'acte'?" *Malraux par lui-même, images et textes présentés par Gaëtan Picon* (Paris, Editions du Seuil, 1953), p. 122.

blossom into admirable exploits . . . but they are nonetheless the guarantees of his humanity."[17]

If primacy is given to life over literature, still another consequence will ensue for the writer: the problem of form loses the importance it possessed for previous generations of writers. Long years of apprenticeship are required to study the models of the past, to master the technique of a genre, and in a time of bad grammar and inaccurate use of the vocabulary, to recapture the purity of the language. "I grant that one cannot understand and dominate life unless one has at one's disposal a solid language, a meditated syntax, conditions of firm thinking. But nonetheless one must first live."[18]

Problems of form and style have always provided lively issues among French writers. In recent years the tendency has been to reduce language to the role of an instrument and to distrust artistry or even too much concern for form as such. In the controversy which recently opposed Albert Camus to J. P. Sartre and his team of *Les Temps Modernes,* it was revealing that one of the indictments against the author of *L'Homme révolté* was that he wrote too well and was too much of an artist.[19] In other times no greater compliment could have been paid to a writer. Taste may change again and future generations will probably judge differently but in 1930 Drieu expressed what was to be the general feeling of his generation.

Life is short and one has many things to do. . . . This dead language, the French language, demands, in order to be recaptured in its past maturity, the patience of a philologist; to be a complete novelist similar to some in the nineteenth century in England, in France, and in Russia, one must wait and gather a long experience of life and art.

But there is something much more urgent than the art of composing a book or even than the art of composing a sentence, it is life. Because, after all, one does not live for the sake of writing and one writes only because one must write in order to live.[20]

---

[17] "Malraux, l'homme nouveau," *op. cit.,* p. 882.
[18] *Ibid.,* p. 880.
[19] See *Les Temps Modernes,* No. 82 (August, 1952), 317–383.
[20] "Malraux, l'homme nouveau," *op. cit.,* p. 880.

what is literature?

It is easy to detect in this article on Malraux the traces of quite personal preoccupations. As with most creative writers, Drieu's judgments throw more light on himself than on those he judges. More exactly, he isolates and emphasizes in those writers what they have in common with himself. The study he wrote on Diderot in 1939 is a further evidence of this tendency. To anyone who is familiar with Drieu's works and capable of making the necessary transpositions, it reads like a self-portrait.[21]

What Drieu sees mainly in Diderot is the man full of curiosity who refused to be enslaved by any given genre, who was too much attracted by the diversity of his interests to adopt the selfish attitude of the great creative artist, indifferent to anything that is not his own universe. He partly sacrificed higher artistic ambitions to insure a liaison between different disciplines. He lived from his pen and accepted well-paid writing assignments without sacrificing literary ambition which relied mainly on posthumous works. Drieu compares Diderot's leading role in the publication of the *Encyclopédie* to that of the editor of a great review and his contribution to Grimm's correspondence as superior journalism. While Voltaire and Rousseau exiled themselves, Diderot remained in Paris. Although the violence of his temperament and his desire to enjoy life in the forms of love, friendship, and conversation made him place life above literature, the great adventure of this adventurer was purely intellectual.

How can one explain Drieu's predilection for a younger contemporary like Malraux and his sympathy for a great model of the past like Diderot? Malraux offered an original solution of the contemporary intellectual's dilemma (as the Nietzschean Drieu saw it): he had engaged his life and his art (literature) in action. Diderot offered the example of an intellectual who had sacrificed a great part of his time, talent, and energies to the worldly problems of his day and had managed to pass to posterity through the most lasting part of

---

[21] Drieu La Rochelle, "Diderot," in *Tableau de la littérature française—17ᵉ-18ᵉ siècle*, pp. 331–339.

his production: dialogues, tales, and novels, which benefited from all the experience acquired by the author in more ephemeral activities.

Very early Drieu discovered that he was interested in nearly all the aspects of his time. His formal studies had centered on political science and he thought that politics (in its broadest, Aristotelian meaning) was, temporarily at least, more worthy of his attention than pure literature. He was particularly aware of the metamorphosis that France, Europe, and the world were undergoing and he first thought that intellectual advisers, endowed with the prophetic insight of artists, were needed side by side with politicians and men of action. He decided later that treating political subjects in essays and articles was not an efficient way of influencing the course of events. He tried to found his own review, but the problems of finding journalistic collaborators, of reaching the public, involved too many practical problems for a man who was apparently not gifted as an administrator. In 1927, Drieu's political position was rather an isolated and mainly a negative one. He knew better what he was against than what he was for. His review, *Les Derniers jours,* appeared for only seven issues. He tried to interest himself in existing parties but they were all disappointing and only confirmed his basic distrust of parliamentarian liberalism as it was practiced in France. European and world problems interested him more than purely internal French politics; he felt that most parties in France were, at least from the point of view of foreign policy, shortsighted and demagogic. On the contrary, he thought that the French should be awakened from their complacency. He had made in *Mesure de la France* (1922) a realistic, almost alarming appraisal of a France dangerously misled by her victory of 1918 (won only with the help of a world-wide coalition) and actually weakened by the loss of a million and a half men; a France in a critical demographic situation dangerously isolated in a world in which the emergence of the United States and the Soviet Republics with their territories as wide as continents and with their populations in the nine-figure bracket had dwarfed the little nation of forty million Frenchmen encamped in a Balkanized Europe. Five years later the situation was even more alarming and Drieu openly preached European unification. In *Genève ou Moscou* (1927) he asked his countrymen and other Europeans to forget their obsolete nationalism in order to become European patriots. The unification of Europe was a necessity; spiritually, the individual nations were exhausted; the very stiffening of the nationalist attitude in various European countries was one more symptom of their approaching agony; economically, the pooling and exploitation of resources on a continental scale was so obviously the only intelligent solution that it made the old system of twenty-odd individual nations fenced in with trade barriers, custom officials, and waging a devastating economic warfare tragically foolish; finally, it was imperative to avoid the suicide that an internecine European war under the conditions created by modern warfare would involve. If the Western democracies, England and France, did not create a unified Europe through the League of Nations at Geneva, Moscow would do it, said Drieu. The victory of communism would result only from the lethargy of the West.

In a third essay, *L'Europe contre les patries* (1931) he addressed the Germans to show them how obsolete it was for them to hope to extend their frontiers by wars of conquest or by assimilation. Breaking the artificial and antiquated barrier of national frontiers in order to merge into a Europe peacefully unified provided the only means for an already exhausted Europe to survive. Distinguishing between an old Europe of the West where the nations as such had reached their full development and a young Europe composed of the eastern, mostly Slavic states created or resurrected by the Versailles treaties and still in the process of asserting themselves, Drieu listed some of the problems presented by those young nationalisms and offered specific suggestions to integrate them into a complex Europe. Finally, he announced that in the event of a European war he would not answer the mobilization call: as a man, he considered that modern warfare was a betrayal of the species; as a European, he gambled his life on the bet that Europe could survive and he saw its only chance of survival in a peaceful unification.

By 1931, the position of Drieu in French letters was original: parallel to the publication of these three political essays, and the venture of *Les Derniers Jours,* he had continued his purely literary production. In that decade ending in 1931 he published five novels, a collection of short stories, and even a play.[22] Two other books which could not be classified in any traditional genre puzzled the critics: *La Suite dans les idées* (1927) and *Le Jeune Européen* (1927).

The political essays were of a theoretical nature but revealed a few central preoccupations which reappeared in the novels. In *Etat-Civil,* for instance, Drieu utilizes his own case history as a "testimony" which can be of value for a whole generation. As the title (vital statistics) implies he centers his self-study on the consequences that socio-historical conditions had for his private life. It is an effort, sincere but not always successful, to break away from the romantic self-complacent analysis of an irreplaceable ego. The author tries to ascertain how much of himself has been shaped by the fact that he was born a Roman Catholic in such and such a family, in the bourgeois class, in France, at the end of the nineteenth century. He attributes a purely empirical, experimental value—not an exemplary one—to this exploration of his ego. It is another way of "measuring" France by giving the more subtle measurements of the Frenchman the author knows best: himself.

Blèche and *Une Femme à sa fenêtre* offer two concrete images of contrasted reactions to the challenge of communism: conservative reaction and participation. *L'Homme couvert de femmes, Le Feu follet, Plainte contre inconnu* expose the decadence of the modern world and especially the decadence of sex through two parallel means: pitiless introspection and satire of the ambient society.

---

[22] Novels: *Etat-Civil* (1921); *L'Homme couvert de femmes* (1925); *Blèche* (1928); *Une Femme à sa fenêtre* (1930); *Le Feu follet* (1931). Short stories: *Plainte contre inconnu* (1924). Play: *L'Eau fraîche* (1931).

what is literature?

It is characteristic of Drieu that all these works, both in their political and literary aspects, should be marked by a tone of urgency and concern for the great problems of the day. Earlier than the writers slightly older who had already published books before World War I, he was passionately interested in the political problems which were later to be so hotly discussed by intellectuals, especially at the time of the Spanish Civil War. As early as 1920, he observed that the intellectual could no longer ignore the world around him: "As late as yesterday some could still afford not to be concerned by worldly matters."[23] In 1927 he justified his writing a second book on political matters even more clearly in defining the role he assigned to himself in his generation: "I have written this book impelled by a pressing necessity: although a man of letters, I have to muddle through this world like everybody else; I have to find its direction in order to orient my own conduct. Others, more entirely artists, find this direction in their work; it seems that my mission is less discreet, more crude. I am one of those who, in a generation, make the liaison, at their own risk, between politics and literature."[24]

The risks Drieu spoke of were those that would threaten his full development as an artist. The danger was not so great for him as it would be for writers, less genuinely interested in politics, who would meddle with politics only because it became fashionable to do so or because of the pressure of events. Since for Drieu a writer should remain primarily a man, if politics holds a greater and greater place in his private life, why should he not talk about politics in his writing and since he is also an artist why should he not make of his political passion a subject for art? Problems which had been for Drieu a lifelong concern were becoming the concern of more and more readers. In a world in which individual destinies were being affected more and more directly by such great collective phenomena as economic depression and revolutions, where

---

[23] "Le Retour du soldat," dated May, 1920, in *Mesure de la France* (1922), p. 4.
[24] *Genève ou Moscou* (1928), p. 208.

threats of civil and foreign war were becoming more precise, where conflicting conceptions of man were embodied by powerful empires and supported by huge armies thoroughly indoctrinated, the interest of the reading public could be expected to shift from the psychological, moral, intimate dramas of the individual to the social, economic, political problems of mankind. These problems led naturally to the reexamination of the human condition as a whole and to the basic metaphysical questions: What was man's fate? What was man's hope? The writer could not remain neutral like other men; he had to take a position and even his abstention became a choice.

To be authentic, however, the political ideas of a man and therefore of a writer had to correspond to a lived experience. He could participate directly, physically, in action in the form of war or revolution. But if he remained in France he was sure to become more and more involved in purely political action, and to be efficacious this action would necessarily be shaped by an organized party.

For a long time Drieu was proud of the fact that he had not joined a party. In the first place, all existing French parties had disappointed him. In the second place, he thought that an intellectual, an artist, could not feel comfortable in a party. In an essay of 1934, at a time when well-known writers were beginning to enter parties with great fanfare, he thought that he was entitled to warn them against the dangers of this new mania of adhesion since he had engaged in politics more than any of them and he could talk with the authority of experience. After recalling what his successive political positions had been, Drieu, with a lucidity which was to prove prophetic, analyzes the contradictory situation of an intellectual in politics: the intellectual's attitude is essentially ambiguous and not very different from that of the mass of the people which supports a regime for a while but reserves its independence and eventually gets rid of it. Politics does not exhaust the human experience. The work of an artist, since it is immersed in the depths of nature, is not affected by politics. Even if he shouts loyally at political meetings, when he returns home how far has this affected his work? Drieu realizes that engagement in politics endangers one's work as an artist; yet he says that neutrality is impossible. A political tendency emerges from the writings of any artist. Still the artist's roots are deep and too much grounded in total life to satisfy the hard and fast classifications of a party. Writing in 1934, Drieu claims that he would rather keep his intellectual independence than be "trapped" in a party: "I prefer to be disdained by the partisan writers as a vain amateur or even despised as a coward. . . . Deep down, I have always had the sense of the differences, the hierarchy of responsibilities."[25]

If the intellectual enters the arena of action, he is the victim of a temporary impulse, according to Drieu. He is welcomed by men of action in the party with a warmth which is either naïve or deceitful. He tries to use the same words they do, but he makes a new language with them. He leaves the party as suddenly as he had entered it. If instead he solidifies his adherence, he is faced by a dilemma: either he becomes mediocre as an artist and writes nonsense for propaganda or he cheats with his official faith and translates it into his work. If the writer is an older man (Anatole France, André Gide), the danger is not so great: his past work constitutes a safe refuge; whatever position the writer may take, the multiplicity of aspects of his work will be a protest against the excesses of the partisan.

In the latter case, however, the adhesion of the artist to a party has little meaning even though it may be exploited by the propaganda of the party. In 1936, when Gide, disappointed by his voyage to Soviet Russia, published his *Retour de l'U.R.S.S.*, Drieu chose this recent example to illustrate the undue importance attached by Frenchmen to the political judgment of their writers. He could not see why a novelist or a playwright's adhesion to such or such a political party should have so much meaning: "In his work, he is uniquely concerned with the *intimate* life of men and women, with their individual

---

[25] "Itinéraire," in *Socialisme fasciste*, p. 241.

and sentimental destiny and not their social, collective destiny. All his sensibility is in that direction, as well as all his thinking and all his study." Drieu then listed some of the requirements he considered necessary to express a valid judgment on political questions: "One must have worked and meditated a long time in the fields of history, economics, sociology, one must have traveled for the sake of inquiring into definite problems, one must have compared not only countries but classes with each other." Far from meeting these requirements, most French writers, according to Drieu, "are interested in individuals and in individuals belonging to the generally narrow social milieu in which they are placed."[26]

To be taken seriously in politics, a writer must specialize. To remain an artist and transpose his political experience into art, his political position must correspond to passionate preferences—and therefore have deep roots in his personality. This is why it is impossible to understand Drieu's idea of literature without understanding his idea of politics. For an adept of an irrationalistic philosophy, ideas cannot form a neat, well-classified series of defined, dead concepts. Anything that can be well-defined belongs to the past and is already dead. According to such a philosophy, the artist rather must have an intuition of "tendencies," the revelation of great movements under the chaos of appearances. In any artist who considers himself a prophet, as Drieu did, there exists a mystic who believes in deep, hidden significances. In a universe thus conceived, the artist is the elect, the priest, who is able to decipher these hidden meanings which escaped the great majority of mankind. This was the belief which already underlay the aesthetics of romantic and symbolist art. Drieu transposes this belief to what is the great experience of his time: politics, war, revolution, the movement of the masses. He thinks he is one of the privileged persons who feel in a mass experience the pulse of a period, the great trends which dominate humanity. He had this intuition for the first time during World War I. His system of aesthetics rests mainly on this initial intuition:

---
[26] *Avec Doriot* (1937), pp. 85–86.

The artist masters ideas only if he finds them in the destiny of characters born from his observation and his imagination, or in his own fate if he is a lyricist. He catches ideas in the most lively moment of their earthly incarnation . . ."[27]

There is a strange parallelism between the spirit of fascism and Drieu's war poems. He was to recognize it himself seventeen years later: "In my first civilian suit, holding the passionate ideas of *Interrogation* (1917), the collection of my war poems, I was entirely fascist without being aware of it."[28]

This may explain his latent hostility to French parliamentarianism and his refusal to join any of the traditional parties. He was in favor of radical change but he could not join the Communist party because he did not believe in Marxist philosophy; he thought that the proletariat was a myth—at least as far as Western Europe was concerned—and he saw in communism a purely Russian phenomenon not applicable to the West. The rise of fascism in Europe in the early 'thirties gave him the idea that the socialist revolution could be accomplished outside a Marxist orthodoxy. It was not in contradiction with his nationalism and his European patriotism. The philosophy of force and violence underlying the fascist movements was in his eyes necessary to counter efficiently Russian communism which had first practiced it and had provided the school for all the "new Machiavellians."

We can see that Drieu despaired too quickly of democracy and that his considerations were too narrowly centered on France and Europe (continental Europe at that); but nonetheless one must try to understand why this intellectual who seemed to have seen so clearly the incompatibility of his freedom of thought and party discipline called himself a fascist in 1934[29] and joined the newly founded fascistic party of Doriot in 1936.

Drieu believed that a complete renewal of political values was taking place in Europe under the labels of communism

---

[27] *Genève ou Moscou*, p. 12.
[28] *Socialisme fasciste*, p. 220.
[29] "La République des indécis," article dated June 10, 1934, in *Chronique politique* (1943), pp. 23–26.

in Russia and fascism in certain other countries. This renewal of political values, as radical as the *Umwertung aller Werte* of which Nietzsche had been the prophet, could be traced back to Lenin's portentous decision in 1903 when he created the Bolshevik party. Then and there the extreme left had broken with the liberal, democratic, parliamentary system. Lenin, in breaking from the Russian social-democratic party, created the first totalitarian party. All the conventions of a liberal system of ethics were abandoned; it was understood by him and by his followers that they would seize power and maintain themselves in power by any means whatsoever. Force and ruse were openly set as the only rules. Elections and parliamentary means would be used only incidentally along with riots and coups. Lenin was more familiar with Clausewitz than with manuals of constitutional law. After he came to power he confirmed the method which had brought him there. His successor, Stalin, had practiced the same methods with even more cynicism. This revolution had opened a new era of authority which put the regimes of Western Europe, still clinging to liberal methods, on the defensive and the weakness of their reactions made them appear hopelessly obsolete. Although in 1914 or even in 1917 liberalism was either firmly established or accepted as a desirable aim, the system seemed to have broken down in the 1930's. The old liberalism of the West was still practiced in England and France and in smaller democracies: Switzerland, Belgium, Holland, Scandinavia. But it was under attack nearly everywhere.

In eastern, central, and southern Europe, "strong men"—all of them, except Horthy in Hungary, socialist renegades—had practiced the terrible pragmatism inaugurated in Russia and had amalgamated what doctrinarians considered irreconcilable: socialism and nationalism, social democracy and political autocracy. These strong men included Mussolini in Italy, Pilsudski in Poland, Kemal Ataturk in Turkey, Hitler in Germany, the semidictators of the Baltic and Balkan states, Primo de Rivera in Spain. Portugal, practically under a British protectorate, could afford a neat intellectual rationalization of the same system of government.

In Asia one could perceive signs of the same totalitarian trend; South America had never known any other principles. Even in the United States, the stronghold of liberalism and of democracy, the depression was forcing Roosevelt to break with economic liberalism.[30]

Thus Drieu brought to the interpretation of politics and history the same Nietzschean sense of the tragic that he expressed in literature.[31] He was entirely aware that it was only one aspect of his time. As early as 1928, he had warned his readers against the dangerous incursions of artists into the domain of great social hypotheses: "There is too much individual sensibility in a poet, even in a novelist, not to fear that he will take shortcuts to reach supposedly objective conclusions.... What constitutes the value of the artists' incursions in this domain [of the great social hypotheses] is the intuition by which the sympathy of their temperament illuminates one aspect of their time."[32]

Drieu wrote those lines in 1928. It was in the logic of his philosophy that he would become more and more deeply committed to politics. Drieu used the word "engagement" long before it became the fashionable motto of certain writers and before its prostitution made it sound rather cheap and meaningless. Not only his writings but his own life testify that he had a tragic conception of engagement. He offers the original example of a *littérateur engagé*. He is different from a Malraux spectacularly engaged in wars and revolutions (but Drieu was a little older; for him youth had coincided with World War I where he had proved that he did not lack physical courage.) He is different from Louis Aragon, his best friend of the early 'twenties, his "enemy brother," who had chosen the way of

---

[30] These views of Drieu, scattered in many articles, are summed up in a longer article "L'Actualité du 20ᵉ siècle," in *Chronique politique*, pp. 197–203, which I have paraphrased above. See also "Nietzsche contre Marx," in *Socialisme fasciste*, pp. 63–75.

[31] "Le Sens du tragique" is the title of one of the articles collected in *Chronique politique*, pp. 324–329.

[32] *Genève ou Moscou*, p. 15.

communism and who, after sacrificing his great talents to the chores of journalism in the service of the communist press, undertook a series of lengthy novels devoted to a Marxist criticism of capitalist society, and who has now become a strictly orthodox, official, consecrated figure of the French Communist party. Sartre and Camus do not belong to the same generation (they were respectively twelve and four when Drieu published his first book) but they may have learned a few lessons from the example of Drieu's political involvements—and it will be interesting to see what solution they will eventually find for the dilemma of the intellectual engaged in politics. Drieu was most of all different from the slightly older group of writers who had published books before World War I and became more or less involved in politics shortly before, during, and after World War II. Their most distinguished exponent is probably François Mauriac, now a regular contributor of editorials in different papers and magazines, an influential "conscience adviser" of an important fraction of the French public. In an article on Mauriac, published in 1941, Drieu expressed his impatience with the refined game between literature and politics indulged in by "literary politicians" and "political men of letters" in Paris in the years before World War II.

It was a sweet commerce (in which I have shared, as well as anyone). And the atrocious drama which was more and more pressingly extending to the four corners of Europe was causing only a few harmless ripples in this academic debate...[83]

One senses Drieu's fear of becoming himself a literary mandarin and of being caught in the trap of a polite but meaningless battle of "penholders." This fear may explain Drieu's defiance in deliberately choosing for himself after the revolutionary days of February, 1934, the label "fascist," because it was the most disreputable one in the eyes of his confrères. It partly explains also why he joined Doriot's party in 1936. He was the only intellectual of any caliber in Doriot's party

---

[83] "Mauriac," in *Le Français d'Europe* (1944), pp. 64–65.

and his fellow-intellectuals—communists or liberals—were all on the other side of the political fence. His disillusion must have been great; in the first place, his role seems to have been purely intellectual, in the form of a two-year journalistic campaign in the *Emancipation Nationale* until he resigned in October, 1938;[34] in the second place, the Parti Populaire Français turned out to be not much different from the innumerable other French parties: "After a few months, it was obvious that France would not be fascist. There were a few dozen fascists, ex-communists for the most part. We were lost among old-fashioned royalists, vague Catholics, vague nationalists without mentioning pacifists and other jokers. France was lost. We fought until Munich, under sordid conditions, disgusted with friends and foes, in the inversion of all feelings."[35]

The same fear of "moderateness," the same defiant attitude opposed to the cautiousness of many literary men, partly explains why Drieu after the French collapse of 1940, silencing "the dwarf who sometimes inhabited his tall carcass" contributed his first article to the collaborationist press in September, 1940,[36] and accepted the direction of the *Nouvelle Revue Française* to be published in occupied Paris until June, 1943.[37] As Daniel Halévy has pointed out: "There were very few avowed collaborators; there was perhaps only one and he was this man most sensitive to nuances [cet être infiniment nuancé]: Drieu."[38] Here again, disillusion was to come quickly. Mauriac's testimony on the subject is particularly interesting: "Drieu's eyes opened very quickly ... I am sure that by 1943, he had understood. German censorship, whether from indifference, neglect or stupidity, let pass in Drieu's articles in the *Révolution Nationale*, judgments reflecting hopeless lucidity.

---

[34] The very title of his last weekly article, dated October 28, 1938, sounds both defiant and ominous: "Mourir en democrates ou survivre en fascistes."

[35] "Entre l'hiver et le printemps," first published in *NRF* in April, 1942, collected in *Le Français d'Europe*.

[36] "Un Homme marche dans Paris," *La Gerbe*, September 15, 1940.

[37] After leaving the *Nouvelle Revue Française*, Drieu contributed political articles regularly to *La Révolution Nationale* until his first attempt at suicide in August, 1944.

[38] Preface to Pierre Andreu's *Drieu, témoin et visionnaire*, p. 12.

At one of the last clandestine meetings of the [underground] National Committee of writers, a typographer brought us from the printing house the proofs of an article by Drieu rejected by the censorship. It was nothing but a barely contained cry of anger and disgust."[89]

Several interpretations have been offered to explain Drieu's suicide in 1945. Along with other factors, a desire to authenticate a political position taken by himself as a man of letters must have had its place. It was a deliberate gesture to assume responsibility for his acts. Drieu could have avoided the legal consequences of his collaborationism as many did or he could even have reversed his position in time to save himself. In the winter of 1943–1944, Drieu went to Switzerland where he could have remained in safety. He said himself in a posthumous text:

> I could easily have withdrawn myself in time, ceased writing, manifesting, all the more easily that my perspicaciousness had early exercised itself against the deficiencies and the errors of Hitlerism and that it would have been legitimate to disengage myself from the so poorly defended European cause ... I had an opportunity to leave France; I went but I came back. It was in Geneva, well received by the Swiss, well sheltered, well provided with enough money to remain two or three years that, in the autumn of 1943, I decided to go back and, thereby, to kill myself [*me donner la mort*] when I would see fit."[40]

Drieu's gesture corresponded exactly to his ideas of the writer's responsibility. In a chronicle, published in the *Nouvelle Revue Française* in December, 1942, he reasons in the following manner. A writer is *never* a true political leader: the complete man in him is necessarily diminished since he devotes himself to representing man rather than living what he represents. But to maintain a connection with the complete man, a man of letters does not have to be a leader: he

---

[89] "Drieu," *La Table Ronde*, No. 18 (June, 1949), 915–916.

[40] "Récit secret," first published by Drieu's brother, Jean Drieu La Rochelle, in a limited edition in 1952, appeared in the *Nouvelle Nouvelle Revue Française*, No. 9 (September, 1953), 391–419. The passage quoted is on p. 406. (The *Nouvelle Nouvelle Revue Française* is hereafter cited as *NNRF*.)

can take his responsibilities at a more modest, more efficacious level: as a soldier—a soldier assigned to a special function but not immune from risk and death. He can join a party like any man—although even in a low position the daily routine is likely to be more boring for him than for the ordinary man. Since, in the last analysis, he cannot be engaged fully in political action he must not wish then for the death of writers in the opposite camp "even if their activities seem to constitute a mortal danger to the cause he upholds; but *he* must accept death as the sanction for his own words."[41]

This uncompromising notion of engagement was not new; it can be traced back to his 1921 novel, *Etat-Civil*.[42] In the evolution of this idea, war experience again seems to have played a decisive role. Drieu wrote in one of his autobiographical short stories about World War I:

> I was twenty-four; in a few days I was going to enter life through the gate of the armistice. I foresaw dimly what I have felt since: that the same deliberate abandonment to death would be the basis of all my actions.... In any love, any work, one must go to the limit, toward the sanction of death."[43]

Perhaps Drieu felt all the more the need to engage irretrievably his action because he knew how uncertain he was at bottom. This perpetual advocate of trenchant positions was always prone to understand, even to espouse, the position of the adversary. This artist who had to sacrifice to the necessities of political journalism fine distinctions of thought had the most developed sense of the nuances. This writer who despised intelligence was preëminently intelligent. This man who envied and admired men of action was a man of letters through and through. This Parisian who denounced the decadence of the megalopolitans of his day exposed pitilessly the progress of that decadence in himself. This Frenchman, who tried so hard to be a citizen of Europe and of the world, who

---

[41] "La Fin des haricots" first published in *NRF* in December, 1942, collected in *Le Français d'Europe*, p. 203.
[42] See *Etat-Civil*, pp. 21–22.
[43] *Comédie de Charleroi* (1934), p. 248.

so pitilessly criticized his own country, loved France with an almost carnal love. Malraux understood this ardent nationalism of Drieu's: "It is for France that Drieu fought—to his death—"[44] he said. This Nietzschean has left in *Gilles* the portrait of a twentieth-century Adolphe.[45] This author, haunted by the mirage of a life lived on the limits of total risk has left a work which instead offers the negative aspect of Malraux's novels of heroic transposition. This man who would have liked so much to be a participant in the events of his time was more than anything else an observer, a witness.

The value of his testimony is guaranteed by his almost compulsive sincerity. Drieu was in many ways the victim of this sincerity. As Gaëtan Picon points out: "He was never able to deceive himself either by making a value of his availability, or in reducing himself to one part of himself, chosen once for all, and tenaciously developed. An uncertainty which knows itself and hates itself: such was Drieu."[46]

He also encouraged the patronizing tone that most critics use toward him by what he termed himself his "masochism," his "passion to plead guilty," a display of his intimate weaknesses.

All these contradictory aspects of an unusually complex personality, necessarily repressed in the political writings, constitute the richness of Drieu's literary work, particularly his fiction. The human experience gained in the world of politics enriched the novelist. Without his participation in the domain of politics, it is doubtful that he would have been able to write such novels as *Gilles* (1939), *L'Homme à cheval* (1943), and *Les Chiens de paille* (1944) in which we find the artistic transposition of politics by an artist more and more sure of himself and of his craft. The temporary sacrifice of the *clerc* was certainly not in vain. The lamentable failure of Drieu's political career should not influence us when we read these

---

[44] Picon, *Malraux par lui-même*, p. 90.

[45] Jacques Bompard in his introduction to *Adolphe* had already pointed out in 1929 the similarities between Benjamin Constant's hero and those of Drieu's. See Benjamin Constant, *Adolphe* (Paris, Les Textes français, éditions Fernand Roches, 1929), introduction, p. lxiv.

[46] Picon, *Panorama*, p. 88.

novels. He possessed the saving virtues which permitted him to remain an artist in a time when it is difficult to do so—at least according to the traditional notion. Drieu spoke justly when he wrote, on the eve of his death in the preface to *Les Chiens de paille:* "I have remained an artist and I have even become a better one by asserting myself elsewhere in my passionate preferences.... An artist is in turn detached and committed, rich and poor; he makes his richness of tomorrow with his poverty of yesterday and reappears more secret in a novel after a campaign in the press."

two

THE NARROW, INERADICABLE SELF

Pierre Eugène Drieu La Rochelle was born in Paris, in the tenth *arrondissement*, on January 3, 1893. He was a second-generation Parisian, still aware of family roots in the provinces. His father was from Coutances in Normandy, and his mother was from a family, with ancestry from Normandy, Brittany, and Valois, that had settled in Neuilly, the residential suburb of Paris. His family name was Drieu, but his paternal great-grandfather, an officer in the wars of the Revolution and the Empire (1793–1814), had been given the nickname of "La Rochelle," which the family thereafter retained as part of the last name. There is no indication of his father's profession.

At eight, Drieu was sent to a private school, Sainte-Marie de Monceau, conducted by the Order of the Marists. When he was eleven, his only brother, Jean, was born. At sixteen, Drieu made his first trip to England, and lived for a time with an English family.

the narrow, ineradicable self

These are the few verifiable facts[1] we possess about the writer's early life: all the information generally collected as vital statistics—what the French call *état-civil*. These data have little intrinsic importance because they are taken for granted by most people. Most writers fail to tell us what these facts signified for them and let the critics speculate at will about the possible influences of family, racial origins, environment, and historical background. Drieu was more conscious than most people of the limitations imposed upon him by the chance factors which constitute the situation of any man in this world: family, class, nationality, religion, education. Considered from a certain angle, Drieu's whole life appears as an effort to liberate himself from these limitations—or at least to transcend them, since they cannot be rejected or ignored. His works constitute, in a way, the record—sometimes pathetic, but always interesting—of his efforts in that direction.

---

[1] Drieu was fifty-two when he committed suicide in 1945. Consequently, it is too early to exhume all the documents, correspondence, and intimate journals that would make possible a critical biography. Too many people involved in the story of his life are still living. For different but understandable reasons, they are all opposed to the publication of documents which would be indispensable for elucidating details of his private life. Drieu married twice, divorced twice, and his former wives both remarried. His only brother, who inherited all Drieu's manuscripts and papers, sued the *Nouvelle Nouvelle Revue Française* when it published in September, 1953, "Récit secret," an essay on suicide, written by Drieu after his first attempt at suicide on August 12, 1944. Gallimard, the publisher, agreed to withdraw this issue from sale and to have the remaining copies destroyed. Drieu's brother also refused to permit the publication of a novel left unfinished. (*Derrik Raspe* is the title of this novel as it is given in Pierre Andreu's *Drieu, témoin et visionnaire*. However, in a letter to me, a friend of Drieu's spells the title *Erik Raspe*.)

It is difficult to procure two books, *Le Français d'Europe* (1944) and *Les Chiens de paille* (1944) which clarify Drieu's attitude during the most controversial part of his public life: his collaborationist career under the German occupation, 1940–1944. The printing of these books coincided with the liberation of Paris, July, 1944; they were never put on sale although a few copies escaped destruction.

Even Pierre Andreu, who, in 1952, wrote the first book on Drieu and knew him personally, has used, in the biographical sketch which opens his study, mainly what Drieu reveals of himself in his works. (Andreu, *op. cit.*, pp. 19–89.) This sketch is useful as a friend's testimony. Since Andreu knew some of the actual events of Drieu's life, his acceptance of elements of the confession is in itself a guarantee of their authenticity. The method, however, presents a serious danger because elements of the confession are to be found in fictional works and it encourages the assimilation of the author with some of his characters.

At the very beginning of his literary career, he must have felt that the best way to get rid of the young man he had been on the eve of World War I was to put on paper what it meant to have been born in the early 1890's of a French family belonging to the Catholic, republican, nationalist lower middle class. Drieu's first book in prose represents that effort; its title, *Etat-Civil*, is a fair description of the contents. He later referred to this book as a "study," a "confession," and even as a "novel." He described it more accurately when, in 1940, collecting his early writings (1917–1927) he decided to abandon to its fate what he called this "curiously premature autobiographical essay."[2]

We can utilize this unique document as long as we do not forget what it is: the lucid meditation of an author about the mythology of his origins, giving probably a distorted picture of those origins but the only one that counted for him.

"I was born too old, in a world which—I want to believe it with a desperate fanaticism—will be tomorrow very young again; my parents, old French people from an old France which heroically we could forget."[3] This passage taken from *Etat-Civil* sums up Drieu's feelings toward the family's inheritance: a sense of personal decrepitude, the rejection of a dead past, but a rejection which requires heroic effort because the author still belongs to this past, is marked by it. He suffers from seeing around him the death of an old form of life to which he is still attached; at the same time he desires this death as the unavoidable condition for a renewal. He looks, almost compulsively, for symptoms of decadence in himself and in everything he loves. His sincerity is sometimes carried as far as exhibitionism: "My glance was like a knife held by the blade with which I wounded myself while I plunged it in the clothes, the flesh, dull and humiliated rags covering shriveled bones, pitiful muscles" (p. 149). This compulsion will turn Drieu into a specialist in unpleasant subjects and make of him more particularly the hound of decadence. From

---
[2] Drieu La Rochelle, *Ecrits de jeunesse*, 1917–1927 (1941), preface, p. 7.
[3] *Etat-Civil*, p. 179.

his very first book in prose, he exercises this cruel lucidity against himself and reveals the weaknesses that others try so hard to hide or to forget, but he will later also denounce the hypocrisy of the social comedy around him, disturb the smug complacency of the pharisees. Drieu's particular brand of satire is always combined with a personal self-accusation: his public confession is an invitation for everyone to examine his conscience, to drop his mask. He has said himself that the lucidity of an artist is always, to a certain extent, that of an accomplice: the observer is not entirely detached from the object of his observation.⁴ In that respect, *Etat-Civil* foreshadows a basic trait of the rest of Drieu's work. "A writer must efface himself. And here is the fatal literary illusion to which I fall a victim: I write these pages [*Etat-Civil*] to fix in permanent form outside myself all the things from which I want to disassociate myself" (p. 178). Thus, he devotes his first book in prose to his past in the hope of getting rid of it. This first step will be endlessly repeated. The same pattern applies to the other objects of his satire. Drieu will remain glued to whatever he denounces. Later he will adopt this role as his own and make the most of it as an artist. In *Etat-Civil*, he even refuses the consolation that, as an artist, he could have found, in the literary transposition of a disappointing reality. "Utilizing myself as a character in a novel is no consolation to me for not being a complete man" (p. 178).

Drieu uses the fictitious name *le petit Cogle* (the little Gallic rooster) in portraying the child and adolescent he has been. The portrait is not flattering: at sixteen—the book leaves him on the eve of the "unavoidable romanticism of his eighteenth year"—the young Cogle is prisoner of a narrow universe. He is walled in by prejudices and inherited notions. He has lost touch with life. He conceives of a possible liberation, but he lacks the courage to accomplish it—except in imagination. He lives on languidly but complacently in the "old and dilapidated prison of disembodied thought." Everything in the early life of little Cogle has contributed to a divorce from the real

⁴ *Le Français d'Europe*, p. 66.

by the development of daydreaming and of imaginary compensations for a disappointing reality.

The book has three parts, which correspond to the three main periods of that early life: life in the family from Cogle's earliest recollections at the age of three, which he considers the time of his birth since it marks the limit of his conscious memory, to the time he is sent to school at the age of eight. The second part is the school years (eight to fifteen), and the last one describes the young adolescent meeting the outside world (fifteen to eighteen). The central figures in the story are the members of the family, but also there are heroes and imaginary companions which the child found in books.

Among the creatures of flesh and blood, the person Cogle seemed to love most was his maternal grandmother. He spent a great deal of time with her in endless conversation. She had been brought up according to the ideal of *Emile* by a father who admired Rousseau, physical vigor, and a republican form of government. Her own mother had given her a Catholic education and had taught her to admire the exploits of the "chouans," royalist rebels of Brittany. She respected only men and the great thing in her eyes was to be *un homme réussi* "a complete man." Neither her father nor her husband corresponded to her ideal of men and she transferred all her hopes to her grandson, the only son of her only daughter. Unfortunately, her enthusiasm for masculine action was mainly verbal. She suffered from the very defect she denounced in others: "a minute after she had repeated some bellicose sentence, she would protest loudly if I exposed myself to a minor risk, she would call me back beside her so that we could resume the dream of my future in perfect tranquillity" (p. 57).

She had a cult for Napoleon who became the child's hero very early. Abundantly illustrated albums, as well as the first books she gave him after he could read, made of the national hero a very real person to the imaginative child. The emperor-soldier was for him the embodiment of kindness, strength, power. He was more real than God or country: "I believed that he was wed to France. France? When did I find out what it was? Much later. I knew Napoleon before France, before God, before myself" (p. 45).

Cogle's grandmother read mainly historical books and she considered literature beyond her reach. She gave him the memoirs of Marbot, Coignet, Bourgogne in which the child found nourishment for his military fantasies. Another person in the house encouraged his dreams of military glory: the servant Joseph who enjoyed the prestige of a soldier who had served with the colonial troops and had taken part in the expedition to Madagascar. He represented for the child an authentic hero even though he had been only a colonel's cook for a few months.

Deprived of companions of his own age, the child spent his time with older people. Cogle's grandfather, a printer, was a hard worker. Work and thrift were the only traditions of the bourgeoisie that he had maintained. But he was a creature of fears; by oversheltering his grandson, he prevented the latter's normal development and growth: "He was creating a vacuum around me with an atrocious zeal. Depriving me of everything, reducing my life to the thinnest by keeping away from me so many imaginary perils, he did not really think of me; he no longer saw in my place anything but a mysterious abstraction" (p. 145).

Cogle's parents were young and seem to have given very little time to him. His mother was pretty and he expresses sensuous attachment for her. When she went out at night, as she frequently did, he experienced terrible anguish at her departure, but he had been told that he should be brave and he made a point of hiding his feelings from his mother. The repetition of similar occasions in which the child had to repress the expression of his emotions led him to be withdrawn and to worry by himself.

The father, far from restoring the child's confidence in himself, would mock him. On a rather pathetic occasion (the child had killed his pet hen by maltreatment), the father uses his authority only to make Cogle feel unbearably guilty. The portrait of this father is remarkably vague, almost absent, as a matter of fact: "I rarely saw my father. I was afraid of him with the cowardly feelings of a slave secretly cherishing his master" (p. 38).[5]

Brought up by women, the little Cogle is thus condemned to the most sedentary life. Until he was thirteen, he was never allowed to go out by himself. The child was forced to compensate for the immobility of his body and the monotony of his life by great activity of the mind and especially of his imagination.

The tales told by his grandmother and the pictures in his albums had already provided him with an exalted idea of life far above the dullness of his daily reality. Reading offered the perfect escape. It plunged the child for years into the realm of illusion. While his body languished in a passive inertia, his imagination became too familiar with exploits of all kinds: military exploits of war memoirs, sentimental daydreaming about the languid heroines of the novels by the Countess of Segur and by Zenaïde Floriot, exotic travel adventures and improbable exploits of the child heroes in the novels of Boussenard and Paul d'Ivoi. Thus the child's craving for real adventures is satisfied by cheap substitutes. The indignant author compares the writers of those books of adventure to "agents provocateurs who attract children into the trap of imagination." The immediate result of so much reading was for Cogle an increased solitude. To perpetuate the dream life of his readings the child indulged in fantasies of his own invention which he would tell to himself, every evening, by installments.

The gap between the exalted idea of courage and the natural fears of the youth would create painful and perplexing

---

[5] The author's half silence about the father in *Etat-Civil* assumes its full significance on reading *Rêveuse bourgeoisie*, a later novel (1937), in which most of the characters of *Etat-Civil* reappear with fuller treatment. The father, Camille Le Pesnel, is one of the central characters: weak, irresponsible, and sensuous, he is a bad father and a bad husband, he married for money, has a mistress, and wrecks his family. With mounting horror, his son, Yves, obsessed by the fear of resembling him, discovers in himself his father's basic defects. See below, chap. vii.

conflicts. A more permanent tendency was born from frequenting an illusory world: the habit of considering thought as sufficient in itself, of enjoying it for its own sake as a retreat from the outside world. Cogle's inner life tended very early to be divorced from the world. And once more the author, forgetting his fiction, intervenes in the first person to denounce this nascent "romanticism": "I proclaim it loudly to commit my future: I loathe this innate disposition (e.g., to divorce oneself from the world) I intend—through study and art—to banish it from my nature. This romanticism which was already threatening, I defy it" (p. 141).

Another way to escape from the mediocrity of his family or at least to seek reassurance against the fear of resembling them is for Cogle to look in the family past for adventurous ancestors. He questions the right of his father, because he happens to be the immediate progenitor, to represent and talk in the name of all those ancestors. He dreams about the ideal situation which would consist in not knowing anything about one's origin: to have been an infant abandoned by his parents at a border post; any fantasy would then be legitimate. The next best thing is to select from family traditions the most glamorous ancestors. Although he could not go much further back than the third generation in the "mute comedy of his origins," there were enough characters to represent the chief embodiments of the conflicting tendencies of Cogle's inner drama. Politically, all the French traditions were represented. Together with those who adopted a timid, neutral or opportunistic attitude, there were those who took sides and maintained a passionate loyalty to the king, to Napoleon, or to the Republic. Sailors and corsairs represented the adventurous elements of the family settled on the shores of Normandy and Brittany. Around 1850, four of his uncles had left their native province for California. Even among the more commonplace members of the family, historical events had brought out traits of heroic courage in otherwise uneventful existences. A vivid anecdote illustrated the repercussion in Cogle's family of France's occupation by the Russians in 1814. One of Cogle's ancestors, seeing a Russian officer making advances to his wife in the garden, took his gun, aimed it from a window and killed him on the spot. In retaliation the Cossacks choked him to death with pigs' food.

In the recent past, however, the family had not shown much vitality. Cogle feels that all those older people are transmitting to him a tradition which was already dead in their own time or which died with them. They belong to a dying class and their morose view of French history points to the country's decline. Little Cogle calls himself the "grandson of a defeat," which is chronologically true in reference to the French defeat of 1870 in the Franco-Prussian war but even more true in the sense that a defeatist spirit colors the views of the older generation around him. Sedan marked the lowest point in French destinies but the child had been made aware that the descent had begun long before. He was familiar with all the French defeats since the Middle Ages and each of them marked a more irreparable decline of French power: after the three major defeats of the Hundred Years War, Crécy, Poitiers, Agincourt, the French kings and Napoleon had little by little given up the control of the sea and lost overseas territories. Trafalgar marked the end of imperial ambitions; Sedan was even more alarming: part of the very territory of France had been surrendered and France had been defeated on land by a single country while until then a coalition of all Europe had been necessary to defeat it.

There was little hope in the future to counterbalance this catastrophic view of the past. Cogle's family belonged to that part of the French bourgeoisie which still sulked at the Third Republic. It was overcritical of the young regime which illustrated in their eyes only the vices of the republican form of government. They kept their eyes turned toward a vague past and imitated the disdain of the aristocracy and of part of the clergy for the politicians coming from the lower middle class who were then building the belligerently anticlerical "Parti Radical." Their defeatism naturally reflected the tone of the defeated Right and they justified their nonparticipation in

French politics by denouncing the errors and corruption of the regime and forecasting its imminent doom.

Here again the young man found an attitude of ineffectualness, of divorce from the real. He felt that he was sick, and he was made to feel that it was "the sickness of a whole nation." His family had taught him to detect signs of weakness everywhere: "Weak people make of weakness an idol. They explain everything by it." In the moment of acting, "they sacrifice their action to that image" (p. 162). He saw his country under the mark of destruction and yet could not tear himself away from it: "I doubted the cause which a desperate passion (I knew it) would force me to defend" (p. 161).

France is the object of Cogle's anxious love and any sign of weakness on its part produces deep repercussions in his personal life, especially if they are such tangible, physical signs of weakness as the defeat of French teams in international football contests with Anglo-Saxons. By a curious reaction of anger at such collective defeats, the young man sulks at his youth and considers all efforts useless. He does not want to disturb the process of death which he even solemnly desires at that time.

During his "pilgrimage to England," a trip which was becoming traditional for the sons of the French bourgeoisie to the country they both admired and hated, because of its recognized supremacy, the young man has the revelation of a harmonious civilization. He becomes painfully aware of all the things he has been missing in his own country. Oxford, by contrast with French universities, offers him an image of the reconciliation of body and spirit. The individualism of the French appears to him now as "this subtle isolation of everyone which is the law of French life" (p. 174). In a way he feels more at home in England than in France. His physical appearance itself is more British than French: "I was tall, blond, blue-eyed, white-skinned. I belonged to the Nordic race" (p. 167). At seventeen, Cogle was tempted by what he calls the "mythology" of Gobineau which saw in this Nordic race the "masters of the universe." His trip to England helps him to situate himself more accurately: he is a Frenchman born north of the Loire River.

He would not dream of emigrating: "One cannot go away, change one's soul, one cannot break a category of the mind" (p. 21). In spite of his lucid recognition of the shortcomings of his country, his nationalism seems unshaken. The fact that one happened to be born in one country rather than in another is purely fortuitous, it is true, but this chance factor becomes part of one's destiny: "I love France like a woman met in the street—it is disturbing, fascinating, like chance. Then I love her forever, her face becomes solemn: it is that of Destiny" (p. 19).

Patriotism seems to the author a fundamental, inescapable passion of mankind: the need to commit oneself to a group of men such as the nation or party creates the strongest ties. The author reveals in this first novel what is perhaps a trait typical of a "fascist personality." The following passage provides an illuminating insight into a brand of fanaticism peculiar to our time. It is a rather naïve but all the more telling expression of the totalitarian notion of the "pact of blood," the unqualified commitment to a party or a country:

> A country is for some people a way of acclimatizing, of domesticating inhuman ideas, it is a habit, a concern, a passion, the key to all the pretexts of living.... When one leaves countries for a party which both includes and denies them, one still adheres to what in patriotism is the essential complacency: to be with certain men. And when one is with certain men, one is against others. When a man makes a movement of friendship toward another man, either this man commits himself to this last, this supreme gesture which alone is patent, conclusive: the proof by blood, to be killed or to kill; else this man stops halfway, holds to a mental reservation and then he takes refuge in nothingness, he does not exist (pp. 21–22).

This violently nationalistic or partisan passion is all the more significant in that the child and the young man in Cogle could make a mystic association with other men but not with God: he was unable to experience any religious emotion. His family had emphasized the social aspect of religion. A few priests at school and more particularly a confessor had aroused

Cogle's interest in a mystical approach and he had tried with real zeal to know the love of God. In spite of his efforts he could not get beyond intellectual curiosity. He deplores having lost at fourteen or fifteen "the secret of God." He has also rejected without ever knowing it the "spiritual athleticism" of prayer.

He lacked the compensations that physical athleticism could have offered. He has witnessed the renascence of sport in France but he was born a few years too early to participate in it. Here again the enthusiasm for physical training remained purely cerebral: "I was not ripe for the resurrection of the flesh, the reunion of body and soul, separated for so long by the misunderstanding of a certain civilization" (p. 158).

Cogle's anxious love for his country does not permit him to indulge in dreams of individual glory. He has known the ambitions of the Romantic heroes: "Even though I was born in 1893, I took walks with the maniac phantoms of Rastignac and Sorel" (p. 158). But their notion of "success" seems petty and anachronistic to his generation. "Grandson of a defeat," Cogle seems to feel that only a collective redemption can restore individual pride.

Thus Drieu leads us to the great crisis of his generation: the collective experience of World War I. Through the eyes of the isolated, dreamy middle-class boy, one is helped to understand why later the author came to see war as a chance for personal and social redemption. It provided an escape to some sort of reality. One understands also how the author of *Etat-Civil* could be stirred by the nationalism of any fascist party and how commitment to a political party, involving submission to a firm discipline, might look like an unpleasant necessity but a sure way of being in contact with the "real" world.

Drieu's self-analysis in *Etat-Civil* provides certain clues that partly explain his later life. It constitutes a testimony which even illuminates some of the attitudes of a generation. But now we must go back to the meager facts of Drieu's life and return to the young man of sixteen, who has just completed the usual French secondary studies.

II

He entered in 1910, at the age of seventeen, the Ecole Libre des Sciences Politiques, apparently to prepare for a foreign service career. The main subjects that he studied, history, diplomacy, geography, law, and economics, developed an early taste in him for political thinking. His scholastic record for the years 1910–1912 is excellent. In 1913, at the final competitive examination, in which many expected him to rank first because of his brilliance, he failed. This particular failure is almost symbolic of the way in which Drieu repeatedly disappointed those who had high expectations of him. The pattern of brilliant beginnings followed by unexpected failures or at least incomplete success was one he repeated in his life and even in his fiction.

In 1913 he went to Germany for the first time. This country which was to play such a great role in his life, does not seem to have made as strong an impression on him as England. He was never able to read German authors.

In the same year he was called to military service, for he did not avail himself of his student status to ask for a deferment. His infantry regiment was stationed in Paris. He had received about a year of military training at the outbreak of World War I. Three weeks after the declaration of war, on August 23, 1914, during the battle of Charleroi in Belgium, his unit came into contact with the enemy and Drieu took part in a bayonet charge. He was wounded by shrapnel. A month later, back in action, he was wounded a second time, in Champagne (September, 1914). In 1915, he participated in the Dardanelles expedition in which he contracted dysentery. At Verdun, in 1916, he was seriously wounded. During the long interlude that ensued, the war poems of *Interrogation* were published, in 1917. Although serious wounds had caused Drieu's transfer to the auxiliary service, he applied toward the end of 1917 for active service again. In October, 1918, he was attached as an interpreter to an American division in the region of Verdun. This is where the armistice surprised him in November. He was then a sergeant.

Drieu's truthfulness about the facts of his life is attested by his rather scrupulous efforts to set the record straight in the particular case of his war experience. In an open letter published in the *Nouvelle Revue Française*, November, 1929, Drieu himself pointed out the transitory character of his actual participation in the war:

> It is true that I owe to three wounds and a bad case of dysentery this privileged situation of a "transient": but it is nonetheless obvious that this de facto privilege renders suspicious the accesses of lyricism which from time to time swell up in the lyrical journal of *Interrogation* written in hospitals in 1915, 1916, and 1917...*

In 1919 Drieu married a young Jewish heiress. He was divorced in 1922. He was to marry again in 1927 and be divorced again in 1929. The first marriage had deep repercussions in his life as is evidenced by its literary treatment in Drieu's fiction. It seems to have enabled him financially to pursue a literary career. He had many contacts with the Surrealist group until 1925. His friends, Louis Aragon, André Breton, Paul Eluard, were dedicating poems to him in "Littérature." Conversely, "La Valise vide" was dedicated to Paul Eluard, *L'Homme couvert de femmes* (1925) to Louis Aragon, "Le Sergent de ville" (collected later in *La Suite dans les idees*) to André Breton.

Daniel Halévy, who met Drieu for the first time around 1920, was struck by the contrast between his external appearance and the conception one formed of the young author from his books.

> ... when I met him on the sidewalk of Saint-Germain-des-Prés, supple and tall, with an air of grace and ennui on his face, I wondered whether this was the same man who had carried a military pack at Charleroi and at Verdun. So the author of *Interrogation*

---

* "A propos d' 'A l'ouest rien de nouveau,'" *NRF*, No. 194 (November, 1929), 725–730. Sartre, in an issue of *Les Lettres Françaises* published clandestinely during World War II, wrote: "He [Drieu], like Montherlant, played at the game of war in 1914. His influential protectors sent him to the front when he asked them and would call him back as soon as he was afraid of getting bored."

was this dandy prophet who became very quickly a Parisian figure!"

Drieu began publication, in 1927, of a strange political magazine to which he was, with his friend Emmanuel Berl, the only contributor. They explained in a prospectus, the meaning of the name they had chosen for it: *Les Derniers jours:* The "dangerous economic situation of Europe" and its "miserable spiritual condition" made them feel that modern civilization had reached a dead end. The conditions of its renewal had to be examined critically and freely. The new publication was justified because there was no longer any free press: "There are no longer any individuals; there are only groups which have their systematic views printed by their employees every morning, or every month."⁸ *Les Derniers jours* achieved only seven issues, which appeared irregularly in 1927.

In 1929 the Argentinian author Victoria Ocampo met Drieu in Paris for the first time. She was struck by the youthful appearance of the man, now thirty-six, by his punctilious elegance and tidiness, and by his voluble conversation.⁹ They were to become very good friends; she was one of the few persons to whom Drieu wrote shortly before committing suicide. Her essay on Drieu represents a most sympathetic attempt to understand a friend whose ideas she did not share. *Drôle de voyage,* published in 1933, is dedicated to her. Drieu was for several years a contributor to *Sur,* the Argentinian literary magazine founded and directed by Victoria Ocampo.

In 1932, Drieu gave a series of lectures in Argentina on the international situation. *La Nación* published articles signed by him. Analyzing for his audience the crisis democracy was then undergoing in the world, he became himself more aware of the growing importance of fascism and communism as the two most dynamic forces competing for world domination.

---
[7] Andreu, *op. cit.,* p. 10.
[8] "Prospectus des Cahiers 'Les Derniers jours,'" in Appendix to *Genève ou Moscou,* pp. 258–259.
[9] See Victoria Ocampo, "El Caso de Drieu La Rochelle," *Sur,* No. 180 (October, 1949).

the narrow, ineradicable self

Upon his return to France, he learned as much as he could through books, travel, and conversation about fascism; in 1935, for instance, he went to the Nazi congress of Nüremberg and immediately afterwards to Moscow.[10]

On the French scene, the antiparliamentary riots of February, 1934 in Paris, following a political scandal, made a strong impression on him. It was for him not only one more symptom of the corruption and weakness of the existing regime, but an indication that certain elements of the population wanted a change, and were prepared to obtain it through other than parliamentary methods. In numerous articles, he took a position against the old French parties of the right and of the left; examined critically the newborn antidemocratic French movements; explained what the confusing term fascism meant for him, and warned against artificially imitating foreign solutions.[11] Finally, when the former Communist, Jacques Doriot, founded in 1936 the anticommunist Parti Populaire Français, Drieu joined it. Until November, 1938, he was to contribute regularly a weekly article to the *Emancipation Nationale,* the organ of the party. An expression of Drieu's bitter disillusionment with this French "fascist" party has been quoted previously. See above chap. i, p. 26.) It is noticeable, however, that Drieu, who had been sworn into the party, never expressed in print his feelings toward Doriot. He seems to have been freer in private conversation, and Andreu relates what Drieu told him in 1943: "For five years now I have no longer had any illusions about Doriot; at heart, he is a politician, of the radical-socialist type ..."[12] To appreciate this judgment, one must remember that for Drieu, the radical socialist party and its longtime boss, Edouard Herriot, represented all the worst traits of the French Third Republic. For a few months in November, 1942, Drieu joined again Doriot's disreputable

---

[10] For Drieu's impressions of 1934 Germany, see his "Mesure de l'Allemagne," dated March, 1934, first published in *NRF,* collected in *Socialisme fasciste,* pp. 201–216, and "Souvenir d'hier," collected in *Chronique politique,* pp. 204–206.

[11] See "La République des indécis," in *Chronique politique,* pp. 23–26.

[12] *Op. cit.,* p. 77.

party. This gesture contributed toward making his attitude during the occupation appear more extreme and uncompromising than his deepest convictions warranted.

After his first withdrawal from the Parti Populaire Français in November, 1938, Drieu kept out of active politics. The outbreak of World War II must not have come as a surprise to him. A strikingly prophetic article, "La Prochaine guerre," published in 1934, opened with the word: "In five years, the war breaks out."[13]

Drieu also predicted in this article one of the major events which marked the beginning of World War II: "Whether Poland fights with or against Germany, Russia will invade Poland. And this is what will give its main character to the new world war."[14]

His prediction in the same article concerning the situation within France shows considerable insight: "There will be in France a pro-German party and a pro-Russian one. This will bring the most surprising turnabout of accepted positions and traditional classifications. Communism, so weak in France, will resume some strength, thanks to the confusion of its aims with nationalistic aims, an element of appeal which it has strongly lacked. On the other hand, some bourgeois middle-class people, until then nationalists, will realize that nationalism is not so much as they had believed the soul of their lives. They will suddenly justify German aspirations and accept concessions that the leftists had never dreamt of. Hitler has beautiful days ahead of him."[15]

During the first months of the "phony war," Drieu wrote only a few articles, for papers or magazines of varied shades of opinion: *Nouvelle Revue Française, Je Suis partout, Figaro, Esprit.*

To understand Drieu's reaction to the French defeat of 1940 it is useful to consult a section of a book published in 1941, entitled "Ecrit en Juin 1940" and dated January–July,

---
[13] *Socialisme fasciste,* p. 162.
[14] *Ibid.*
[15] *Ibid.,* p. 170.

the narrow, ineradicable self

1940. It contains some of his reflections on the defeat.[16] He saw in the collapse of France, after thirty-eight days of battle, the collapse of a disembodied, blindly optimistic rationalism, which had permeated the Third Republic. In this dream world of optimism the efforts of a minority at the extreme right and at the extreme left had been unable to reintroduce any sense of the tragic and of harsh realities. Drieu wrote: "The France which read Sorel, Barrès, Maurras, Péguy, Bernanos, Céline, Giono, Malraux, Petitjean was not strong enough to impose itself on the France which read Anatole France, Duhamel, Giraudoux, Mauriac, Maurois."[17]

The reasons for Drieu's collaboration, the nature and extent of that collaboration are complex problems which would require considerable study to be fully understood. *Les Chiens de paille,* Drieu's novel on the German occupation, will be examined later, both as a novel and as a documentary record of his attitude. Here it will suffice to summarize his activities during the occupation.

He had called himself a fascist since 1934. In 1943, in a rather disillusioned summing up of his experiences called "Bilan," Drieu wrote that he was a fascist because he had measured the progress of decadence in Europe. He had seen in fascism the only way of containing and reducing this decadence. Not believing in the political resources of France or England and being opposed to the intrusion of the extra-European empires (U. S. A., U. S. S. R.) in Europe, he saw no other recourse than the existing German hegemony. He added: "This seems to me, besides, a very unfortunate position. To put one's salvation in other people's hands is the sign of the worst human misery for nations and for individuals alike. . . . What does the lazy begger receive? Alms, at best."[18]

He expressed his regret that Hitler was postponing the socialist revolution in Europe for so long. Drieu had first seen in fascism a short cut to the socialist revolution. Furthermore,

---
[16] *Notes pour comprendre le siècle* (1941), pp. 171–186.
[17] *Ibid.,* p. 173.
[18] *Le Français d'Europe,* p. 212.

48

in his eyes it represented the last defense of freedom against the Russian attack in Europe, as well as against the destruction that would result from a final conflict on European soil between the Soviet Republics and the United States: "Hitler, for me, is the fatality of socialism accomplished through a lesser evil. This evil is still enormous, if measured by the standards of our old usages, our old ways of living and thinking; but it is certain that who fights against the ever-recurring violence from the East must participate in that violence in order to oppose it. Lenin prepared the way before Mussolini and Hitler."[19]

Drieu's first collaborationist article, "Un Homme marche dans Paris," appeared on September 15, 1940, in *La Gerbe*, directed by another novelist, Alphonse de Châteaubriant. Drieu later recalled the nature of his impulse: "In 1940, when at the end of August, I came back to Paris, the dwarf who at certain hours roosts in my tall carcass (here is a little phrase which can always be of some use) whispered to me Oh no! You'll never write for the Paris press. People would hate you too much in your district. A month later, I brought an article to Châteaubriant. His solitude attracted me."[20]

In October, 1940, Drieu, in an interview given at Vichy, announced that he was taking steps to resume the publication of the *Nouvelle Revue Française* in Paris.

The first issue of the *Nouvelle Revue Française* under his direction appeared in December, 1940. Jean Grenier has given an account of a conversation he had with Drieu shortly before the review resumed publication. It reveals some of the difficulties Drieu encountered in obtaining the participation of his first contributors: Gide, Giono, Jouhandeau, Alain, Audiberti, Morand, Ramon Fernandez. Jean Grenier notes that Drieu emphasized the fact that France had to adapt, without wasting any time, to the newly created situation in Europe brought about by an "historical fatality." Grenier explains Drieu's acceptance of the defeat by what he calls "this syphilis of

---
[19] *Ibid.*, p. 213.
[20] Quoted by Andreu, *op. cit.*, p. 75.

intelligence: a certain Hegelian philosophy of history."[21] Jean Grenier refused to particiapte in the new undertaking.

Most of the older writers who had at first agreed to contribute soon withdrew. The remaining contributors were mainly poets. In the "balance sheet" established by Drieu after two years of operation, he was pleased to note that the review had given an audience to a new generation of poets: Audiberti, Guillevic, Rolland de Renéville, Follain, Fombeure, Henri Thomas, Armand Robin, Fieschi. Few authors had expressed their ideas on the events of the times: Petitjean, Chardonne, Drieu himself. Drieu expressed the regret that only one current of opinion had been represented in the journal. He had desired a more varied expression of views: "I think it would have been possible for some authors, if they had wanted it at all, to express discreetly but substantially, if not their refusal, at least a good part of the reasons which led them to these refusals."[22] It was an admission of the fact that French men of letters were not collaborationists. Drieu, while admitting the failure of the undertaking, said he did not regret it: "Undoubtedly, I could have succeeded better, but what would have been a success? A neutral review, a purely literary review, as they say. I do not believe in neutrality nor in purity nor, by that very fact, in success."[23]

His own contribution consisted of twenty-four essays and chronicles in which literary considerations are mixed in about equal proportion with political ones. They express the nonconformist views of an outspoken critic, judging authors mainly from the point of view of *littérature engagée* of a man irretrievably committed to a cause. Some of the authors considered include Mauriac, Aragon, Montherlant, Chardonne, Fabre-Luce, Pierre Emmanuel, Péguy, Céline, Léon Daudet, Maurras, Bernanos, Audiberti, Guillevic.

After he abandoned the *Nouvelle Revue Française* in June, 1943, Drieu contributed purely political articles to the *Révo-*

---

[21] "Une Conversation avec Drieu La Rochelle," *NNRF*, No. 9 (September, 1953), 387–390.
[22] "Bilan," in *Le Français d'Europe*, p. 211.
[23] *Ibid.*, p. 209.

lution Nationale. Out of a total of thirty-five articles contributed until August, 1944, sixteen have been collected in *Le Français d'Europe.*[24]

Drieu's last article, "Lettre à un ami Gaulliste" appeared in the *Revolution Nationale* on August 12, 1944. This was the date of his first attempt at suicide. He swallowed what should have been a mortal dose of phenobarbital. Saved in extremis by a chance visit of his *concierge* to his apartment he was transported to the hospital and survived. Transferred to the American hospital in Paris, he opened the veins of his wrist in the bathroom but was again rescued.

He spent the following months in hiding in the country. He came back to Paris and hid in a house belonging to his first wife. On March 15, 1945, the papers announced that an order had been issued for his arrest. He killed himself during the following night with gardenal and gas combined. An open copy of the *Upanishads* was found lying beside him.

He was buried in the Neuilly cemetery. According to Pierre Andreu, there were only a handful of people at his burial: Jean Paulhan, Jean Bernier, Audiberti, Léautaud, Gaston Gallimard, and a few women.

III

It was in the logic of Drieu's life and work that even his first attempt at suicide should constitute an experience which he analyzed in the posthumous "Récit secret." Instead of writing in the abstract about suicide, Drieu was able, with a firsthand knowledge, to describe the feelings and thoughts of a man who was sure he was going to die. For a long time, he had trained himself to look at people, things, and events with the complete detachment of someone who is ready to leave this world at any time. But however often one imagines a given situation, it can never have the authenticity of the lived experience: "What is the most acute philosophical thought compared to the glance of the condemned man who smokes his

---

[24] See the Bibliography below, for the dates of the last nineteen articles.

last cigarettes and knows that it is really the last glance coming from his eyes?"[25]

In this autobiographical study centered on suicide, Drieu traces the fascination suicide had for him back to his childhood as a form of intense metaphysical curiosity, the temptation of the unknown. At around eighteen he had decided to put an end to his life when he would reach fifty to avoid the degradation of old age. The predictions of a friend added an element of superstition to the adoption of this fatal limit. Later he used the thought of suicide as a remedy for disappointments and failures in life: failure at an important examination, sordid dullness of war before the first engagement, failure of love, grief, and other wounds from life.

But, above all, suicide was for him the ultimate form and the guarantee of solitude, a way of escaping society, of getting rid of his social self: "What I felt in me that was spiritual, immortal, inexhaustible, was precisely that which was not peculiar to me. I had always had the feeling that in my moments of plenitude, of lucidity, what counted for me, in me, was that which was not myself; it was that which in me participated in something other than myself and even completely foreign and contrary to the self."[26]

The solitude he had spontaneously chosen had taken on a different character by his own choice during the German occupation. He was now threatened, condemned, in the situation of an outlaw, because of his collaborationism. The outside pressure coincided with the secret wish of his life. This new situation, however, risked making the reasons for desiring suicide seem less pure. Instead of being the ultimate form of detachment, suicide might now be a form of fear: fear of having to pay for one's worldly faults rather than suffering with equanimity the inconveniences resulting from a course of life freely chosen. Drieu is aware of this possible rationalization: "Writing these pages, I am often tempted to exclaim: 'All this is a lie; it was not a question of philosophical con-

---

[25] "Récit secret," (1953), p. 414.
[26] *Ibid.*, p. 407.

siderations, nor of age, nor of anything so distant; I was simply afraid, afraid of being beaten, torn by the crowd; afraid of being humiliated by policemen and judges, afraid of having to explain to vile men my reasons, my beautiful reasons.' "[27] Whatever Drieu's motivation may have been for committing suicide, "Récit secret" shows the author's desire to be honest with himself, so characteristic of all his works.

"Récit secret" indicates clearly that Drieu, in spite of his apparent commitment to worldly causes, was more and more attracted by a life of contemplation. He says that since 1938, politics and love were further and further away from his interests, while his religious studies became more and more absorbing. The two simultaneous planes of action and contemplation on which Drieu was living lend an essentially ambiguous aura to his suicide; it provided the sanction of death which he considered indispensable, for the responsible writer who could not remain neutral, but it is also the last step in the personal odyssey of an individual who had already tried to cast off successively the different social ties of his *état-civil*—family, class, nationality, religion. His recourse to suicide may be interpreted as a sign that Drieu had not completely succeeded in liberating himself. Almost twenty-five years after the "curiously premature autobiographical essay," *Etat-Civil*, he could see that the "narrowest but most ineradicable part of himself" was still there. One of his last heroes, Constant Trubert, expresses his desire to kill himself at fifty for reasons strikingly similar to those developed in "Récit secret": "I want to kill Constant. Is killing Constant Trubert the same as killing myself? No. I kill only this individual, this bore, I have been dragging around after me for fifty years. I kill my shadow, everything in me that is superficial and cumbersome."[28]

Perhaps Drieu felt that he could at last rid himself of the burden of his narrow, decadent bourgeois French "self" only by a death that so many of his fictional heroes had already contemplated or experienced. In a way, he had already died

---

[27] *Ibid.*, p. 419.
[28] *Les Chiens de paille*, p. 228.

the narrow, ineradicable self

in his bourgeois French "self" on the battlefield of Charleroi, at twenty-one, when he had experienced a "moment of plenitude" to which he referred later as a mystical ecstasy. Compared to such a moment the trivial and unheroic everyday life of the postwar years was a kind of death in life. It is time we approach this moment at Charleroi which provided the central experience of Drieu's life.

three

WAR AND REVOLUTION

"There are events which exhaust at once, in an essential experience, all the possibilities of our being."[1] Such privileged moments can be endlessly relived and examined; their lesson is almost inexhaustible. They reveal to us unexpected aspects of our own self and are at the same time the basis of our philosophy of life, of our *Weltanschauung*. For Drieu this supreme experience was war. "La Comédie de Charleroi," the title story of the collection published in 1934, reminds the reader of those moments of mystical intuition which great philosophers sometimes experience and on which they construct their whole system of thought.

The difficulty for the artist is to translate into communicable terms this mystical experience. It was sixteen years before Drieu described the essence of his war experience in the concrete, apparently effortless prose of the six stories of *La Comédie de Charleroi* (1934). It is around the same time that his political and philosophical views crystallized in the essays of *Socialisme fasciste* (1934). An ideological drama, *Le*

---
[1] *La Comédie de Charleroi*, p. 40.

Chef first produced the same year, shows the link connecting Drieu's war experience and his "fascism," a term which should be used with caution to describe the author's qualified position. The purpose of this chapter is to show how the war as Drieu experienced it, led him to a fascist position. The works directly inspired by war in their chronological order are: *Interrogation* (1917); *Fond de cantine* (1920); *La Comédie de Charleroi, Socialism fasciste,* and *Le Chef* (all 1934).

I

By comparison with the short stories, the war poems of *Interrogation* (1917) appear strikingly juvenile. Yet they contain some of the main themes of the stories and already reveal an underlying fascist philosophy. The young man of twenty-four expresses antibourgeois sentiments, hatred for the old, a basic antirationalism, a decided misogyny, an obsession with death, and tries to convey to the reader the content of the mystic experience he has known on the battlefield.

In the first place, the young Drieu, in his revolt against rationalism, welcomes in the war poems the reign of the senses and of action:

> Others know spiritual strength in houses which are far from the war. I hate to hear them called cowards by the herd.
> But I must feel war in my entrails.[2]

Thought and action are considered inseparable. The young man of the war poems cannot be satisfied by dreams and abstract constructions:

> The boldness of a generation has arisen, seduced by the ambition of wedding by its will dream and action.
> No, I cannot be one who gives up one of the glories of life and who is satisfied by the secret magnificence of a dream confined behind the eyes.[3]

These enthusiastic outbursts may sound a little rhetorical,

---
[2] *Interrogation*, p. 10.
[3] *Ibid.*

nor do they always avoid the bombast of youth, but they reflect a deep conviction: action and thought must support each other, problems must be lived. We have already seen in the first chapter how this pragmatism and the nostalgia for the "lived experience" of war had contributed to the development of a new concept of literature.

In *Interrogation* Drieu also refers to the war as a mystical experience: "In the trench is revealed the unsuspected reverse, the frightening sun of the mystics."[4] Although the combatants may appear to act as the slaves of the noncombatants only they possess truth and life. The author-soldier feels sorry for the civilians, "stricken by death, cut from our time, precipitated into nothingness." The "ineffable revelation" is reserved to those who are cut off from the rest of the world in the trenches.

Fighting soldiers are like initiates of a spiritual congregation and the different branches of the services are compared to holy orders:

Enter the orders: infantry, artillery, engineers, air corps.
Take a cell in the observation post or the sap: there you are in presence of death, there the abominable suffering threatens (pp. 11–12).

This monastic aspect of war has been expressed by other war writers. Montherlant in *Le Songe,* his war novel, refers to the military overcoat of his hero as a "cassock." The fact that the front line is purely a man's world where women have no place, contributes greatly in the eyes of both Drieu and Montherlant to the prestige of the virile "order" of the warriors. Georges Bernanos compares the impact of the war experience on the fighters to an indelible sacrament which creates a lasting and unmistakable difference between the war veterans and the other civilians, a difference which makes the veterans feel like exiles in the atmosphere of peace, "because one is a demobilized soldier only for a few days but one remains unfrocked for the rest of one's life."[5]

[4] *Ibid.,* p. 87.
[5] Georges Bernanos, "Nous retournerons dans la guerre," *NRF,* No. 320 (May, 1940), 580.

France itself is personified; it becomes the object of a discreet but passionate cult. This articulate and deep love for the country is expressed, however, with reserve as befits a soldier who has been in the front lines. The patriotic literature of the *arrière* had indulged in sickening rhetoric, thus inspiring the greatest discretion in those who had proved their love by facing death.[6] Drieu's nationalism does not preclude respect for a courageous enemy and the French war censorship had barely authorized the publication of the poem entitled "A vous, Allemands" (pp. 63–68).

Paradoxically, the war poems published after the war in *Fond de cantine* (1920) are more "patriotic." The exhausted France of the end of the war inspires in Drieu a tender, anxious feeling.

> J'ai vu la face endolorie
> De mon aimée, de ma patrie
> O grands yeux que remplit
> Quelque larme eau claire
> O lac comble urne amère.[7]

The American soldiers are greeted as crusaders landing in a holy land of tombs, and the sacrificed country is compared to Christ rising again:

> Ça de la tranchée sépulcrale
> ressuscite d'entre tes morts
> O peuple Christ
> mon peuple triste.[8]

The holocaust of so many of his companions makes the author's love for the country all the more sacred. He feels that he is inhabited by their souls. The parapet of the trenches was the "modest altar" on which they sacrificed themselves to the common deity and, although his own body has survived, he senses around him the escort "sweet and severe" of his friends

---

[6] See Emile Villard, *Guerre et poésie* (La Baconnière, Neuchâtel, 1949), for examples of the ridicuolus extremes of patriotic literature.
[7] "Romance," in *Fond de cantine* (1920), p. 23.
[8] "Croisade," *ibid.*, p. 11.

who died at war. By a sort of metempsychosis, a companion whom he has seen killed even survives in him:

> Metempsychose ardente, il m'a dédié son âme
> Le regard immortel, la contagieuse flamme
> Il vit. J'ai recueilli la prompte migration
> De son éternelle passion.*

This soldier who so deeply feels the communion of his dead companions is lonely with women because, he says, they do not understand the self-sacrifice of a man for an idea, for a country, for an emblem.

Action, Sex, Death, recurring themes in the work of Drieu, are already closely connected in his war poems. For he has heard the call of death:

Your shadow is necessary for light to burst out by contrast.
O death, you are the secret of life.

This constant meditation on death isolates him:

When I pass through the city, I taste bitterly the laughter of women who never think of death.
... And yet those women look at me curiously, tenderly. But no one suffers from not understanding my secret destiny.

This "secret destiny" lies beyond the grave where he will be reunited with his friends.

Call of the distant kingdom where there are other joys.
My tenderness is elsewhere, beyond all sight, where my friends are.

He is no longer of this world and wishes to join his comrades:

... you are under the earth, you my dead brothers. One against another just as in life you kept each other warm in the shelter. I shall join you and I shall lie in your midst on the day assigned to me.

He even imagines his death and describes it:

From the trench of the last meditations, I jump
I feel eternity pass, animating current, in that instant
Shock.

---

* "Metempsychose," *ibid.*, p. 15.

I fall in the wires and the barbs bite on my muscles, drawn taut by such a beautiful paroxysm.[10]

A general expression of praise for war emerges from the "lyrical diary" of *Interrogation*. Although an element of questioning anxiety is present and gives the book its title, the note of exaltation predominates: "No, we cannot deny our war. Through it life seemed to us more adorable, our ecstasies were renewed."[11]

This enthusiasm springs partly from gratitude: war gave Drieu the chance to break away from his family as soon as he came of age and to fulfill some of the aspirations of his youth:

War for us, born in a time of long peace, appeared as a wonderful novelty, the fulfillment which was not hoped for in our youth.
It is doubtful that peace would have satisfied us so magnificently.[12]

This attitude toward war was to change considerably when Drieu went back to the theme of war after the passage of time had given his war experience and his own personality more depth.

II

The portrait of the chief character, the narrator, as it emerges from the six stories of *La Comédie de Charleroi*, is certainly more substantial and more complex than that of the young author of *Interrogation*. The general point of view about life—and war—has also changed. This change had been anticipated by Drieu himself in an open letter to Benjamin Crémieux, published in the *Nouvelle Revue Française* November, 1929. He protested in this letter against a tendency to contrast the attitude of himself and of Montherlant toward war with that of authors like Erich Maria Remarque whose *All Quiet on the Western Front* had just been translated into

---
[10] "Triptyque de la mort," in *Interrogation:* "L'Annonciation de la mort," p. 13; "La Commemoration des morts," p. 15; "L'Accomplissement de la mort," p. 18.
[11] *Interrogation*, p. 88.
[12] *Ibid.*, p. 86.

French and was a literary sensation, as well as a popular success. Crémieux's review of the book made Drieu realize that he was in danger of having his war poems interpreted as an unqualified exaltation of war. After re-reading the poems he was forced to admit that their testimony might be misleading. He wrote: "My reflections end up in a serious recantation: I do not think that *Interrogation* is a fair testimony about war."[13] At the end of the letter, after many interesting remarks about the war experience and its potential literary transmutations, Drieu announced a new work destined to offset the impression left by *Interrogation*, "a somewhat questionable piece of writing, which I shall have to correct by writing another one."

The choice of the short story as the most suitable literary form for the new war book must have been the result of many hesitations. Reviewing in 1923 Montherlant's war novel *Le Songe* Drieu wished the plot had been less important and considered that the best pages were those in which the autobiography appeared stripped of all adornment.[14] This was in 1923. The autobiographical element in a novel was, at that time, Drieu's central preoccupation. In 1929, his views seem to have changed to a certain extent: he is now convinced that sincerity without art is of little avail: "... the decisive and complete works on war will not be a patchwork of subjective notations but novels of composition and imagination, based, however, on memories just as Tolstoy's *War and Peace* is based on impressions of Sebastopol."[15]

In a way, the short stories of *La Comédie de Charleroi* constitute a rather original compromise between the two forms of purely autobiographical memoirs and a novel "of composition and imagination." Even though the total effect of the six short stories is one of great unity, they vary greatly in length and tone. They correspond also to the fragmentary nature of the war experience. Except for the personality of the narrator, there is little in common between the first contact with actual combat which is, in essence, the subject matter of the first

[13] *NRF*, No. 194 (November, 1929), 726–727.
[14] *NRF*, No. 113 (February, 1923), 455–456.
[15] *NRF*, No. 194 (November, 1929), 729.

story, "La Comédie de Charleroi" (reminding us often of Fabrice del Dongo at Waterloo in *La Chartreuse de Parme*), and the end of the war in the headquarters of an American general ("La Fin d'une guerre"). Very different also are the stories concerning the emotions of an infantryman under bombardment at Verdun (in "Le Chien de l'ecriture" and "Le Lieutenant de tirailleurs") and concerning the war of movement of the Dardanelles expedition ("Le Voyage des Dardanelles"). A few essential problems raised by modern war are discussed in more abstract dialogues: the problem of the deserter, or conscientious objector, is discussed in "Le Déserteur"; and the condemnation of modern warfare appears more specifically in "Le Lieutenant de tirailleurs." The personality of the narrator is, however, a powerful tie which links all the episodes together. It constitutes the main interest of the book. We share the ironic or passionate interest with which the mature man of forty looks back at the young man he once was. The author thus achieves unity on at least two planes. The unity of mood proceeds from the fact that the narrator is always looking back. Everything is seen in the perspective of a retrospective account. The unity of subject proceeds from the development of the main character, the portrait of the young man as a soldier exploring all the different aspects of himself during a supreme experience: war.

The war stories of *La Comédie de Charleroi* are as lyrical in many respects as the war poems of *Interrogation* and *Fond de cantine*. War, France, death always arouse the author's deepest emotions. He even manages to convey a greater feeling of authenticity than in the poems: the perfect harmony of form and content contributes greatly to that effect. Drieu has acquired a style of his own and no longer needs to imitate the form of the Claudelian "verset" used in *Interrogation*. He has acquired a better knowledge of himself and no convention, no censorship, prevents him from admitting sentiments of which professional patriots would not approve. He is not blinded by his early nationalism; at least he thinks he has transcended it. Also he has become clearer about his political position. By 1934, glancing back at his successive political attitudes, he recognizes that when demobilized, he was already a fascist without being quite aware of it.[16]

Being more self-aware, Drieu can be more sincere even though the honesty of his testimony in the war poems is not questionable. The end result is a total condemnation of modern war. War is only another symptom of the general decadence of our present civilization:

"Men have not been human, they did not want to be human. They did not want to go beyond this war, to reach eternal war, human war. They have missed something like a revolution."[17] And the following "stanza," which by its accumulation of words and its rhythm is worthy of being compared to the great lyrical prose of a Rabelais or a Victor Hugo, is even more truculent:

They have been defeated by this war. And this war is bad which has defeated men. This modern war, this war of iron and not of muscles. This war of science and not of art. This war of industry and of commerce. This war of offices. This war of newspapers. This war of generals and not of leaders. This war of prime ministers, of union leaders, of emperors, of socialists, of democrats, of royalists, of industrialists and of bankers, of old men, of women, and of little boys. This war of steel and of asphyxiating gas. This war made by everybody except by those who were actually fighting it. This war of advanced civilization (p. 61).

The narrator of the short stories is all the more aware of that decadence and bitter against it because in war itself, before his disillusionment, he discovers what he feels to be his true vocation of hero and leader of men. This revelation of his true self and of the nature of eternal war constitutes the climax of the first story: "La Comédie de Charleroi." In this climax is the description of the charge in which the narrator spontaneously takes the leadership:

Then, all of a sudden, something extraordinary happened. I had risen, risen from among the dead, from among the larvae. I understood the meaning of grace and miracle.

---

[16] "Itinéraire," in *Socialisme fasciste*, p. 220.
[17] *La Comédie de Charleroi*, p. 61.

war and revolution

All of a sudden, I knew myself, I knew my life. So this was myself: strong, free, heroic. So this was my life: an elan which was not to stop, ever.

Ah! I had foreseen on certain occasions this boiling over of young and warm blood—puberty of virtue; I had felt, pulsating within myself, a prisoner, ready to rush forth. A prisoner of the life that had been made for me, that I had made for myself.

... I was a leader. I wanted to take hold of all those men around me, increase myself with them, increase them through me and launch ourselves all together with me at their head through the universe ... (p. 57).

The manner in which Drieu builds up the story to this central passage constitutes a tour de force of technical skill and composition. He manages to create the mood, makes the reader share the emotions of a young man seeing fire for the first time, gives a very intelligible account of a battle, sketches vividly a few secondary characters and describes all the different persons he has felt himself to be on that day. The philosophy of life of the narrator is implicitly or explicitly indicated at the same time that some of the experiences which have determined that philosophy are related. This masterly piece of writing deserves close analysis.

The choice of the point of view is very happy. In a war story, the author is in danger of placing the reader either too close to the events of the story or at too great a distance. In the first instance, one is confused; in the second, one gets a conventional picture like a neat historical painting. In *La Comédie de Charleroi* the main story line is built around an incident which took place in 1919, which leads the narrator to recall a personal experience of 1914. Briefly, after the war, in 1919 the narrator accompanies to Charleroi, as a secretary, the mother of a fellow soldier who was killed at the battle of the same name in 1914 and he explains the battle to her on the battlefield. This double perspective works as a double screening process allowing only the essential events to enter the story after their full meaning has been extracted. The danger of an oversimplified and lifeless picture is avoided by the structure of the short story, rendering, in its apparent disorder, the confusion of events and emotions of the day of the battle in 1914. It is not a straight-line narration. The main events of the day are announced, then barely indicated, then handled in detail but not in chronological order. Each development corresponds exactly to the tone of oral narration with its shifting in time, space, and emphasis. The total effect is that in spite of the concrete and intelligible details, the whole narrative assumes the timeless quality of an epic. Any grandiose quality is avoided by the simplicity of the language adapted to the elementary reactions of a soldier and by using the soldier's vocabulary, rich in slang and colloquialisms.

The experience related reaches at certain points the level of a mystical experience, incommunicable in terms of the intellect. It has to be suggested more than described and the reader must be placed in a state of active sympathy. Drieu achieves this by a striking contrast. Madame Pragen, whom the narrator accompanies and to whom he tries to explain the battle, is the person the least likely to understand the true nature of war. We suffer for the narrator, who encounters only misunderstanding in her—and we follow him with all the more sympathy in his own stream of consciousness. She is a woman, in the first place, and we have already seen that Drieu does not believe that a woman can understand anything of the world of war. He says of Madame Pragen: "She did not know what war was, and she did not want to know. That was part of this domain of men for which women have so little curiosity" (p. 47). She is impressed only by titles and notoriety. She is continuously acting in a self-staged show and is so used to pretense that it is impossible to detect when she is sincere. What insures her authority and inspires a respectful devotion in everybody is her money. Madame Pragen displays her decorations and her army-nurse uniform, her "costume"; she has exploited the death of her son *mort au champ d'honneur* to gain as much glory for herself as possible. It is on the battlefield, *"les champs de bataille,"* as she says, of Charleroi, that she has staged the *comédie* which gives the title to the story. She is full of distrust when her secretary tries to give an accurate account of the battle; she is the prisoner of preconceived notions, *beaux sentiments* and clichés.

Her son, Claude, is the touching embodiment of the young "bourgeois," unprepared for war, completely lost and inefficient on the battlefield in spite of his exalted patriotism. The narrator in a few touches paints a suggestive picture. In a manner typical of this story, Claude's portrait is given piecemeal and blends with other themes to give an impression of the more general theme of French unpreparedness. He is introduced on page 12 as a victim of his mother:

> This woman, all dry vanity, had had a son.... One day she amazed me by telling me that she had breast-fed Claude. Poor little Claude: she had made him very thin and yet, very early, she had wanted to launch him in a brutally rapid career... Ignoring his frail constitution, she had wanted him to be a soldier.

When next we see Claude, it is the beginning of the day at Charleroi in 1914 when the French are expecting the attack of the Germans. Here is the graphic description of Claude in which every physical detail is symbolic:

> Upon entering the lines, I had seen Claude, kneeling on the freshly dug earth, his pince-nez on his nose, holding his shovel in his frail and awkward hand, watching his companion, a raw recruit, working for him as he had done at the barrack and finishing the individual hole of the young bourgeois.
> "Ah," he had said on seeing me.
> "They are coming," I had answered.
> And he had remained, kneeling, open-mouthed, quite pale, his pince-nez awry, doomed (p. 21).

Claude had given a "helpless, exalted gesture" the day before the battle to express his impression of a very light encounter with the enemy. On page 34: "I saw Claude again toward noon. From quite a distance. He was kneeling, shooting. He looked blind and bewildered. He must have lost his pince-nez." On page 36: "Then I saw in passing Claude who did not see me and was shooting, with a terrible shaking of his whole frail body at the moment of recoil. He was pale, surprised, lost."

Through another shifting of time, on page 40, we have another sketch of Claude a few days before the battle when the colonel wants to evacuate him because he has been a laggard, unable to carry his heavy bag, and his feet are bleeding:

... I had seen him, very short, pale under his tan, his pince-nez in distress, hunchbacked and tense, at attention, begging his colonel not to evacuate him.... "But, colonel, we are going to fight." But all that was still peacetime imagination. What would he have done with his bayonet? Absurdity of universal conscription.

On the last page of the story (98), the narrator poses a final question concerning the meaning of Claude's sacrifice: "By the way, for what had Claude died? Do I know? For France. Perhaps he had fought for France because he was Jewish."

Madame Pragen was Jewish, and a Catholic convert. Thus, another note of ironic comment on Claude as the defender of France is injected. For if Claude Pragen is doomed, according to Drieu, it is because war is the testing ground of elementary values where all the artificialities of civilization are worthless, where the primitive man—the animal—reveals himself under the imprint of advanced civilization. There is no doubt that Claude Pragen is what the narrator himself might have been if he had not kept alive in him a spark of that primitive man that is prisoner in every one of us, although most of the time nearly extinct. War unleashes all the instincts or reflexes which the life of modern men in cities has not completely destroyed, according to Drieu. The narrator, although he is himself an intellectual and a bourgeois, feels a strong respect for all those elementary forces—and he points out the irrational behavior of men around him as well as the awakening of another man in himself.

This theme of the basic irrationality in men is introduced on the very first page of the story when the narrator evokes the enthusiastic departure of the *réservistes* in August, 1914, singing the *Marseillaise*, while the very same people were singing the *Internationale* at the May first public demonstration.

Men love to get drunk and sing; it does not matter to them what they sing, provided it is beautiful; and immortal songs are always beautiful (p. 19).

Even if, with his critical intellect, the narrator is able to judge the unreasonable character of such an *élan*, he enjoys it as a form of communion with others: "A certain part of myself was inebriated by this loud spectacle, this facile departure, this thoughtless *élan*." On the last page, the narrator admits that aside from any other rational justification or motivation, the ultimate experience he was seeking in war was this communion with other men:

I fought to be with men. The men I despised in Charleroi. I went back to them. And again I left them. I looked for a balance between them and me, between my pride which they needed and their humility, which is my basis.
It took me years to understand (p. 98).

This climate of irrationality is highly favorable for the birth of the hero, who is by definition the one who acts beyond and above the requirements of duty. The inertia of the mass accepts and even expects this call to break the limitations of human condition, this call which awakens *inquiétude* in them. "Men cannot refuse anything to a man who has a high idea of mankind" (p. 34). It is in the most pragmatic fashion that the narrator finds, when he spontaneously leads the charge in battle, both a way of wielding the conflicting parts of his personality and of raising his fellow men above the mediocre level of average humanity: "Just as I had recognized myself they recognized themselves in me. Soon they were running, as if they had never been anything else, noblemen. Nobility belongs to everybody" (p. 60). Man is contradictory because life is made of contradictions and those contradictions cannot be solved by abstract reasoning but only by action. It is the great lesson drawn by the narrator from that memorable day at Charleroi which taught him more than all his previous life as an over-intellectualized, individualistic bourgeois had done:

... later, during the day, when I made movements in turn to save or to lose my skin, I was not involved; it was only a matter of reflexes. A reflex is one of the great principles of life imposing itself. Principles, not my little person, were involved. Crossed reflexes, contradictory principles: "A man is made to live" and "A man is made to die." "When there is no leader, there must be one" and "I do not want any leader" (p. 26).

The importance of that theme is so central that it determines the inner structure of the story. In order to describe what takes place in the mind of the narrator, which is only a reflection of what was going on in his blood, his nerves, his muscles, the author is obliged to use abstract means of expression and has recourse to intellectual analysis, but in order to recreate life, in its movement which escapes logic, he uses a "ballet" technique to introduce his themes: "All the themes were going back and forth, facing each other. My blood was carrying this ballet" (p. 94). Hence, the fragmentariness with which each theme is introduced again and again, sometimes in almost identical terms, at an interval of a few pages. All these different themes are connected with the character of the narrator, which undergoes several metamorphoses during the day. For instance, the theme of French unpreparedness, symbolized by the conspicuous red trousers of the French uniform, appears at least twelve times in the course of the story.[18] It is accompanied, each time, by an emphasis on German efficiency and comes as a justification of the pessimism of the narrator, confirming all the predictions he has always heard in his family about French decadence.

The advantage of the retrospective narrative is that the errors of perspective of that day are corrected. It turns out that the losses were about equal, on both sides, and in the cemetery which he visits in 1919 there are five hundred Frenchmen and five hundred Germans. "After all, the French 75-caliber gun had done as much harm as the German ma-

---

[18] See for example, p. 22: the captain; p. 24: the archaic character of the French army; p. 30: the impracticality of French military service; p. 31: the bayonet; p. 36: the load of the sack; p. 42: the French machine guns don't work; p. 45: the weakness of the French artillery; p. 46: the "carapace"; p. 62: the awkwardness of the French uniform; pp. 64, 88, 90 ff.

chine guns and their heavy artillery, and the green trousers had not saved more soldiers than the red trousers had lost" (p. 51). At the moment of the bayonet charge, the narrator has the simultaneous revelation of the eternal urge for war and of the nature of authority. Beyond the immediacy of the Franco-German war, the battle of Charleroi becomes "the eternal battle in the plain."

... Was there anything else in this rush but itself ... Why did we fight? For the sake of fighting ... We did not have any aim; we had only our youth.
We were shouting. What were we shouting? We were howling like animals. We were animals. Who was leaping and shouting? The animal who is in man, the animal in which man lives. The animal who makes love and war and revolutions (pp. 58–59).

All his doubts about himself disappear and his ideas about true aristocracy are confirmed when he, an enlisted man, leads the charge in a spontaneous burst of courage:

All my strength was surging in hope. And this hope was that the event was going to condemn the old stupid hierarchy, established in quiet times. God was going to recognize his own; this plain was the field of Judgment. War interested me because I was going to appoint myself a Captain, a colonel, much better than that—a leader (p. 56).

But modern war is bound to be affected by all the vices of modern civilization. The contact with the enemy, which would have been the normal, human consequence of the charge, never takes place: the Germans stop the charge with their machine guns. This is only the first sign of the degeneracy of an old instinct. The machine industrializes war and the values of courage are of little avail: "It is easy to tear a square centimeter of flesh with a ton of steel" (p. 63). How can one be a hero on a front line of several hundred kilometers where generals, separated from their troops, send trainloads of soldiers into battle like herds of cattle to slaughter? Everything is anonymous. The pride of the hero is broken: "War today is to be lying, crouching, flat on the ground. Formerly war meant standing men. War today is all the postures of fear"

(p. 27). What disappointment for the young man still haunted by the dreams of glory of his childhood! His patriotism is submerged by the revolt of the species against the devilishly inhuman character of guns, artillery, gas attacks.

When I wanted to commit suicide, when, later, I wanted to go away, there was also in me the Species acting in self-defense. It was the man in me who was throwing away his rifle, who was casting off this excessive machinery, the man who was denying the big guns and the sadistic machine guns ... Modern war is a malefic revolt of matter enslaved by man (p. 72).

Besides, the narrator is himself a victim of modern civilization, so far from the source of elementary life. ("Modern men are so far from death, suffering, nature.") He is aware of the limitations imposed on him by the education of his class ("I was a bourgeois, sensitive to cold, parasitic, pessimistic"), his nationality ("It was really no fun to be a Frenchman: since I was born in that country, I had not had one good moment"), his family ("I did not owe more allegiance to my country than to my father, this braggart who was talking of being the first one to enter Strasbourg and who, right now, was waiting for the result of the battle in his armchair.") He has inherited from his family a "theoretical nationalism" which is in conflict with an individualistic education:

I was oscillating between the theoretical nationalism I professed before joining the army and my practice of avoiding work, escaping responsibility, defending myself minute by minute, steeping myself in dreams or getting a book out of my pocket as soon as I could (p. 30).

The different themes of *Etat-Civil* are recognizable, including the refusal to be an anonymous unit in the big herd doomed to butchery:

What resemblance was there between my childhood dreams in which I was a free man in command risking his blood only in a great action and this reality of my identity tag labeling me, a calf branded among ten million other calves and oxen ... this Chicago slaughtering place was not the glorious career the pride of my youth demanded (p. 28).

This explains why, after the charge has been stopped, the retreat has started, and he has been wounded, the narrator separates himself violently from his countrymen. It is pride much more than fear: danger and death have on the contrary a great attraction for him, are indispensable to his really living: "What is the use of living if one does not use one's life to strike it against death as against a flint? War—or revolution which is war again—there is no way out of it" (p. 70).

The theme of suicide appears when the narrator explains that at the beginning of the war, before he had had a chance to feel the attractions of war, that is, to share the sufferings of peasants and workers, to discover the true leaders and to feel in himself the deep urge of eternal war, he wanted to commit suicide on August 20, 1914. He analyzes the reasons for despair: his eternal melancholy, an all-pervading "ennui," and, above all, the prophetic impression that war in the midst of those enormous mobilized herds would preclude any glory. He suffered at sharing with mediocre people under officers he despised what should have been a unique adventure. Actually, he despised all the men around him. The *délicat* had not yet shed his bourgeois skin or found a *modus vivendi* in this new milieu. The chance encounter and gaze of a fellow soldier served to reëstablish the connection with life, when he was on the very point of suicide. He had related the same attempt at suicide in *Mesure de la France* and added: "From then on I decided to live in order to die better." Thus the leitmotiv which was to reappear in most of Drieu's books finds its place in his war book and announces the act which put an end to the author's life. The two dates of August 20, 1914, and August 12, 1944, are worth noting: the whole productive period of a man's life is inserted between those two attempts at suicide which coincided with the beginning of one war and the end of another.

Is it pure chance that Drieu's fate was so closely linked to the fate of his country? Drieu certainly did not think so. This explains the personal tone of the political essays, where the ideas are so impassioned, and, on the other hand, the impossibility for Drieu of not weaving political ideas or reflections into his fiction. From that point of view, the stories of *La Comédie de Charleroi* offer an excellent example of how Drieu understood and realized the integration of ideas in fiction.

III

If we want to know what were, in the mind of Drieu, some of the metaphysical suggestions contained in *La Comédie de Charleroi*, we should analyze the collection of political essays of *Socialisme fasciste* published in the same year, 1934.

What distinguishes Drieu's particular brand of fascism is that it sprang from ideas about man and about society that were deeply rooted in his own personality and in his own experience, particularly the war experience. There is a latent fascism in Drieu's first book in 1917: "There is a pact, which nobody mentions, between all leaders: maintain life against the will of the people who would like to go back to nothingness."[19]

In *Socialisme fasciste*, he says: "Freedom is exhausted. Man must go back to his dark roots. I am saying that although I am an intellectual and therefore an eternal libertarian."[20] He knows that what is going on in Moscow, in Rome, or in Berlin is a reaction, more thoroughgoing than anyone could ever have dreamt of: "Because it is a pure theocracy in which the spiritual and the corporal are finally fused."[21] Drieu established a connection, on the political level, between this return to the dark roots of man's being and the rigorous and essential antirationalism of Nietzsche. In a remarkable article, "Nietzsche contre Marx," he tries to show that Lenin behaved more like a Nietzschean than a Marxist, at least in his seizure of power. He sums up the philosophy of Nietzsche—the Nietzsche of the last period, the author of the *Will to Power*—in the following manner:

---

[19] *Interrogation*, p. 35.
[20] *Socialisme fasciste*, p. 102.
[21] *Ibid.*

war and revolution

Man is an accident in a world of accidents. The world has no general meaning. The only meaning it has is the one we give it one moment, for the development of our passion, of our action.[22]

A few propositions can be deduced from this metaphysical basis which, according to Drieu, characterize the "fascist era."

1) If this world has no meaning, it cannot become the world of the Marxists, the world that is progressing toward the triumph of the proletariat. Drieu had written in 1917 essentially the same thing: "War made us believe again not in progress but in the noble effort, aimless and free from hope."[23]

2) The constant call on the unfolding of passions and of action which is in every page of the *Will to Power* has found an echo in the fascism of Mussolini and in Hitlerism. "First action and then thought" could also be the motto of *Interrogation* and of *La Comédie de Charleroi*.

> Strength is in front of me, foundation stone. I must feel its resistance....
> I want to understand it with my own body. Alimentary necessity: I seek my life over there, the life of my thought.[24]

3) By emphasizing man's autonomy in the universe and the autonomy of man's action, Nietzsche stresses that the chief element of human energy and of social movement is that individual capable of the maximum of action, the elite individual, the master. Thus he poses implicitly the dual social element on which fascism rests: the leader and the group around the leader. Drieu had had the fulgurating revelation of this during the charge at Charleroi.

These are the tendencies which Drieu had in common with the Italian or German fascist movements. A certain harmony can be explained by the common Nietzschean inspiration, strengthened by the influence of thinkers like Vilfredo Pareto and Georges Sorel. But most important of all was the fact that the core of those movements was constituted by men who were veterans of World War I. Drieu trusted that anyone

---
[22] *Ibid.*, p. 70.
[23] *Interrogation*, p. 87.
[24] *Ibid.*, p. 9.

who had seen closely the horror of modern war would be an antimilitarist. In *La Comédie de Charleroi*, he addresses to the fascists of all countries a prophetic warning:

War is no longer war. You will see it one day, fascists of all countries, when you'll be hiding flat on the ground, with diarrhea in your pants. Then there won't be any more feathers, gold tassels, stirrups, horses, bugles, words, but simply an industrial smell devouring your lungs.[25]

His fascism was extremely critical of the notion of dictatorship. In two essays of *Socialisme fasciste*, "Mériter un chef," and "La Dictature dans l'histoire," he traces the romantic origins of the concept of the "great man" and shows that an individual cannot be greater than his time and cannot create out of nothing: "He can only take in hand the collective *élan*, bind it and project it." This was exactly the pattern of the charge at Charleroi. The leader only gave shape and significance to the expectation of the men. It is a lazy and catastrophic conception to expect the strong man to be a panacea.

The rigid nationalism of the fascist movements in Europe did not please him any more than their militarism. The deserter who talks in one of the stories of *La Comédie de Charleroi* and sounds so much like the alter ego of the author, refuses the ready-made ideas which are provided by the modern state and the cheap "mystiques" distributed by the newspapers, radios, and politicians.

The same deserter, whom he imagines he has met in South America, denies that politics deserves the engagement of the whole mind and spirit. When he writes in his own name, Drieu is just as severe in his condemnation.

Politics is the crudest game of all the games this planet has to offer. Everything that pertains to the State is a valet's task. Valets are necessary and some are picturesque but I despise them and I am not impressed by them.[26]

And yet Drieu entered political action openly by joining the Parti Populaire Français in 1936, accepting Jacques Doriot

[25] *La Comédie de Charleroi*, p. 72.
[26] *Socialisme fasciste*, p. 226.

as his leader. Did he feel doubts about his talent or how to fulfill it? He says himself: "My desire to join a party had often coincided with my moments of depression."[27] Or did he decide then to live on two levels: on the level of engagement in the world, in the crude game of politics with its sometimes picturesque "valets," and on the heights of contemplation? In March, 1940, prefacing a collective reprinting of his early writings (1917–1927), he said: ". . . my philosophy and my religion were ravishing me in the solitude of an inalterable sphere."[28]

IV

One can find further reasons why Drieu decided to enter politics actively and for his choice of an authoritarian party in his play, *Le Chef*. *Le Chef* shows how fascism can derive from war in an even clearer way than *La Comédie de Charleroi* and *Socialisme fasciste* had done. It dramatizes Drieu's inner conflict through two characters, the man of action and the intellectual. It expresses the belief that there are times when liberty is not the supreme good and must be sacrificed: the libertarian intellectual must then be silenced, even though he may be right in a world of absolutes. The timing of its production indicates that Drieu meant it to be not only a profession of faith but an act, with potential political repercussions.

In 1925, Drieu had announced as forthcoming "an unpublished tragedy in four acts," *Le Chef*. It was not produced until 1934. It is likely that he made several changes to bring it up to date with events. He attached great importance to it and wanted young men from both the extreme right and the extreme left to see it.[29] He must have thought that the political events of February, 1934, in France lent his play timeliness. What did those events mean for Drieu? Mainly, they aroused in him the hope that the welding of the active elements among

---
[27] *Ibid.*, p. 242.
[28] *Ecrits de jeunesse*, p. 9.
[29] See the testimony of Pierre Andreu, *op. cit.*, p. 68.

the nationalists and the socialists in a dynamic national-socialist single party was possible. On the 6th of February, the nationalists of all denominations, and on the 9th the leftists, had defied the bullets of the police in an instinctive revolt against the vices of the parliamentary regime revealed in the Stavisky scandal (this being the meaning that Drieu saw in those two days). In *Gilles*, Drieu later described the emotions which assailed Gilles Gambier the 6th of February on the Place de la Concorde. The notes published by Drieu in the *Nouvelle Revue Française*, the articles from *La Lutte des Jeunes* collected in *Socialisme fasciste*, show that they were also his own: "In one moment, he was transfigured, looking at his right and at his left, he saw himself accompanied by the divine couple resuscitated, Fear and Courage, who preside over war."[30] February 6, assumes in the mythology of Drieu the same importance as the battle of Charleroi. The events of these two occasions are like revelations for Drieu: revelations of the essential nature of war and revolution, his two ideological preoccupations. War, for Drieu, is the test and purging of individual man; revolution is the test and purging of society.

War and revolution are intimately connected in *Le Chef:* the first act takes place during a war in Macedonia, in the front-line area of an elite brigade in which men and officers have unusual courage and an unusual contempt for headquarters. Jean, the officer in command, and Michel, the intellectual, are in conflict about whether they shall desert their post and their comrades. This is one of the first examples of the splitting into two characters of Drieu's personality: already in "La Fin d'une guerre" there was such a distinction between an idealistic self and a cynical one in the narrator.[31] Jean, fed up with war ("All this routine. This endless war. Those morons above us"), decides to leave and to learn more about the city crowds now that he has understood the army.

Two years later, in the second act, we find him again, in a

---
[30] *Gilles* (1942), p. 418.
[31] *La Comédie de Charleroi*, p. 245.

political meeting, at the head of a revolutionary movement. Michel, now a journalist, overcomes his misgivings and joins the party. This party constitutes the tie—the religion—of those lonely men who no longer believe in gods or ideas ("We believe neither in Jesus Christ nor in Karl Marx"). It is the "tower of their despair and their pride." Their program is an echo of the complaint of European soldiers in *Interrogation:* anxiety to do away with the old order:

> Farewell, generals who were losing wars. Farewell, princes losing their crowns. Farewell, bankers losing their money. Farewell, socialists losing their revolutions.[32]

They will build a strong national community:

> We must in the sweat and blood of all classes,
> Build such a country as has never been seen,
> One so compact, a block of steel, a magnet. All the rest of Europe will aggregate to it, willy nilly.
> And then, in front of that block
> Of our Europe
> Asia, America, Africa, will fall to pieces.

The third act, a year later, takes place in the headquarters of Jean's party. There is no longer the pure atmosphere of nascent revolution. Compromises with the representatives of the old order arouse the indignation of Michel, who has become the chief of the war veterans. He threatens to resign from the party and is characterized by another character as a *délicat:* "Of course, not to live is the only way not to get dirty" (p. 233).

The situation prefigures, in many respects, Sartre's *Les Mains sales.* Michel, in a fascist totalitarian party, like Hugo in a communist totalitarian party is decidedly not *recupérable:* he is too idealistic to accept the compromises imposed by the seizure of power by the party.

Jean makes Michel realize that there is some hypocrisy in his refusal to face the dirty side of any seizure of power, and reveals at the same time the solitude of the dictator:

> The world is divided into hypocrites and cynics. You are a hypo-

---
[33] *Le Chef,* p. 211.

crite. You tell me: ... our cause is good. But *I* tell you, our cause is already rotten. Already, we have received money and we have given money. Already we have a police forging grotesque lies. Already we spare some people who do not deserve it and we condemn some who have excuses. For you, is not that the eternal rottenness you have repudiated for ever, hypocrite? ... I am a cynic, an active cynic. My activity has already started. I will continue it through the death of others and my own. My work is my fidelity (p. 249).

In Anouilh's *Antigone,* Créon will use exactly the same language with Antigone, the uncompromisingly idealistic adolescent. Hoederer in *Les Mains sales,* or Olga would have said the same thing to Hugo.

A month later, after he has failed to kill Jean, Michel, wounded, has a discussion in which he stigmatizes dictatorship. He realizes that his failure to murder Jean, the "great man," is symbolic. How could the great men be killed by those who have made them? There is a frightening weakness in men who surrender themselves to another man:

You wanted everything for yourself; well, they have given you everything. Your heart is the only one to beat in Macedonia; the other hearts are empty. They have emptied themselves into yours. It is too much blood for a single man. One heart is not enough for a whole nation to live: they will notice it, twenty years from now, when you'll have a stroke (p. 269).

The mechanism of the wars of conquest in a dictatorship is analyzed, not without irony:

—Europe will be one, poor and Macedonian.
—And this is why the Macedonians have sacrificed their liberty to the pride of being Macedonians. What does it matter to a Macedonian to have nothing and to obey, if he knows that Jean lives on his behalf a prodigious destiny. Hating our mediocrity, we have thrown our insufficient strength into the fire of your genius. Live for us, we shall live for you (p. 265).

But man-made gods are only mortal. They make mistakes. They become ridiculous. Their followers cry then of shame and despair for having believed in them. But one of the characters remarks: "When liberty is killed it is usually because it lived poorly. There are seasons. Season of liberty. Season of authority." The intellectual Michel, the "last republican," was right yesterday; he will be right tomorrow. Jean, however, has the last word for the time being; "I am right today" (p. 273).

It is interesting to note that Drieu had no illusions about dictatorship, even before seeing more closely the intrigues of a fascist party from inside its ranks. One could also point out that shortly after he had demonstrated in *Les Mains sales* that he had no illusions about communism, Sartre did not hesitate to align himself with the Communist line on certain issues when it seemed to him efficient to do so, risking accusations of blindness or stupidity or betrayal by people who did not believe in compromising one's ideas. A reviewer, commenting recently on the baffling contrast between the lucidity of a man of letters in his writings and his political blindness in real life, remarked about Sartre: "How strange that this acute mind should be such a baby in actual politics, stupidly allowing himself to be used time and again by the Communists!"[33]

It is tempting to direct toward a writer the severity that one feels for the man, especially when one violently disapproves of his political position. However, Drieu's autobiographical essays such as *Etat-Civil* and some of the essays of *Socialisme fasciste,* along with works in which the direct testimony is artistically transposed (*La Comédie de Charleroi, Le Chef*) contribute greatly to explaining some of his attitudes.

---

[33] William Barrett, "Sparks from the Mind of an Idea Man," *The New York Times Book Review*, October 23, 1955, p. 28.

four

THE EMPTY SUITCASE

In a recent book on the new American novel, *Le Nouveau roman américain*, a French critic and novelist,[1] trying to make his countrymen understand the phenomenon known in American letters under the rather vague term of the "lost generation," uses Drieu La Rochelle to illustrate this complex state of sensibility characteristic of the 1920's. This comparison is valid so long as one does not carry it too far. One can turn it around to explain Drieu to Americans.

Drieu shares with his American contemporaries, Hemingway, F. Scott Fitzgerald, and the early Dos Passos, certain traits: a vague feeling of nostalgia toward the war years which were, in a way, the "best years of their lives" since they were all born around 1895; a sense of emptiness and unreality in the materialistic, mercantile atmosphere of the prosperous postwar era; a hunger for new values, an urge to start afresh after the liquidation of a lingering but dead past; an effort to forget their fundamental quest for an absolute in the follies

[1] Michel Mohrt, *Le Nouveau roman américain* (Paris, Gallimard, 1955), esp. pp. 18–25 and *passim*.

the empty suitcase

of the "happy" 1920's; an ironical "pursuit of happiness" through alcohol, women, drugs, and all the Baudelairian artificial paradises; and, finally, an obsession with sterility, impotency, leaving a taste of ashes in their mouths and the realization that they had been failures.

Drieu is, with F. Scott Fitzgerald, perhaps the most tragic, authentic embodiment of that lost generation. Not only their work, but their lives are marked, like stigmata, by the main themes of that generation. A parallel might be seen in their destinies: Fitzgerald dying at forty-four after drinking himself to death and Drieu committing suicide at fifty-two. They had both had their doubts about their literary talents: one prostituting his pen in movie-writing, the other one in political journalism.

The great difference between Drieu and the Americans of his generation, however, is that they had a desire to leave their country. Drieu could not disassociate his fate from that of France and his pessimism about France extended to the rest of the planet. He had not the illusion that there was any refuge for him outside the "old" world. Being a Frenchman, he was also more interested in abstract thought and generalizations than American writers. He made an effort to systematize his views and finally saw in decadence the "crushing fact" facing the contemporary French writer.

We must proceed cautiously in approaching the notion of decadence in Drieu. The word itself is ambiguous and Drieu used it to explain so many different things that distinctions must be made. Before trying to clarify Drieu's idea of decadence, we shall examine in this chapter the concrete picture of decadence offered by his fiction in *Plainte contre inconnu* (1924), *Feu Follet* (1931) and *L'Homme couvert de femmes* (1925). Because *Feu follet* deals with the same character as the central story in *Plainte contre inconnu,* we discuss it before *L'homme couvert de femmes,* although it was actually published six years later.

I

"La Valise vide," one of the short stories collected under the general title of *Plainte contre inconnu* first appeared in a summer issue of the *Nouvelle Revue Française,* in 1923. It met with immediate success. Its title became the symbol of the younger generation, for it expressed an inner emptiness that many felt at the time, as well as a sense of rootlessness and a quest for new values, coupled with an urge to travel in the hope that "elsewhere" a solution might be found.

To feel keenly the "emptiness" of the symbolic suitcase one must, paradoxically, have a strong sense of the lack of something which might make it "full." The sense of a lack of something can become so intense that the "absence" assumes almost a positive value: one can talk without paradox of the "presence of the absence." The best illustration of this in poetry is *Les Fleurs du Mal.*

The cruelty with which Drieu makes his characters open their empty suitcases reveals the bitter disappointment of someone who has glimpsed the absolute. The author feels keenly the absence of the intensity and heightened vitality which paradoxically he had experienced only at close quarters with death. In these stories there are constant references to the war, still so recent. The drama, for some of the characters, is to find their energy and thirst for action unemployed. They talk ironically about their war feats, but this irony should not deceive us; a sense of grandeur has undeniably been awakened in them by the war:

> In a narrow but deep domain, we had accomplished deeds. In the blood we had shed we had seen a prodigious love. It was not exhausted. We would have liked to do more.[2]

The author's sense of the tragic appears in apparently innocuous statements when, for instance, describing the pointlessness of one of the character's daily occupations, the narrator notes: "What is the point of it all? Nobody knows. But,

---
[2] *Plainte contre inconnu* (1924), p. 13.

for lack of wars, famines, plagues, the human race must be kept busy."

Most of the characters seem to be busy at destroying themselves. But we must bear in mind that many of Drieu's companions in the early 'twenties, then turbulent dandies of the Dada and surrealist group, were to commit suicide a decade later—Jacques Rigaut, René Crevel. What might be interpreted as a predilection for depicting the morbid aspects of life and of suicidal types of personality may be a faithful portrait of a certain kind of youth in the early 'twenties.

As the title of the collection of short stories indicates, Drieu has no firm belief on which to base his satire. Who or what should be blamed for the ambient decadence? He seems to be as unhappy about himself as about the people he frequents. He instinctively recoils from these people, but he is attracted and repelled at the same time by something which he senses in the atmosphere around him and his friends. He despises the existence he leads but cannot escape it. He knows that something is wrong but cannot define it.

Liessies, in "Le Pique-nique," senses everywhere the smell of death. This makes him angry with his degenerate companions, to the point of desiring their death. His mood is much the same as the one expressed already in a poem of *Fond de Cantine* entitled "Vengeance." It is the mood of a man who has lost all self-respect by permitting his companions to soil with disdain the things he holds sacred:

> The heroes and the saints
> And the pride of dying
> Grave frivolousness
> For an idea.

He feels himself to be even more of a buffoon than his companions. They do not respect him either because they think he is only pretending; they cannot believe that, being "intelligent," he could be that quixotic. He smiles maliciously, and with a benign look makes his secret prayer to the "god of war and revolutions," dedicating to the "just" mouth of powerful guns his good companions.[3]

Liessies foreshadows in many respects the Gille of *L'Homme couvert de femmes:* he is disturbed by the ambient decadence but he is part of it. He is attracted by it. He explains his fascination by his *inquiétude:* he is a hound on the scent of decadence: "... it is impossible to separate Liessies from his restlessness. He must enslave himself to the task of a dog sniffing and uncovering death everywhere." Drieu gives us here one of the most accurate descriptions of the particular aspect of his talent as a *moraliste*.

If Liessies is uncovering death everywhere it is because society around him is attached to obsolete values having too weak a hold to bring about any accomplishment but still strong enough to produce a bad conscience and to prevent a frank exploration of new values. The result is that any enjoyment of life, or blossoming of the personality is spoiled.

Guy La Marche, for instance, an ex-lieutenant in the story "Nous fûmes surpris," hesitates until the last minute between reaction and revolution when faced by the general strike on May 1, 1919. He thinks he is a reactionary. But he does not share the beliefs which were the foundation of the conservative principles of his parents. He does not permit anyone to mock priests in his presence, but he would not dream of going to church. He never talks against the army, but his eagerness to serve is as anachronistic as the parade guard in front of Buckingham Palace. He still reacts according to those principles only as a kind of defense, but his senses are undisciplined and lead him into dangerous experiences in complete contradiction to the principles to which he renders lip service.

Nobody has been more severe in judging his first writings than Drieu himself. From the stories in *Plainte contre inconnu* he intended to reprint in a collection of his early fiction only "La Valise vide," "the only one which was read then and is perhaps still readable."[4] It is very readable indeed, but more

---
[3] "Vengeance," in *Fond de cantine*, p. 38.
[4] Preface to *Ecrits de jeunesse*, p. 7.

as a witty commentary on the early 'twenties than as a short story. There is something of the slidefilm technique in the composition of "La Valise vide": slide after slide gives us the evidence of Gonzague's emptiness, as if a case history were being unfolded. Meanwhile, the commentator seems to tell the audience: "This may seem to you a rather poor comedy of manners. It is not my fault. This is what I see, and I have strictly recorded the facts." A few conversations are also faithfully reproduced. A remark of the author here and there, "He was unknown to me only because of my indifference" (p. 80), shows that he is aware of the limitations of his technique: "I preferred justice to charity" (p. 68). However, under the apparent impassivity of the observer in "La Valise vide" there is more sympathy (or should we say complicity?) than first appears. The warmth of this human reaction is undoubtedly what maintains some life in this tale, even for readers thirty years later. Indeed, Gonzague, the hero of "La Valise vide," must have exercised a fascination on the author, because Drieu found in him—to his horror—certain common traits. One feels all along in the narrative an implicit and anxious comparison in the mind of the narrator: "In what respects am I so different from this monster of weakness and emptiness?"

Gonzague is introduced to the narrator by Gertrude, an affected and snobbish girl, the 1920 version of the eternal *précieuse ridicule*. She is a caricature of all the fads of the time. A great liberty of speech on sex matters is used as a cover for an equally great ignorance and innocence in those matters. She continually uses clichés to praise the poetry of the avant-garde, the cult of the sun bath and of Swedish calisthenics. She expresses a blind admiration for Gonzague, who is "different" and so difficult to define! At first sight, Gonzague, who is very handsome, does not seem witty to the narrator—but then, nobody is. Gonzague goes with the narrator to bars, a circus, other bars. They exchange confidences. He is suffering from a venereal disease and talks about the drawbacks of his situation.

The next time we meet Gonzague, it is in another bar with

a group of men of letters, smoking and drinking. Everybody talks admiringly of Gonzague's new tricks and pastimes. These include kleptomania (involving thefts of the most bizarre objects), alcoholism, cards, and races. He does not know anything, does not read, does not enjoy painting or music. The narrator wishes somebody would oblige him to open this "empty valise" with which he intends to perform magician's tricks.

Gonzague is the secretary of a famous journalist, of whom the author paints a satirical portrait. But he is soon dismissed because he cannot spell. He becomes then the right hand of a businessman, "active in the stock exchange, the press and politics." He loves to gossip with the narrator about their companions but his observations are rudimentary.

A mutual friend expresses some surprise at seeing the narrator often with a young man who is not at all *drôle* and who has a reputation for homosexuality. Two long digressions analyze what is meant by *être drôle* and the nature of the concern with the sexual life of our neighbors. The author thinks that this excessive concern reveals a deep anxiety: people look in each other for the deficiencies which threaten everyone; normalcy has become the exception.

Gonzague does not like his work and seeks only the sensation of passing quickly from one thing to another. He remains outside everything he does. His constant lack of money adds to his anxiety. The final result is that he lives a more narrow life than his bourgeois parents whom he despises. His various attempts at making a fortune, which include writing a pornographic best seller and marrying an heiress, all fail for lack of perseverance.

And yet his life expresses some of the trends of his generation:

The attributes of personality were broken or perverted. The mind created every morning and devoured before evening its daily fad. The will was dodging, seemed to disappear, then suddenly would surge up in some outburst. The passions were not fought but deviated toward unexpected outlets. Unity and continuity had

the empty suitcase

to be broken at all cost. Any violent motion was good provided it gave the sensation of energetic stir: negation, paradox, illogicality, contradiction, all the possible combinations of abstract thought, which are not more numerous than those of love (p. 88).

The fashionable game is *le jeu du chat perché*, where mobility is of the essence. The point is to hop from the extravagant to the bizarre, trying always to be ahead of the next one by a second. All these experiments leave Gonzague sad and he imagines new extremes of action, of which suicide is one. He ridicules the notion that suicide is anything unusual. He says: "On going to bed, instead of turning the light off, absent-mindedly I make a mistake and press the trigger" (p. 92).

The last episode gives the key to the character of Gonzague, and it is characteristic of Drieu's ideas on decadence that it should concern his sexual life.

Gonzague drags the narrator to a sordid brothel, which is the occasion for him to confess the inanity of his love life: he narrates at length the love affair he had during the war, when he was eighteen, with a Madame Lemberg, lamentable *éducation sentimentale* of a third-rate Frédéric Moreau. He had, besides, adopted the worst habits in the army. His captain, who was a pederast, had introduced him to cocaine, and Gonzague cannot remember exactly what happend when he was under the effect of the drug. A whole side of Gonzague's personality can thus be explained by drugs: "Not that he had ever taken much of it, but drugs favor in the milieu in which they are used a great indifference to sexual matters" (p. 118). He has not experienced the great adventure of war: "He had lost a petty little game in a bar or a boudoir, while others were having their great game elsewhere, in heaven and in hell" (p. 119). He exercises no real sensuous attraction for women. The only time he had a normal sexual life was when he lived in a district frequented by prostitutes who solicited him and to whom he could not say "No." Since he moved from that district—even masturbation has become superfluous! Here, the author implies, is the ultimate in emptiness.

II

There is no doubt about the identity of inspiration which dictated "La Valise vide" and *Le Feu follet*. The young man who had served as model for Gonzague in 1923, Jacques Rigaut, committed suicide on November 5, 1929, and Alain, the hero of *Le Feu follet*, does so at the end of the novel. Drieu himself established the connection between the two stories in the Preface to *Gilles:*

> I had begun with a short story "La Valise vide" which was immediately a minute and implacable analysis of the character of a young man molded by the mores and the literature of 1920. I resumed this portrait in a little novel, *Le Feu follet*, in which, in accord with the fatality as I saw it, the traits were accentuated and the logic of the character resulted in suicide.[5]

Again he blamed the times for the somberness of the picture in his novel; he had only reported faithfully on what was happening to a part of French youth.

The title was equally symbolic, with an even more definite reference to decomposition and decadence. Alain shares with the will-o'-the-wisp a certain lack of substance, a lightness and a fleetingness not without charm. He is the emanation of a rotting society. He seems sometimes to be one of those "flowers of evil" imagined by Baudelaire, who had placed drugs, suicide, and alcohol among the forbidden means offered to man to break the walls of his prison.

The technique used to present Alain is very different from that of "La Valise vide." The author adopts the omniscient point of view and we follow Alain's intimate thoughts and reactions. It is a picture from the inside. The author has imagined with a horrified fascination the situation of a man who has decided to end his life and who sees everything and everybody in the special light of impending death. There is such an appeal for Drieu in this particular situation that his imagination goes back to it again and again. In one form or another it finds a literary transposition in all his novels.

---

[5] Preface to *Gilles* (1942), p. iv.

the empty suitcase

The theme of suicide is the most important one in the book and drugs are only an expression of it. It is the first step on the way to self-destruction, and Alain keeps in the same place the syringe and the pistol. He knows that they are inseparable and that one leads to the other. For Alain is attempting for the third time to be cured of drug addiction in a sanitarium. The episode of heroin injection means the final surrender of his will to live. Drugs are only the symbol of his refusal of life. Alain does not want to make the compromises which are indispensable in order to live: compromises with women "who are neither very beautiful nor very kind," or with work, "this boring and mostly useless work which fills our cities with its vain agitation" (p. 111). Drugs are for him a form of mystical revolt against death, an adoration of nothingness. Thus, drug addicts are the necessary product of a deep human urge in a time of general fatigue.

The drug addicts are the mystics of a materialistic age which—not having any longer the strength to animate and sublimate things into symbols—undertake the opposite work of reduction, wear them down and gnaw them to their core of nothingness (p. 112).

The outside world seems hardly to exist which is in keeping with Alain's character. He has never paid any attention to the décor: "He was living in the empty rooms of ethics: the world is imperfect, the world is bad. I disapprove, I condemn, I annihilate the world" (p. 140).

When the book opens Alain is already at the end of his rope and the narration of the last three days of his life has the simplicity of an ancient tragedy progressing without any relief to an ineluctable denouement.

Alain is a product of a society in the state of decomposition already mentioned in reference to *Plainte contre inconnu*. Alain has rejected with horror the traditions of his family but he has inherited the prejudices of his bourgeois background, especially about money. In the lower middle-class family to which he belonged, a quiet, leisurely life was necessary to cultivate the ego. Money came from inheritance, a sinecure, and marriage. Caught between two sets of values, Alain refuses to adapt to the law of "forced labor" imposed by modern life and clings to the tradition of money coming from other sources than work. He is lazy and so far he has exploited women, not without a sense of guilt: he is a *bourgeois désaffecté*. "Alain was indeed the disaffected bourgeois denounced by his friend: seeing the vices germinated by his prejudices but unable, because of his prejudices, to enjoy his vices" (p. 115).

But Alain has no longer any hold on women. He cannot make Lydia, an American divorcée, stay in France and he is in the process of being divorced from his American wife, Dorothy. He is left alone with his worst enemy, himself, and a ten thousand franc check which Lydia has just given him after making love in a shabby Parisian hotel room. She has insisted that they ought to get married but he has sensed that she is afraid of his drug addiction.

An interruption of his terrible habit had permitted his marriage to Dorothy. But he relapsed, and this time the hold of the drug was stronger, with unavoidable regularity, increased doses, and closer intervals. Frightened, he had tried a thorough cure of disintoxication. Besides the humiliation of the sanitarium, the cure was illusory. What was left of life in him was impregnated by drugs and led him back to drugs. And yet he had no longer any pleasure in taking the drug, for he recognized the mediocre trap it was. The life of drug addicts had all the characteristics of the kind of life he hated, "settled, sedentary, sedate." "A routine of old maids, united in a common devotion, chaste, bitter, gossipy, turning away with a scandalized look when their religion was criticized" (p. 56). The terror he had of that life gave Alain enough courage to try one last time to get rid of the drug habit.

The description of the patients in Dr. de la Barbinais' rest home is a striking picture of decadence. Mademoiselle Farnoux, a rich heiress, has so little vitality left that she has to retire half of the time to a sanitarium to recuperate from an already rarefied existence. The Marquis d' Averseau, scion of a family belonging to the highest nobility, has written a book the title of which indicates clearly where his interests lie: "Histoire des Princes français qui furent sodomites." Mademoiselle Cournot is another example of sexual abnormality: enormous, monstrously tall, she is continually devoured by a desire for men. M. Moraire and M. Brème are both financiers; one is Catholic, the other Jewish, and they perpetually discuss points of religion together. Madame de la Barbinais, the doctor's wife, is really mad. Their conversation around the dinner table is not calculated to cheer Alain! When he retires to his own room, it looks like the "ideal prison." "The door and the window did not open on anything. The mirror opened only on himself."

He sees through the doctor's illusory reassurances: "The doctor, in order to get away from lugubrious thoughts, turned toward a future in which everything would get better." Alain sees only hypocrisy in the doctor's calling on his will power, since modern science denies the existence of will power: "Individual will power is the myth of another age: a race worn out by civilization cannot believe in will power" (p. 57). Finally, how could the doctor convince Alain that life is good? Is he convinced of it himself?

Literature cannot be his salvation. We see him, at his desk, tempted to do some writing; a title on a sheet, "Le voyageur sans billet," reminds him of a confession he has started. But people in the literary circles among which he has spent his youth have taught him only contempt for literature. And since he has experienced little of life, he can see in it nothing but a pointless exercise: "He had no idea of a deeper, necessary quest in which a man needs art in order to fix his traits, his directions ... he might have conceived ... the function of writing which is to put some order in the world so that one can live." Alain added a few paragraphs: "For the first time in his life, he put a semblance of order in his feelings and immediately he breathed a little, he ceased to choke under those feelings which were simple, but which had become entangled, knotted, for lack of being delineated" (p. 82). But Alain is quickly tired and stops writing.

One of his friends, Urcel, is a writer and an opium smoker, who rationalizes his situation. Alain's bitter irony pierces through all the sophisms with which Urcel tries to dupe himself. Urcel claims that drugs are a form of risk, at the limit of life and death; life itself is a horrible intoxication and drugs introduce human beings into another world. At least, Alain does not want to go through such reasoning to make of his weakness a kind of strength: "He preferred to stiffen to the point of breaking." His only consolation for being in such a company is the certainty of dying soon.

Alain's other friends cannot relieve his solitude. Dubourg, for instance, who shared with Alain a rather dissolute youth, is now married, has two daughters, and devotes himself to the study of the ancient religions of Egypt. To Alain, this retreat among papyri looks like a slow, dull death. Dubourg tries to get to the root of Alain's despair and indeed he can explain Alain but he is unable to make the effort of love which would recreate Alain in his heart. He cannot admire Alain or approve of his life, but then he should offer him an example of greater strength, something to admire. He fails to do so, and therefore Alain's failure is his own failure: "Dubourg's attitude, among other pretexts, gave Alain every reason to die: life through this example had not managed to justify itself" (p. 120). Dubourg represents only a barrier of words between Alain and death.

People who are successful in terms of the world like the brutal adventurer, Marc Brancion, back from Asia, whom Alain meets at his friends, the Lavaux, do not offer a model of humanity either. And the Lavaux themselves, so full of solicitude for him, how indifferent they really are. What brutes men are. Men attached to their tasks: Egyptology, religion, literature, or men attached to money, men who attract women. Always lucid, the *bourgeois désaffecté* confesses to himself his own weakness: "If I kill myself, it is because I am not a successful brute."

But Alain has to see a picture of himself, an even degraded version of himself to get thoroughly disgusted with his last

the empty suitcase

illusions of *dandy spleenetique*. He meets Milou, a kind of Parisian bar-fly, and they meditate on their fate: they are not taken seriously by other people because they are too sensitive, thinks Milou. But Alain is aware that his solitude comes from his inability really to love.

How is it possible to love other people? They like to lie too much. Everyone is the dupe of some illusion. Those who have a profession are the dupes of their profession; those who do not work, like themselves, secretly believe that if they do not work, it is because they are more *délicats* than the others. They are now walking along the Champs-Elysées and a curious reference to Baudelaire subtly indicates that art only could justify their parasitic existence. They meet an old prostitute and Alain tells her: "In case you see M. Baudelaire, say good night to him" and she replies: "M. Baudelaire! Who do you think I am? He is an artist" (p. 204).

When he wakes up the next morning, Alain, who has again taken some heroin without the least pleasure, sees the prospect of the same routine repeating itself over and over again: "Life was not going fast enough in me, I accelerate it. The curve was bending. I straighten it. I am a man. I am the master of my skin, I prove it" (p. 213). He sits down on his bed, his breast bare: "A revolver, that's something hard. At last, I'll get in touch with the object" (p. 213).

The plot is not very important. What matters is Alain's quest for a reason to live and his failure to find any reason. In that respect *Le Feu follet* opens the series of the great books of the 'thirties sounding the depths of the more somber side of man's fate. Alain, being a kind of outlaw who refuses to follow the rules of the social game, sees through the lack of sincerity of people around him. Everybody is vaguely frightened by Alain's possible outburst of truthfulness—a truthfulness which does not admit any compromise since it measures everything with the authentic detachment of someone who has chosen death as the alternative to an unsatisfactory world. Alain—although he is a social nonentity—denounces the world of *salauds* in which he lives: "Liars, liars!

They know that sincerity is not possible and yet they talk about it. They talk about it, the bastards" (p. 195).

The fascination for death must have been what interested Drieu in Jacques Rigaut's fate and what allowed him to reconstruct with so much sympathy the last hours of that almost perfect case history of decadence in its most virulent form: self-destruction. Although *Le Feu follet* represents one of his major efforts at fictional objectivity, one can see that Drieu had injected a large part of himself into the character of Alain. Although in "La Valise vide," he had given a portrait of Gonzague in the tone of a comedy of manners, Alain is a tragic figure sympathetically treated.

The characters in later novels will have wider scope and meaning for the average reader. Gilles, in his many incarnations will reveal more facets of contemporary society and therefore more facets of the decadence, corruption, and hypocrisy which Drieu hated. But none of the later characters or novels will have a more chilling impact. The narrowness of *Le Feu follet* that Drieu imposed on himself by following rather closely the *fait-divers* of Jacques Rigaut's suicide, lends it a certain effectiveness. The smell of death is there.

III

L'Homme couvert de femmes (1925) is a bad novel but a good document about the early 'twenties and an illuminating presentation of the main symptoms of what Marcel Arland around 1924 called *"un nouveau mal du siècle."*[6]

Drieu's first novel gives the impression that the author is groping to find himself, just as he is groping to find a formula for his novel. Drieu was aware of the danger which threatened him as a novelist: his irrepressible tendency to write only about himself. He admitted this defect in a manner characteristic of him by writing about himself in the act of writing, by making a confession of how he had written a confession and had failed to write a novel. It is the "L'Histoire d'un

---

[6] Marcel Arland, "Sur un nouveau mal du siècle," *NRF*, No. 125 (February, 1924), 156.

roman" inserted in *Le Jeune Européen,* published two years later, in 1927.

Drieu's account tells how, after writing about himself, about his past, the desire came to him to write about someone else. He was disturbed by his solitude, by his inability to reach women whom he loved to madness. The basic theme, therefore, was "I don't know how to love women"; but through his pedantic habit of "explaining things before looking at them," he generalized the theme into, "Men don't know how to love women," and he soon added, "Neither do women, men." And finally, following the lessons of his "old teacher," who had crammed dried-out notions into his head, he decided: "I am going to demonstrate why a man and a woman of today do not understand each other."

As Drieu himself comments: why "why"? And why "of today"? He chose as his heroine a type of woman he knew very little and did not particularly like, so that he would be obliged to invent her almost entirely and thus enter into the realm of the imaginary, where he could find at last a refreshing change from his egocentrism. Unfortunately, he did not do the same for his hero: he was unable to escape from his own personality. He intended to modify the traits borrowed from himself or from his past.

But as soon as he started thinking about himself, he was unable to think about anything else and things got out of hand.

As soon as I got close to the paper, my pen started to run, and, overflowing the barriers I had planned, an imperious confession swelled its impatient stream. At the end of three days, I had written a hundred pages, two hundred pages after seven days. My whole sexual odyssey unfolded itself, bold, miserable, every one of its sordid or sumptuous episodes was related with a naïve desire to be complete.[7]

Gille's confession of adolescent experiences which explain why he feels that he cannot have love relations with anyone but a prostitute is actually a continuation of the experiences

---

[7] *Le Jeune Européen,* p. 66.

of the boy in *Etat-Civil*. The author had left little Cogle, at the age of eighteen, on the eve of the "unavoidable crisis of romanticism." He takes up this story with Gille, showing the shattering of a young man's dreams of love when in his eighteenth year he experiences physical love with a prostitute.

Gille's romanticism is essentially the same as Cogle's: it consists of a dissociation between dream and reality. In the matter of love, an unbridgeable gap between aspirations for unsubstantially pure vision and the garish reality of a sordid prostitution establishes itself in him. Deprived of any contact with women outside his family, he has been reduced to dreaming and reading about them. The absence of social life in his home has deprived him of the two usual "safety valves" of a young bourgeois: the "ice box" constituted by social life, such as dancing with some "jeunes filles," or the comfortable adulterous love affair with an older married woman. Abandoned to the resources of a big city, Gille develops an early taste for brothels. He seems to enjoy there a masochistic humiliation of his pride:

> Children are like barbarians: skipping all the degrees of depravity, they are capable of going straight to the lowest one and feed on it with great appetite. I was possessed by a fulgurating desire for ugliness (p. 118).

Gille's access of impotence when trying to make love to a "respectable" woman, his hostess Finette, is only one symptom among many in the book illustrating the various disorders of sex. Gille has been invited to Finette's luxurious country house by her brother Luc, who is a homosexual. Guests come and go and engage in amusing love affairs. The novel starts in the light tone of the early Huxley novels with the same set of rather empty characters who cannot take anything seriously. But Gille introduces a tragic tone: he is not satisfied with himself nor with his companions. His curiosity about all forms of humanity, his desire to be liked by everybody, his liberal attitude lead him to mix with corrupt people. The fascination of destruction explains even better his choice of companions.

the empty suitcase

... because he preferred a virulent vice which showed vivaciousness and the rapidity of violent death to a virtue made of vital fatigue which made him think of an endless old age (p. 63).

But when he sees with his own eyes the perversion of basic instincts, Gille, like Liessies in *Plainte contre inconnu,* cannot help cursing the devilish distortion of human nature. He is all the more upset about sex perversions because he wonders if his sterile quest is not very similar to Luc's. His own sexual life, considered "normal," if excessive by his contemporaries, presents a strange resemblance to Luc's homosexuality.

On the physical plane, Gille is obsessed by the images of feminine shapes, Luc by masculine ones. The idolatrous cult for those images is basically the same. The form of a body is only a sign, associated with sexual gratification. The sign has become more important than the pleasure for Gille. Originally, the sexual pleasure was the main thing, because it meant a participation in creation: "The enthusiasm of God, the thunder of inspiration from which surges the world, the frenzy of Creation go through man in this formidable instant of the deluge of blood" (p. 189).

To refuse, or to be unable, to conceive the "act of life" in all its implications, breaks the connection of man with trees and stars and makes him unable to create either children or gods. The sexual act becomes for Gille—and the modern man—a "meaningless prayer." "The prayer has no longer any sap, it is a desiccated formula muttered in a senile way."

It is worthy of notice that in order to describe the decadence of sex Drieu uses some of the key words, or key concepts, which characterize for him all decadence: the words are *résidu* (residue), *desséché* (dried out), *privé de sève* (deprived of sap), to emphasize the idea of something that offers only the appearance of a life vanished long before.

On the sentimental plane, the mad rush of Luc passing from one human being to another, seems frightening to Gille. He must admit that similarly, under the pretext of looking for the right woman, the quick succession of his love affairs looks like a search for the sake of searching. He does not, however, enjoy the multiplicity of his experiences. He would like to escape the "law of numbers," put an end to the list or famous "catalogue" of Mozart's Don Giovanni. After his alarming crisis of impotency—is it merely reëxamination of his past, or because of a need to reassure himself?—Gille establishes his own list.

Gille ... undertook writing on the back of playing cards a complete list of all the women he had had. How poor were the first years, but from year to year how it grew (p. 99).

He wants to find the irreplaceable woman with whom he will escape the tiring and never-ending succession of affairs. He definitely puts permanence above constant renewing: "In this little mirror, I can evoke in depth more diversity of passions than Don Juan in the whole course of his long career" (p. 195). Don Juan must have been desperate to find out that there were so many souls and that he would never exhaust their number. Gille, not feeling that he has Juan's "genius," cannot usurp the privilege of God, "who, alone, can give himself to everyone without becoming thereby the most prostituted as Baudelaire was inclined to believe." He must limit himself to the exploration of one soul. The miracle of the "incredible communication" between two souls which constitutes an opening on eternity is preferable to the endless succession in time.

Without the coming of a child, however, the woman loses her function of "tie between heaven and earth." She symbolizes for Gille the union of body and soul; she holds an essential place in the economy of man.

But the child is the evidence of the reality of love because it is creation of life, "a new and unexpected aspect of the world which is neither one of the parents and both of them." It establishes at the same time a link with the ancestors. Gille uses the vocabulary of religion—in this case the vocabulary of Catholic orthodoxy—to describe this solemn mystery: "And all the ancestors, communion of the three churches, militant, suffering, triumphant, participate" (p. 200). He condemns, therefore, the facility of Don Juan's "conquests": however modest, every conquest must be deserved. Don Juan has not been loved because he never took enough time to love, and one is loved only so far as one is able to give love.

Gille flees Finette's house, in which he senses a putrefaction corresponding to his inner degeneracy. He is going to explore the possibilities of a life centered on one woman, the wife, the mother of his children. The theme of *Drôle de voyage*, which deals with Gille's attempt to love a "jeune fille," is also announced at the end of *L'Homme couvert de femmes*. Gille says: "No, really, I loathe 'bourgeoises' women of the world... I can stand only prostitutes... or perhaps girls? I'll have to try" (p. 207). In the meantime, he goes back to a savage and tortured solitude.

In spite of its unevenness, *L'Homme couvert de femmes* is not without merits. Drieu was more severe in his judgment than any critics had been.[8] All the many descriptions of physical love are powerful and bold in their precision but never lewd nor in bad taste. In later novels, Drieu introduced similar descriptions with more restraint, but gave them greater meaning by making them part of the development of the action. They stand a little by themselves in the first Gille novel and are not always devoid of the defiant tone of "morceaux de bravoure." The very defects of *L'Homme couvert de femmes*, as a novel, turn into virtues if the book is considered as a document on the times. Gille's uncertainty, his contradictions, his unsolved dilemmas, his vague aspirations expressed sometimes in rather obscure jargon, may be considered as defects in a novel; these traits might have been better used as themes of poems in a collection of *méditations*, corresponding to those of Lamartine more than a century earlier. But does not Gille, and, through a too transparent veil, his author, present some of the symptoms of a *nouveau mal du siècle?* The opening of any new age of sensibility is marked by extremes and its literary expression dates quickly. It requires a great effort today to

[8] Robert Kemp pointed this out in his review of *Le Jeune Européen*, *Revue Universelle*, July 15, 1927, p. 243.

read *René* from cover to cover. Marcel Arland, in the article already mentioned, foresaw in 1924 what may surprise the reader of today about the literature of his day:

> It is possible that one day such torments will appear naïve and that people will be surprised by that taste for moral suffering, for this masochism, for this "inquietude" which leads us to rather peculiar attempts.[9]

Marcel Arland considers that the central problem which baffles his generation is the problem of God. One of the words which is most often used in *L'Homme couvert de femmes* is "Dieu." Gille has no opportunity of expatiating on the subject. His interlocutors, Luc, and especially Finette, who is an admirer of *Candide,* stop him when he starts using what Finette terms a "mystical gabble." In spite of his reserve, it is possible to see that for Gille, God is the symbol of all metaphysical research, or a notion of the divine detached from any orthodoxy. He makes clear that he intends first to explore what the earth has to offer: "Gille will finally be able to go to God but only after ploughing the earth for a long time because the soul is, after all, made of two hands" (p. 202). If belated, his surrender to God, his renouncing all earthly ambitions, will be total: "[My wife] . . . will understand that I admit God [in our home] and little by little, He will absorb everything and ravish me" (p. 202). He insists that the "season for God" must come after the "season of souls."

Among other symptoms, Marcel Arland points out the oscillation between the two extremes of anarchy and order. Gille oscillates between two opposite ideals corresponding to those extremes transposed on the plane of love: the ideal of complete freedom ("no woman can reasonably deprive a man of all other women and all other interests"); and the ideal of loyalty to a single woman ("a whole life is not too much to know a single soul").

What also characterizes Gille is his search for the absolute. It explains his idleness, and even his laziness, to which he is so often referring: "I am not doing anything, but let me de-

---
[9] Arland, *op. cit.*, p. 156.

pend on this single word of life, on this tearing hook; only the absolute deserves to live" (p. 154). This search for the absolute is exemplified by the two extreme (and therefore impossible) ideals of love just mentioned. To aim at the impossible leads necessarily to suffering; the hero displays always the same deep-seated masochism.

What distinguishes the twentieth century "mal du siècle" from that of the nineteenth is a frantic attempt to be lucid. In *Plainte contre inconnu* Drieu had already noted: "The fashion is too much to be antiromantic for us not to have our most languid clouds crossed by a lucid flash of lightning." All the characters in the novel analyze in great detail the motivations of their behavior. Even when he does not reach any conclusions, Gille seems to have the impression that by self-analysis he achieves greater insight into himself. He has a cult for sincerity. Marcel Arland had been a good prophet in announcing in 1924: "Toward an absolute sincerity—such is no doubt the orientation of the four or five individuals who suffice to represent, if not express, a whole generation."[10] This sincerity sometimes borders on exhibitionism in *L'Homme couvert de femmes*.

Drieu is not yet reconciled with the limitations that the writer imposed on the man in him. "L'Histoire d'un roman" shows that the composition of *L'Homme couvert de femmes* took place at a time when he was most acutely torn between being a writer and being "a well-rounded man" (*un homme réussi*). In this he was quite representative of his generation, and he would have endorsed Marcel Arland's revolutionary statement: "Before all literature, there is an object which interests me most: myself."[11] Clearly, the man had some difficulty in disappearing behind the author, and this was at the expense of the novel. And yet, we must recognize with Drieu that here and there a page has the stamp of originality because some of his "blood" rather than his "ink" has flowed into it. One of the main defects of the novel is that the various dis-

[10] *Ibid.*
[11] *Ibid.*, p. 155.

orders in love relations between men and women analyzed as a particular aspect of decadence are artificially separated from other forms of decadence. This defect will have disappeared, eight years later, in *Drôle de voyage,* the second Gille novel in which the sexual aspect of decadence will still hold a central place but will be explained and reinforced by a picture of decadence encompassing all the other forms of human activity: art, politics, religion. Between 1925 and 1933 Drieu had meditated on this idea of decadence and had tried to elucidate it in various nonfiction works which should be considered briefly before going on to *Drôle de voyage.*

IV

In *Le Jeune Européen* (1927) Drieu writes: "I suffer to be the man of today, the man who feels threatened ... the man who is going to drown ... I am desperate. I, the European, I still love all the things I despair of." This statement characterizes the mood of most of Drieu's nonfiction works of the decade 1920–1930. In them, Drieu seems to have adopted a more or less Spenglerian view of history. He explains the dissatisfaction he feels toward his time, his contemporaries, himself by the fact that the civilization to which he belongs has entered a period of decadence. This civilization is no longer able to create anything new—its apparent life consists of the last movements of its agony and this agitation is self-destructive. The war experience had confirmed this view. We saw in the previous chapter, how Drieu had been repulsed by modern war as an expression of modern civilization with its devilishly inhuman machinery. As is usually true with Drieu, the exposition of his ideas is mixed with a genesis of those ideas, he tries always to qualify his positions by explaining how he has reached them. His personal problems are inextricably intertwined with the problems of his time. *Genève ou Moscou,* for instance, strikes the reader by its very personal tone and the first title that Drieu had intended for the book is indicative of the method: *Confessions d'un Français.* Constantly the author tries to find an explanation of his difficulties in an examination of the times and, conversely, an explanation of what is wrong with the times in self-analysis. He was encouraged to use this method by all those who saw in him a "witness" of his generation, all the more representative, that he presented an extreme case of the general illness: the symptoms could be more easily identified in him because they were magnified. As early as 1925, for instance, Ramon Fernandez could write:

Drieu is the one who, in an epidemic, is stricken more completely, more definitively than the others—the one we must not leave for a moment if we want to understand.[12]

How did Drieu come to see in decadence the "crushing fact" facing modern man and, therefore, the contemporary writer?

Drieu's own family, from what we read in *Etat-Civil*,[13] had provided the example of people turned toward the past and deploring the present in politics, art, and religion. They were, almost as a matter of principle, against everything modern: democracy as well as industrial plutocracy, the leaders of the Third Republic as well as liberal Catholicism. They were sulking and deliberately ignored the present. They were nationalists and worried about France's international status. They had a vague nostalgia for the past, all the more vague and all the more violent in that they did not participate in the building of a new France. The young Drieu, "grandson of a defeat," had inherited the view that France was on the downgrade and that its future was somber. Thus, the "idea of decadence" which Drieu recognized as part of his *Etat-Civil* and bourgeois inheritance, was rather a complex emotional attitude than an intellectual notion.

His intellectual formation reinforced this pessimistic view of the present. In 1922, the answers he gave to an inquiry about the literary masters of the then young writers help us place him in a certain tradition of thought:

[12] *NRF*, No. 136 (January, 1925), 104–106.
[13] And also in an article, "L'Idée de décadence," first published in 1928 in *La Revue Européenne* and collected in *Genève ou Moscou*, pp. 225–230.

On the eve of my baccalaureate, I read, as a form of relaxation, the *Pages de Sociologie* by Bourget. Suddenly I discovered reaction in them. I read Maurras, *L'Action française*, Bainville, Georges Sorel, and, through them, I got in touch with the long chain of French reactionaries: Bonald, Maistre, Balzac, Barbey, Villiers. All came to multiply the formidable impact made on me at Oxford, when I was sixteen by Nietzsche. Thinking back on it, I admire the way in which everything conspired to give me a reactionary formation.[14]

In the same interview, Drieu notes in the daily life of his contemporaries a contradiction between their conservative doctrines and their licentious behaviour:

I was receiving in books a strong doctrine of conservatism or restoration, but in the mores and in what passes from the mores into books, the most destructive examples of individual folly, of unleashed passions. This contradiction, which was in my masters, in Barrès, is the very portrait of France today.

The main literary influence on Drieu around 1922 was, by Drieu's own admission, Barrès and every year he reread a whole cycle of his works. This admiration was shared then by most of the young writers, Montherlant, Malraux, Mauriac who, like Drieu, had also known the contrasting influences of Maurras and Gide. In Barrès' work, Drieu was particularly sensitive to the obsession with death and the fascination with decadence. And yet Drieu tried to escape the fascination of the man who had said that "there is nothing more beautiful in the world than a man falling to pieces." In a letter to Henri Massis in 1923, Drieu judged the ideological development of Barrès with the severity of one who has thoroughly penetrated a former master.

Each year, I reread a few books by Barrès and the older I get, the more I admire the writer and the less I am satisfied by the thinker. It is most likely because we have entirely assimilated whatever nourishment there was in him. But his subjectivism perfectly sure of itself—I have to make a historical effort to stand it. There is a considerable confusion in his *culte du moi* and also some

---

[14] Henri Rambaud and Pierre Varillon, "Enquête sur les maîtres de la jeune littérature," *La Revue Hebdomadaire*, No. 44 (November 4, 1922), 91.

difficulty in hiding this confusion. Finally, later, the objects to which Barrès attached himself, after he had found a somewhat objective method, seem to me insufficient and poorly related. In his *cult of the dead,* for instance, there remains too much of his romantic taste for death."[15]

André Gide did not think that Drieu had succeeded in shaking off the influence of Barrès. After mentioning in a page of his *Journal* of 1927 a conversation with Drieu about the latter's second marriage, he notes:

> All these young men are frightfully concerned with themselves. Barrès was their very bad master; his teaching leads to despair, to boredom. It is to get away from this that many among them hurl themselves headlong into Catholicism, as *he* threw himself into politics. All this will be severely judged twenty years from now.[16]

It is a fact that Drieu was very much under the spell of Barrès. Like Barrès, he could not resist the temptation to engage in politics as well as in literature. There can even be found a certain parallelism in their political adventures: Barrès' infatuation for General Boulanger can be considered as a manifestation of fascism before the term was invented.

But Drieu refused to play the role of "embalmer" of the past which the president of the Patriots' League had finally played; he preferred the road of destruction and revolution. His attitude was essentially agonistic: even the things he most dearly cherished had to be put to the test of battle and possible destruction. Only what survives is really worthy of life and not a mere pretense. All the rest is decadence, is marked for destruction and should be destroyed.

This French civilization which Drieu felt to be at its height, in which he saw symptoms of decadence, should not be exploited as literature but should rather disappear if it is moribund: violent death is preferable to senility. This attitude explains the severe examination to which he submitted France in *Mesure de la France,* the logical sequence to the anxious

---

[15] Henri Massis, *Maurras et notre temps,* p. 258; for Drieu's attitude at the "Barrès trial," see pp. 141-142.
[16] *The Journals of André Gide,* translated by Justin O'Brien (New York, Alfred A. Knopf, 1948), II, 409.

Interrogation of 1917. What is the exact meaning of the victory of 1918? Is it not a delusion leading to further delusions? Drieu was full of fear but he had not yet given up every hope Decadence can be diagnosed when a country is no longer able to affirm its beliefs by muscular expression and when it enters the road of self-destruction both by sterility and by a suicidal misuse of whatever resources are left, when, in a word, the instinct of conservation is compromised. Just as the author of *Interrogation* wanted his full realization as an individual in both dream and action, a living country must want more than dreams of past grandeur or delusions about its future.

The disciple of Nietzsche is recognizable here: one of the main symptoms of decadence denounced by the author of the *Will to Power* is the search for compensation of present deficiencies or impotence in an "after world," a "world beyond," a metaphysical world where the sanction of the real is avoided. Drieu's lifelong concern with Nietzsche is revealed by references to Nietzsche in almost every one of his books. From *Etat-Civil*, in which he acknowledges with gratitude the debt of his youth to the creator of Zarathustra, to *Les Chiens de paille*, in which he introduces a long meditation on Nietzsche's theory of decadence, Drieu gives evidence that the great German's thought was always a constant ferment for his own.[17] The Nietzschean influence is particularly noticeable in Drieu's ideas on decadence.

For instance, the "pessimism of the strong" described by Nietzsche as a relentless lucidity in identifying the symptoms of decadence applies very well to Drieu. In the *Origin of Tragedy*, Nietzsche wonders whether a certain kind of pessimism is necessarily a symptom of decline, of decadence, of the failure of worn out and weakened instincts. Is there not also a pessimism of the strong, an intellectual predilection for horror, for cruelty, for the uncertainty of existence, owing to an excess of health, of life, of strength? Drieu reconciles both

[17] It is interesting to note the same lasting preoccupation with Nietzsche in Malraux. Nietzsche, already mentioned in Malraux's "D'Une jeunesse européenne" (in *Ecrits, Les Cahiers verts*, Paris, Grasset, 1927), is introduced in *Les Noyers de l'Altenburg* (Lausanne, 1943), as a character.

the empty suitcase

explanations. Since the ambient decadence is inescapable, he finds its stigmata in himself. His drama, however, is to feel more strength in himself than remains in the society around him.

It seems that at first Drieu interpreted very literally Nietzsche's *Will to Power*. He hoped for worldly glory within the framework of the country. For instance, he writes in *Genève ou Moscou*: "As for me, both during the war and since the war, I have sought in the nation a principle which would allow me to live" (p. 104). In *Les Chiens de paille*, Constant, the character who represents best an aging Drieu, identifies with Judas, of whom he says: "In his youth, in his ardor, in his early faith... he had wanted the conquest, the victory, the earthly triumph" (p. 141). His political essay of 1928, *Genève ou Moscou*, shows an important evolution in his thinking. He had to admit that the *patries* as such were dying, even as Rome and Greece and Babylon had died. However painful this might be, Drieu said, we must accept the fact and even accelerate the process; for Europe is to be our new *patrie*.

In *Genève ou Moscou* Drieu admitted that he made of his life two parts. Deep down, he prepared himself to sacrifice the ideal of a unified Europe as he had already sacrificed the ideal of a powerful France; he accepted the mortality of every earthly thing, including the civilization which had given meaning to his life. He retired from the human community in its social and political aspects and he took refuge in contemplation. But this mystical retreat, so characteristic of decadence according to Nietzschean standards, affected only half his personality: the secret, inner one. It was the painful, ardent secret of his heart. In his outward life, he remained passionately interested in the metamorphoses of life, hoping for the renewals which follow dissolutions and decadences. Europe seemed to be the new form adopted by the spirit for its embodiment.

By dividing his life into two parts, one in the world, the other on a contemplative plane, Drieu tried to combine the two attitudes which had the greatest prestige for him: that of the hero and that of the saint. Here again Drieu was following the footsteps of Nietzsche. He was to say of his master in his last novel:

What a marvelous combination Nietzsche had offered of the extreme detachment of Buddhism and Taoism with the indelible pragmatism of the West.[18]

This "indelible pragmatism of the Western world" is seriously questioned by Drieu, at least in its aims. All the traditional values which had so far justified the activity of Western men and insured their supremacy on the planet seem suddenly to be without foundations. In the *Will to Power* Nietzsche had analyzed what he called "the process of decomposition." On one hand, he said, accepted moral values make us condemn existence, because they are contrary to the essence of life; they are artificial rules imposed by the herd and made to flatter its weaknesses (all the analyses of the *Genealogy of Morals* and of *Human, All too Human* tended to establish that fact). On the other hand, when we lose the support of accepted morality (when God is dead) we remain poisoned by it, our psychological reactions being determined by it, and we are not liberated in the least. We have lost our main stimulus, ethics, and especially Christian ethics, the latter being an antidote against practical and theoretical nihilism, according to Nietzsche.

Drieu expressed in all his books of that period, but more particularly in *Le Jeune Européen*, his anxieties about the liquidations of the Western spiritual inheritance.[19] *Le Jeune Européen* is dedicated to André Breton with a quotation from the latter's *Légitime défense:* "Our mission is perhaps only to liquidate a spiritual succession which it would be in the interest of everyone to renounce."

This sets the theme of the whole book, which finds its summary in a dramatic dialogue, "Dialogue de moi avec un autre,"

---

[18] *Les Chiens de paille*, p. 123.
[19] At the same time Malraux expresses very similar views in "D'Une jeunesse européenne" (p. 135); for example, "Of all the marks we bear, the Christian one made in the flesh of our very flesh, like a scar, is the deepest one."

in which the two conflicting tendencies of reaction and revolution existing in Drieu's own mind find their expression: "All the values on which we live, disappear. This system of the world which was perpetuating itself in the mental entrails of mankind is going to be annihilated; it is the very next happening in the cosmic novel," says his conservative self, while his other self is turned toward the future: ". . . in the present state mysterious causes are germinating which will engender unexpected consequences. You cannot condemn absolutely a future which has only surprises in store for you."[20]

Drieu's agonistic conception of life made him wish to put to the test of battle this present civilization, even if it meant his own destruction. This explains why between 1920 and 1925 he was so close to the surrealists with their emphasis on sheer destruction. In *La Suite dans les idées*, which best reveals the evidences of surrealist influence, most of the poems and essays are an invitation to burn one's bridges behind one. "Whether this civilization is dead or alive, we must want to kill it."[21]

It is from this particular point of view of destruction and because of the challenge that it represented for bourgeois civilization that Drieu was tempted by communism. While Blaquans, of *Blèche*, is trying "to perpetuate the principles of the old civilization of Paris," Marcel Boutros, in *Une Femme à sa fenêtre* is a Communist agent.

Drieu wrote later about that period of his life: "I thought of becoming a Communist, to precipitate decadence, the end of everything, to drive everybody against the wall, especially the working class."[22]

The orthodoxy of such a communist would have been most questionable. He may have advocated violence; Drieu was too lucid not to know that it was alien to his true nature. We touch

---

[20] "Le Jeune Européen," in *Ecrits de jeunesse*, pp. 240–241.

[21] *Ecrits de jeunesse*, p. 168. The same book contains, however, an implicit criticism of the *Umwertung aller Werte*: ". . . a city can be razed, a book can be burned, but a brain cannot be turned inside out overnight, nor washed with a single sponge wiping" (p. 169).

[22] *Le Français d'Europe* (1944), p. 127.

here one of the contradictions of Drieu's theory, as well as of Nietzsche's theory, of decadence. The denouncer of decadence is admittedly a decadent himself. When all the categories have been destroyed, when all the values of morality have been refused, on what authority, by what standards can anyone decide what is decadent and what is not? Nietzsche is aware of the contradiction.[23] Drieu is almost obsessed by it. Following the supreme commandment of Nietzsche's ethic, he never recoiled from lucidity about himself, however painful it was. One has the feeling that he paints an even darker picture of himself than was actually justified. Because of his idea of decadence, that is, that a man goes to pieces because society around him does, introspection assumes a moral meaning. By unmasking and denouncing his own weakness and deficiencies, he gives a picture of his times.[24] As he puts it, he does not give an exemplary but an experimental value to his own personality.[25] He believes also—and this may constitute the best answer to the accusation of internal contradiction—that sick people have a better sense of life and health than healthy people. He cites as examples D. H. Lawrence, Nietzsche, Rousseau, and Dostoievsky.[26] He agrees with D. H. Lawrence in emphasizing the sexual aspect of decadence: "Lawrence has struck at the heart of the evil, where all the deficiencies, all the decadences are summed up and consummated."[27]

This may partly explain why such an important place is given to descriptions of physical love and to sexual confessions in Drieu's novels. *L'Homme couvert de femmes, Drôle de voyage,* the short stories of *Plainte contre inconnu* and of

---

[23] For example, "A seer, a purposer, a creator, a future itself, and a bridge to the future—and, alas! also as it were a cripple on this bridge: all that is Zarathustra," *Thus Spake Zarathustra,* in *The Philosophy of Nietzsche* (New York, Modern Library, 1927), p. 152.
[24] See the preface to *Gilles,* esp. p. v and *passim.*
[25] "Itinéraire," in *Socialisme fasciste,* p. 244.
[26] See D. H. Lawrence, *L'Homme qui était mort* (Paris, Gallimard, 1933), translated by Jacqueline Dalsace and Drieu La Rochelle, with a preface (pp. 7–37) by Drieu La Rochelle.
[27] *Ibid.,* p. 37.

Journal d'un homme trompé offer good examples of this predilection.

All the other symptoms of decadence which Nietzsche describes in his "Theory of Decadence" in *The Will to Power* appear in Drieu's novels of that period: vice, sickness, crime, sterility, hysteria, weakness of will, alcoholism, pessimism. The Gonzague of "La Valise vide" and Alain in *Le Feu follet* offer extreme cases of decadence, and Alain, a drug addict, is unable to accomplish any act except self-destruction.

These cruel pictures of decadence should not mislead us and it would be a mistake to identify Drieu with them. He was capable of unfolding these pitiful destinies because he had experienced existential freedom facing death and he felt that people should be awakened to the pointlessness of their dull lives, their lives of "larvae." He had been awakened himself at Charleroi: "I had risen from among the dead, from among the larvae... this was myself, strong, free, heroic... I had felt on certain occasions, pulsating within myself a prisoner, ready to rush forth. A prisoner of the life that had been made for me, that I had made for myself... the event was going to condemn the old stupid hierarchy established in quiet times."[28]

He was always afraid of becoming again the victim of the world of money and dead values, the bourgeois world of the *salauds*. *Drôle de voyage* shows how he preserved the independence of a lone wolf's existence at the cost of a life of emptiness.

---

[28] *La Comédie de Charleroi*, p. 56.

five

THE VOYAGE

By contrast with *L'Homme couvert de femmes*, *Drôle de voyage* is both better focused and broader in its implications. Although the first Gille novel is an excuse for a confession and a pretext for the expression of the author's ideas on a decadent society, the second one develops simultaneously on several planes, with a well-defined conflict arising from a definite situation against a firmly drawn social background. The philosophy of life underlying the narrative is more implicit than explicit. The liberty of structure is compensated by the unity of mood (a bitter, ironic mood, as the title suggests), and the apparently rambling line of the narration corresponds to the basic theme of the book (the voyage, also indicated by the title). The style, sign of supreme mastery, is hardly noticeable. Adapted to the mood, it contributes to the harmony of the whole. Its directness establishes a contact between reader and author. Rather than an author, we sense a man. We can even sense his occasional impatience with the little tricks and devices commonly used by authors. He succeeds in conveying the feeling of "authenticity." In the same way that *La Comédie de Charleroi*, by the very tone of the book and the simplicity of its style, reveals the complex personality of the narrator, *Drôle de voyage* gives the reader the impression that he is conversing with a real person, having a definite "style" corresponding to a style of life. This aspect of the novel is so important that critics who knew Drieu, the man, seem to have seen in the book little but the similarity between Drieu and his fictional counterpart. Marcel Arland, for instance, in his review of *Drôle de voyage*, said:

> It goes without saying that one does not dream of identifying exactly M. Drieu La Rochelle with his hero; but one compares them and one is convinced that it is from himself that the author has created his character and that the great virtue of this book is that in it the author has succeeded in finding himself, expressing himself and, temporarily, getting rid of himself.[1]

After noting thus the close connection between the author and his hero, Arland develops through four pages the conclusion of his review: "It is a book which resembles his hero: complex, subtle, cruel and delicate; one would like to scold him but one cannot help liking him." The disarming sincerity of *Drôle de voyage*, the unmistakable "presence" of the author, are not the least achievements of the book, but they are not its only merits and it would be misleading to emphasize them at the expense of the others. It is not always an advantage for a critic to know personally the author whose work he criticizes.

The plot of the novel is of very general interest and develops one of the situations most frequently treated in fiction or on the stage: a confirmed bachelor of thirty-five meets a rich *jeune fille*, thinks he is in love, half tempted by his own feelings about marriage and half under the pressure of society gets engaged and, at the last moment, backs out.

But the true subject is contemporary decadence and the very plot of the novel resting on Gille's inability to stop moving, his urge to pursue an endless journey, is presented as the tragedy of the modern man refusing the dead values of a

---
[1] *NRF*, No. 237 (June, 1933), 982.

crumbling society. The composition of the novel and its structure are also a reflection of the characters and the society depicted: the four parts succeeding each other without apparent transition may seem at first sight completely heterogeneous. Within each part the composition by short sections, bits of dialogue, stream of consciousness, desultory conversations, description of different decors appear disconnected at times and are meant to produce a disconcerting effect of rupture. Arland remarked in his review of *Drôle de voyage:* "One has sometimes the impression that M. Drieu La Rochelle extends a short story to the proportions of a novel or combines several short stories to make a novel."[2] This is only a superficial impression.

The composition of *Drôle de voyage,* similar in many respects to that of "La Comédie de Charleroi," is thematic and the same basic themes reappear, transposed, in each part of the novel. Apparently nonchalant, the author pursues rigorously his demonstration. The syncopated rhythm is an integrated element of Drieu's picture of decadence in modern society, modern culture, and modern men: this is no longer the time of "calm and full harmonies." We should not expect an author who has an apocalyptic vision of the world to write a majestically flowing novel in the pattern of the Victorian tradition.

As a matter of fact the composition is so tight, the different themes are so successfully integrated in an artistic whole, that to unravel them is not only a difficult undertaking but a betrayal of the spirit of the book. Decadence is within and without Gille; the portrait of Gille cannot be isolated from its background nor from its frame.

The first twenty pages, besides constituting an excellent exposition, offer a good example of Drieu's art in blending the various themes developed in the rest of the novel and connected to the central one: decadence. The appearances are all reassuring: La Béraude, a substantial old chateau in the background, the sedate, leisurely life of a wealthy middle-

[2] *Ibid.,* p. 983.

the voyage

class family (Gille himself mentions that he has a reserve of two hundred thousand francs for his older years), the peace of the countryside, the peasants coming back from the fields, the massive silver teapot on the table. This security is deceptive. Everything is marked by decadence, threatened by destruction. The castle was built in the Middle Ages as a solid block with its four towers. Its decadence has coincided with the development of bourgeois life: the seventeenth century razed the towers and opened the walls for high and broad windows; the eighteenth century covered the walls inside with woodwork and paintings; the nineteenth century only spoiled the furniture; the twentieth century bored holes for the pipes and wires indispensable to modern comfort. But the indefatigable action of nature renders ludicrous the agitations and efforts of human beings. In spite of the repair work, the stone of the castle will go back to ruins before the twenty-second century.

The setting thus takes on a cosmic proportion and, in this new time perspective, the dramas of human beings are dwarfed and do not deserve to be taken too seriously: "Man thinks he disturbs nature, but his activity is only one of nature's circuits: he cannot change its order which is also his own" (p. 10).

Within this broader, cosmic framework, the decadence of the castle can be considered as symbolic of the decadence of a whole civilization. Drieu's views on this subject, expressed more explicitly in other books,[3] encourage this interpretation. According to this pessimistic view of history, the Middle Ages have been a magnificent period of youth, of great enterprises and great adventures—Western man has then written great epics, built the cathedrals, and the imposing systems of Christian philosophy, undertaken the Crusades. The following centuries, far from constituting progress, have shown a gradual degeneracy. What man has lost in the process is much more than what he seems to have gained. "And besides what man has gained until very recently was perhaps nourished by what

---
[3] Especially in *Notes pour comprendre le siècle* (1941).

he was losing only slowly, which was still giving him warmth while being consumed" (p. 27).

The picture of a group of contemporaries still living under the shelter of a roof dating from the Middle Ages is highly symbolical: they are "successors," living on the last resources of a dwindling inheritance. And what degenerate successors they are! Madame Cahen-Ducasse embodies the decadence of a whole class, the bourgeoisie: "Portraits in the drawing room showed that Ducasse daughters, two centuries earlier, did not lack majesty of the flesh. Nature had become tired of always receiving the same traits and little by little had refused the material" (p. 13). The fact that her stepsons are Jewish is not a mere coincidence. For Drieu the Jew is the *decadent millénaire*,[4] he represents the modern world par excellence.[5]

One of the main traits of this modern world is its overintellectualism. It characterizes the three brothers: "What a family, thought Gille, a little ashamed for having talked so much himself. I will become anti-Semitic. The Jews and their ideologies, those speeches which exhaust life" (p. 27). And yet Gille is not anti-Semitic. He must admit that he has himself, and even to a greater degree, the very defects he finds in his friends: he is the one who talks most. He identifies so much with his friends that any form of anti-Semitism in him would be a form of detestation of himself.

About what are these intellectuals talking? The decadence of art as exemplified by painting. Gille explains contemporary abstract paintings as "partial exercises" of painters no longer able to embrace both nature and humanity in their compositions. As for Picasso, who knows how to draw and how to paint, he has too much vigor for his contemporaries. "He has amused himself making a fortune by describing the processes through which images pass through the brain rather than producing the images themselves" (p. 19). Matisse is the only one who recomposes the organic universe.

They talk also of the decadence of Western society's central

---
[4] *Ibid.*, p. 102.
[5] This is, at least, what Carentan says in *Gilles* (p. 99). He is Gilles' adoptive father and intellectual master.

institution: marriage, as illustrated in the Bronsac family. They emphasize the role played by the money of the bride, a rich American, in this marriage. This gives the author an occasion to sketch the contrasted characters of the three brothers, each of whom corresponds to one of the facets of Gille's character. Yves is the *délicat,* the artist who takes refuge in his music and plays Bach, as well as modern music, to perfection; but he is also the egoist and the effeminate who does not like women, while being full of courteous attentions to them; he is a pederast. Baptiste, an air pilot, looks like a brute by comparison: he is straightforward, naïve, has been disfigured during World War I, is a Don Juan of the servant quarters. Gabriel is a businessman in the textile industry and a lover of books; he is violent, loves ideas and is sardonic, paradoxical, iconoclastic. He has married Sephora without loving her and suffers through his mistress, Rose Ramsey, the children's governess, who is sadistically cruel to him and takes pleasure in humiliating him. Like Gille, he is passionate and enjoys reflecting on his passions. The various disorders of sex are thus exemplified in the three brothers: homosexuality in Yves, brutal satisfaction in Baptiste, adultery in Gabriel's loveless marriage.

As for Gille, his heart has been "dried out by Paris" and he is obsessed by images of naked bodies, bodies without faces, even without arms and legs. Since the crisis which struck him two years earlier (in which he lost at the same time the woman he loved and his best friend), he has lost confidence in himself. He is no longer what he used to be. Thus, within the character of Gille we have the theme of decadence like a worm in the fruit. But he feels the ambient decadence even more deeply seated in himself. It seems hard to believe that it is only since the crisis of two years ago that he has been incapable of any reaction but "weak gestures" (*des gestes chétifs*). He says himself that the idea of decadence has weighed on his mind "since his childhood." The adjectives he uses to contrast the present (synonymous with old age, decrepitude) and the past (synonymous with youth) are worth noting.

His mind was used to this back and forth movement from the old age of today with its jerky and meager agitation, to the creative youth of the past with its calm and full harmonies (p. 20).

Distrustful of any conventional thinking, Gille questions the validity of this idea of decadence:

Decadence of whom and of what? Decadence of La Béraude? Certainly, decadence of the Bronsacs and the Cahens? Certainly, Decadence of a whole world around him? Certainly. But did not life reappear at the same time elsewhere? Why was he not there? (p. 21).

Gille must confess the secret complicity he feels for the very things he condemns: "He was complacently enjoying all these old things. His raillery was complacency." The satirist who enjoys unveiling with his iconoclastic friends the make-believe of bourgeois society is himself a bourgeois, a bourgeois to the bones, but a bourgeois with a bad conscience toward his protected life: "In the leisurely garden one forgets life and its atrocious chores. One is far from the cities and their worries as sharp as the whistle of that train beyond the creek" (p. 21).

The Gille of *Drôle de voyage* is thus a much more substantial character than the Gille of *L'Homme couvert de femmes*. He has become realistic enough to see himself and accept himself as he is, without wishing a problematic metamorphosis in some distant future. But if he has no illusions, he is lucid enough to judge his shortcomings, and he has retained enough of a sense of life to feel its absence in the society around him. He does not stand out as a rigid and solitary figure in a hostile world. We hear him in an intimate conversation with friends who are, to a certain extent, his own "harmonics."

Finally, the author, placing his hero in an almost cosmic perspective, shows detachment toward him. He smiles at his weaknesses and manias. He does not take him as seriously as the earlier Gille. The difference is more than one of tone or point of view: the author may have shared some of the expe-

the voyage

riences and reactions of Gille—he is now beyond them. We are not shown only the face Narcissus sees in the mirror of the water; we see Narcissus meditating on the mystery of his inner contradictions.

Besides, Gille's psychological make-up is not given once and for all in a few formulas; it is not already determined by his past. We are going to see him carried away by an effort to break with his past. He seems to be comfortably settled in his bachelor status, not satisfied with it but reconciled to it: "I shall remain a bachelor. I am forever separated from women who are all bourgeoises" (p. 30). The whole novel will be the story of Gille's attempt to take his place in society by marrying a *jeune fille*. But this apparent subject is only a pretext. In view of the fact that, for the author, woman means society, and bourgeois society at that, the indictment of women is at the same time an indictment of society. Thus, the debate takes on a wider perspective. Gille, at the end of the novel, may go back to what he himself calls "the fatal rut" of adulterous love and brothels. His refusal to be committed to a society "based on money," his determination to maintain free his critical sense and his irony toward a society he despises, his urge to go always further, to satisfy his boundless curiosity, express, after all, some of the noblest aspirations in man. The mythical figure of Don Juan exercises an unfailing fascination for us all. Gille, in spite of his efforts to disparage himself, has some of the traits of the eternal hero, if it were only the consistent and courageous defiance of the solitary man for the rest of the universe.

Thus, there is both unity and the diversity that flows from inner development in *Drôle de voyage*. The situation is not deterministic and flat, as in *L'Homme couvert de femmes*. The central character is rounder, more complex, more interesting, more capable of change. But he is still the hound of decadence.

Whether Gille is in France or in Spain, he senses decadence under deceptive appearances. In spite of the complete change of decor, the same central theme of decadence reappears.

There is a subtle parallel between Spain and La Béraude. Both are very old, very beautiful, and very rotten; they show signs of past grandeur, of youth, which emphasizes all the more the contemporary decadence. In the third part, the similar sound of La Renaude and La Béraude seems intentional. La Renaude, the nickname given to Gille's mistress, symbolizes the sexual decrepitude of modern woman. Gille is fascinated by an image of strength which emerges from her physique. But it is only an appearance of force, of the force that was real in her crude grandmother, the charwoman, or even still in her mother, the model of a famous painter.

Gille may be a reactionary; he is not a conservative. He shows the same impatience for whatever is artificially preserved. Of La Béraude, he said: "One cannot demolish anything, everything is rotten. But everything remains standing up ... just like this house. It is pretty and rotten." Now he says of the political regime of Spain (then a dictatorship within a monarchy): "If it is not to last forever, it may end tomorrow."

The opening scene of the second part, in the hall of a big hotel in Granada, is in spite of the appearances, very similar to the opening scene of the first part in La Béraude. We see the "rabble" of tourists in this highly advertised historical setting. Gille, the *délicat*, the man of refined taste, who identifies too much with the past not to be shocked by the intrusion of those busy and ugly people, his contemporaries, remains isolated from the crowd and does not share the enthusiasm of the tourists, Baedeker in hand, for "the things to see." The contrast between the beauty of the past and the ugliness of the present is materialized by the confrontation of the modern hotel and the Moorish palace: "The hotel is built on the hill and stands presumptuously by the side of the palace of the Arab aristocrats who died of refinements" (p 117). What do those tourists have in common with the Alhambra? Only a misunderstanding, a misinterpretation can make them gasp at it.

Gille refuses to be carried away by blind admiration

the voyage

prompted by literary associations and literary illusions. For him exoticism is deprived of any prestige. The Spanish crowd at the bullfight is not different from any other modern crowd: "It was a modern crowd like any other one, humiliated by black and gray colours, as if in mourning, with a smell of barracks, even of convent" (p. 120). This theme is resumed in the last part. In December, Spain appears at its worst: cold, desolate, chilling. Instead of the palms which populated the exotic dreams of Gille's childhood about Granada, he sees everywhere fields of beets. Granada itself is described prosaically as "a provincial town hibernating in the routine of winter" (p. 269).

The bullfight itself is, among other things, an occasion to resume a *motif* already announced in the first part: the intimate connection between love, desire, and murder: "the love of the murderer for his victim, love which—at least as much as hunger—makes the dog bark in his pursuit of the stag" (p. 123). In the first part, Beatrix, during a walk with Gille in the garden of La Béraude "heard in the depth of the woods the cry of the beast of prey, the painful cry of the animal in love with its prey, who, in the moonlight, weeps out of desire" (p. 78). Prefigurations of what will happen between Gille and Beatrix, images of the eternal war of the sexes, all the more cruel as the participants are more sensitive. "The truth is that one is sensitive and, by that very reason, one is more cruel. Because the suffering inflicted on a heart by a sensitive heart is much more refined than the one inflicted by a brute. The sensitive man first caresses the place where he is going to strike" (p. 315). Gille finds everywhere a justification of his agonistic conception of life. Everything looks very tame but the awakening of nature's terrible forces is always possible.

"Peace, the deceptive peace, made of a million hushed murders, the peace of the countryside, just as secretly howling as the peace of a city which, at night, stifles behind its shutters moans and entreaties" (p. 60). Gille seems at times to have a childish fear of the "struggle for life." He is often tempted to flee, flee to solitude, run away from life. But this solitude, the solitude of the "lone wolf" is a frightening prospect: "He would always be threatened by falling back into solitude, a solitude more and more atrocious as age would come because it would become irremediable and he would never get used to it" (p. 133). This fear of solitude plunges him into a state of anxiety. He feels like a shivering child looking for the warmth and protection of his mother's bosom. In those moments, Gille admits to himself what Beatrix means to him: "Undoubtedly he was mixing in her his dead mother and the Virgin Mary" (p. 145). She is a refuge. But she is a refuge because she has society behind her, the institution of marriage and ... the Bank of England. He is then afraid of loving her mainly because of her money. Actually, he is torn by two conflicting tendencies: a regressive search for protection and the desire to awaken Beatrix, to tear her away from Society and the Molochs of the tribe to which she is going to be sacrificed. He does not have the patience and the perseverance to encourage this liberation. He would like to be the Pygmalion of this still unshaped lump of clay but so far he has loved only mature women who had already received their shape from other men: in love, too, he has been a "successor." He lacks the simple faith which is at the root of any creative act. His intellect, demonstrating the pointlessness of any undertaking, surrounds him in a prison of dilemmas.

Gille's attitude toward marriage brings out his basic trait: the violent desire to commit himself coupled with an almost panic fear of committing himself. Under the pressure of society, he finds himself more committed than he would like to be and suddenly exchanges roles or rather divides himself in two: the "spectator" watching with irony and detachment the "actor" without ever endorsing fully his acts and eventually preparing for him an exit. Gille's lucidity in analyzing his weaknesses allows the reader to see that at the root of what Gille considers an intellectual quality, his critical disposition, always avoiding the routines of the mind, is an emotional restlessness, the inability to commit himself.

the voyage

The opposition of stability-movement, both in love and in the realm of ideas, the secret connection between the two attitudes on the emotional and the intellectual levels are strikingly dramatized in the last part of the novel in Gille's meditation in the train. The theme of the voyage is emphasized by the fact that Gille is bodily in a train and that at a certain stop, where a woman awaits him, he is going to get out while the other travelers go on. But the theme is also broadened by the subject of the book he reads: "the memoirs of a man of sixty who had never stopped any place, took pride in it and spat on all those who stop" (p. 241). Although the author of that book is not mentioned, the description of the contents suits almost any of Gide's books.[6] The following indication seems to confirm this interpretation: "The author was telling how, having started in life quiet and married, he had broken his ties" (p. 242).

In a moment of anger, Gille rejects the book. His life has been different. Since he has followed the opposite course, having started with a licentious life, the remedy for his unhappiness should also be the opposite; to become attached should mean for him the beginning of his freedom.

He takes up the book again and experiences a feeling of complicity with the author. The defiance of the solitary man has for him the same irresistible effect as the bugle call: "To go away, always, along the roads, alone."

But Gille, irritated, rejects the book again. He thinks that illusion and self-deceit are at the root of the old man's attitude: "Why always play the toughy while one is sad and shivering deep down in one's heart, like a small child who has lost his mother in the crowd" (p. 243). It is amusing to see Gille outdoing Gide in his sincerity and denouncing hypocrisy in this archenemy of all forms of hypocrisy.

After concluding that, in any case, the problem is completely different now for him, since a wife is like clay in the hands of a sculptor, Gille thinks he can pick up the book in

---

[6] Gide's name has been mentioned previously in the book (p. 157). The age also coincides. In the early 1930's Gide was in his sixties.

all serenity. He is upset again, however, at the idea that his marriage means exclusive choice, final commitment: "to give everything to another human being: what excess, what a lie" (p. 244)! Because of this young girl, he is going to be a eunuch for the rest of the universe.

The dramatic fluctuations in Gille's reactions to the book seem to correspond to Drieu's delicate position at equal distance from Gide and Barrès in their conflicting attitudes regarding the question of whether one should take root or seek uprooting. In an article about Barrès' novel, *Les Déracinés*, in which he posed the now classic question: "Where, Monsieur Barrès, do you want me to take root?" Gide also used the image of the voyage:

> I have ... decided to travel ... I have taken the liberty of advising others to travel ... I went further; I have written a whole book ... to exalt the beauty of traveling, trying, perhaps out of a mania of proselytism, to teach the joy there would be in not feeling any ties, any roots, if you prefer that term (after all, you had written yourself *L'Homme libre*). It is while traveling that I have read your book.[7]

The last sentence makes all the more subtle Drieu's ironic representation of his fictitious hero Gille reading, in his turn, Gide in a train. Even though he is at that time basically in agreement with the spirit of Gide's book and prefers movement to settling down Drieu shows, by making Gille analyze himself, that the inability to become fixed may also result from an inherent weakness and is not a quality to be blindly admired.

In that respect, *Drôle de voyage* marks the passage from an ideal of Gidean sincerity to a yearning for adherence to some kind of orthodoxy. Gille's fear of immobility provokes perpetual movement in him and he is thus a Gidean hero. The climate of destructive irony which permeates the whole novel is also Gidean. In *Les Caves du Vatican*, Gide, a few years before the surrealists, had denounced the dissolution of

---

[7] "A Propos des Déracinés," *L'Ermitage* (February, 1898), collected in André Gide's *Morceaux choisis* (Paris, Gallimard, 1921), p. 14.

morals and proclaimed the final rupture of the individual with society. Similarly, Gille does not want to become the prisoner of a woman because, through the institution of marriage, he would become the prisoner of society, of ready-made values which do not suit his personality. He respects his contradictions and refuses to compromise with any system: "Nobody dreams of being a man, of thinking freely, of confessing his contradictions and of making with them his own personal, living system" (p. 273). He is possessed by a tremendous curiosity and in his desire to tear Beatrix away from society there is something satanic. He is fascinated, as Gide was, by the role of awakener, the role of Satan. He enjoys upsetting the smug, stagnant milieu of the Owens. Sincerity is his only rule. In order to remain sincere, he rejects a pact which would bind him even after his passion has died. His sincerity is loyalty toward an ideal of passionate intensity. Since society is built on fidelity to pacts, a character like Gille, or Don Juan, appears to be diabolical; he creates uneasiness wherever he passes. Denis de Rougemont points this out in *La Part du diable:* "The Devil has substituted in our minds the respect of sincerity for the respect—even distant and theoretical—of the welfare of others and of commitments taken under oath. Supreme astuteness because this sincerity still retains the name of a virtue."[8] Gille experiences the savage joy of being alone, still "available," not yet committed. He feels that no one has any hold on him since the common prejudices on the basis of which his behavior could be condemned are refused any value by him. He is reminded of similar defiances of the laws of society when he was a combatant: "Gille was thinking so intensely in those moments that life was going to end the next day and that he should not deprive himself of anything, of any liberty" (p. 268). Even though this is one of the very few references to war in *Drôle de voyage,* Gille's psychology would not be understandable without the background of war in his past experience. He has preserved something of the determination of those who are doomed to death,

---

[8] Denis de Rougemont, *La Part du diable* (Paris, Gallimard, 1942), p. 162.

to enjoy life and to defy the laws of the ordinary human beings clinging to life.

In a world of counterfeiters, in which bad money is continually driving out good, it seems a sacred duty to individualists like Nietzsche, Gide—and Gille—to uphold the ideal of pitiless sincerity. They may be viewed as traitors by the herd; betrayal, for them, would consist in respecting and maintaining habits from which the freshness of life has fled to be replaced by the rigidity of automatism.

Gille is irritated by all forms of insincerity and sees them everywhere. When Beatrix asks him to explain why he thinks that Madame de Bronsac is not "natural," he says:

Nothing in her is natural; she is an American and she lives in France; she has a husband who does not love her but she is satisfied that he pretends to love her; she reads books she has no need to read; she buys paintings she loathes ... (p. 70).

The same insincerity, born from an insufficiency of life, seems to characterize the thought of the twentieth century:

We are still fully in the nineteenth century, we are still steeped in theories. The nineteenth century has invented theories: they first blossomed with all the life and the freshness of which mankind still possessed great reserves. But today mankind is much more tired and those old theories have become heavy chains ... people adopt one of those theories and try to put all their thoughts in agreement with it (p. 273).

To be aware of this, Gille is one of those who still possess more life than the average person. He suffers and is overcome by *inquiétude*. He frightens those who are afraid to live. Before the official birth of the existentialist hero in French letters,[9] he denounces the "bad faith" in most people, who

---

[9] Not so long before, since *La Nausée* was published in 1938 and *Drôle de voyage* in 1933. Cf. the Sartrian use of *salaud* in *Le Feu follet* (1931) and even in *Blèche* (1928). Nothing is ever born from nothing, at least in literary matters, and we should not be surprised to find "pre-existentialist" elements in the literature of the period 1918–1938. Some can even be found earlier, in the masters of that generation and eminently in André Gide. Irritated perhaps by the excessive publicity surrounding existentialism, Gide himself noted in his diary in January, 1946: "It may happen that, later, an attentive reader will quote one of my sentences which had first passed unnoticed and that, con-

refuse to assume the responsibility of their acts: they cheat, consciously or unconsciously, by following a ready-made doctrine, or conforming to an attitude, or playing a comedy. The "analysis" made by Gille at the beginning of the novel of the situation of the Bronsac couple is a pitiless satire of a comedy invented by husband and wife to avoid being sincere.

Perhaps more than anything what Gille fears is that in marrying Beatrix, he will give way under social pressure to the temptation of stepping into the role of a social personality. In order to exist, that is to say, to avoid becoming a mere puppet, motivated by social values which have not been accepted as one's own, it is necessary to desolidarize one's self from the group, even if one should thus cause suffering to innocent people. Besides, are they really so "innocent"? Beatrix is endowed with the aura of prestige that centuries of culture have attached to the conception of the fiancée. She does so little to be herself, to break away from the routine of life that her parents and her society have made for her. In her letters to Gille, she keeps recalling the time they have spent together. This infuriates Gille, who exclaims, "What matters is not to remember things but to live them" and his judgment of condemnation is already made: "This Beatrix did not exist, would never exist" (p. 189). She is marked too deeply by middle-class timid prudence and she is too much protected by money. Gille would have to undertake too much to give her even "an appearance of freedom" (p. 313).

However, it is only by contrast with Beatrix and the other characters of the novel that Gille is free. He has managed so far not to be trapped by society. He thinks he is liberated from most social prejudices. Even his work is as "pure," as free from concessions to society as possible. He is not duped by social appearances. He is available, *disponible*, but for what? He has avoided all the commitments which bind most men, but he cannot escape the prison of his ego. He some-

---

fronting the hullaballoo which is made today about certain existentialist declarations or manifestations (for which Sartre is not uniquely responsible) this reader will protest with surprise: 'But Gide has said it before him'...." André Gide, *Journal 1942–1949* (Paris, Gallimard, 1950), p. 245.

times even doubts he has a personality: "I am not a person, I am a place. There is an intelligent thought passing through me but I have no hands to retain it, to make of it my instrument. There are people like that. They are called amateurs or failures" (p. 289).

The joy of being without anchorage is not without drawbacks: "One is held by nothing but then one does not hold to anything" (p. 267). Thus the yearning for commitment is in the background of this apology for freedom. Gille's irony is also rooted in an incapacity for affirmation. If the author with whose thought Gille feels so much complicity in the train is Gide, how could he forget that Gide is also the author of *Corydon*, the champion of homosexuality? Gille observes in two of his companions a definite connection between this sexual abnormality and the hesitancy to affirm anything.

Johnny, even more than Yves Cahen loathed this slightly thick affirmation which one finds always in the male pure and simple. And heaven knows how much today pederasts set the tone. How many men, even though they do not belong to their caste, soft-pedal their opinions to avoid displeasing them. Gille was one of these (p. 275).

Gille feels besides that, on the sexual plane, his endless desire, his inability to stop in his quest for women, make him very similar to homosexuals. In *L'Homme couvert de femmes*, as well as in *Drôle de voyage*, we have noted Gille's obsession about homosexuals, which seems to run parallel to his obsessive notions about Jews. He is continually complaining about the decadence around him, but it seems dubious that he could live in any environment but a "decadent" one. Why does he not break away from this little world and go wherever there are possibilities of renewal? All those well-bred, polite, sad people feel the end of something around them, but also a premature old age is creeping within themselves. Cahen has asked why Frenchmen are sad and Gille answers "the Frenchman is frightened: he feels he is growing old and he is afraid of his future" (p. 257). Even though Gille puts his hope in the rising of a young Europe which would replace the obsolete nationalisms, Gille admits, with a nuance of shame, that he cannot escape his personality:

"You are very French, just the same."
"Of course, to the tip of my fingernails, as they say, but I don't brag about it" (p. 71).

But all Europeans are the same. They are unable to have faith in anything. Sometimes Gille must wish he could be a bolshevik. When he is accused of being one by Johnny Hope, he answers with a nostalgic envy:

How could a European be a bolshevik? We have been much too well-bred by our mother Europe. We—Englishmen, Frenchmen, Germans—have invented socialism. It required Russians to believe in it (p. 309).

Fascism appears then to Gille a rather despicable next-best to communism.

No, even the Germans are much too well-bred to be bolsheviks. At most, we Europeans are capable of being fascists, that is to say, to put a little demagoguery in our conservatism (p. 309).

The ideal of "freedom" and constant change is thus subtly undermined. In Gille's case, the emphasis on "freedom" is shown to be a form of anxiety, accompanied by a confused sexual attitude—which is also true of the homosexuals around him.[10]

Like any methodical doubt, Gille's destructive irony is only a preliminary stage preparing the *tabula rasa* on which something new can be built. The time has come for engagement. In *Drôle de voyage*, Drieu sheds one of his skins, the skin of the-man-covered-with-women. He had not succeeded in doing so in the novel bearing that title because the author was too complacent about his hero. Gille Gambier may still

---

[10] Mario Praz writes (*The Romantic Agony*, translated by Angus Davidson, Oxford University Press, 1951, p. 365): "It has always been his [Gide's] chief occupation to avoid any fixed anchorage; whether this inability of his to be consistent, this restlessness as of someone who is always on the point of undertaking a new journey, is not a form of anxiety-neurosis caused by a confused sexual attitude, is a conjecture for which I do not feel inclined to take the responsibility."

correspond to the individuality of the author, but this individuality is depicted and analyzed in order to be judged, renounced, and rejected. *Drôle de voyage*, as well as the essays of *Socialisme fasciste* or *Le Chef*, shows that Drieu has no illusions about his own motivations for committing himself to a cause, or about the values of any cause he may serve. But he is repulsed to the point of nausea by the charming, empty life of a certain kind of society around him and he is disgusted with an irony which for all practical purposes amounts only to complacency.

Even as an artist, the painter of decadence is caught in an impasse. The author puts in the mouth of his hero an accurate description of what he is himself trying to do in the novel. Gille, in a conversation on art with the painter Johnny Hope, which constitutes a resumption of the theme already announced in the first part of the book in a similar conversation on contemporary art with the Cahens, says:

> I am in a very desperate situation; I hate conventional art, I nervously enjoy free art, but I don't believe it has real life. I believe, actually, that it exploits our agony, that it makes a beautiful agony for us. Picasso is the most exquisite, the most joyous sneer that one can see in our times. He is a healthy man who pours for the sick the most beautiful wine in the world. He is a great painter of ruins (p. 156).

In the denunciation of this agony, Drieu cannot help being elegant, elegant and cruel. He notes himself the connection of this aspect of his talent with Gide's:

> What elegance! It is like Gide. What elegance! There will not be, to finish, a Lawrence, in France. I am talking of the novelist. Only elegant ones. Thank heavens, in France elegance can be cruel. How cruel they are, those two or three men (p. 151)!

The meditation on Gide in *Drôle de voyage* represents a farewell to Gide and all the values he had represented so far for the young writer. By criticizing the position of André Gide, Drieu indirectly attacks a certain interpretation of the Nietzschean superman. The "superman" seems to be essen-

the voyage

tially a decadent *délicat* scorning the rest of the herd but retiring in a comfortable ivory tower. Gille takes leave of Gide because the Gidean criticism has led the disciple to a point where he has to go beyond the master. Without knowing it he is more Gidean than ever. Gide himself had felt that he had reached a dead end. In 1932, he proclaims in his *Journals* that he wants to give his life for communism. His communist adventure was to bring him disillusionment just as the fascist adventure did to Drieu. The great difference is that political preoccupations were not new for the author of *Mesure de la France*, and that he had to risk more than his elder in terms of a literary career by engaging actively in political action. The gap between two literary generations is visible here. Drieu belongs to the generation of Malraux, *l'homme nouveau*, and of Louis Aragon, the party man.

Within its limitations, *Drôle de voyage* has a very special place in Drieu's work and in the literary production of the 1930's. It is the supreme expression of what is exquisite in decadence. It shows what a sacrifice Drieu made in abandoning that type of novel. He had found his tone and his style. He displays in this book his major qualities of grace, elegance, refinement, and cruelty. Even in the most risqué scenes, he preserves, as Marcel Arland pointed out, "a perfect, an instinctive decency."[11] In the subtle, delicate analyses of fleeting sentiments, he emulates eighteenth-century *marivaudage*. The themes are introduced in an original manner, and somehow the book is charged with all the things that are absent from it but are suggested, such as the aspiration to a simple life based on firm commitments. Sure of a medium perfectly adapted to his purpose, Drieu takes some liberties with the traditions of the genre of the novel, but he makes us accept those liberties as virtues.

He had not reached such maturity without previous work. *Blèche* (1928) and *Une Femme à sa fenêtre* (1930) mark phases of progress in conquering the problem of form. They offer also the study of bourgeois intellectuals in two con-

---

[11] *NRF*, No. 237 (June, 1933), 983.

trasted situations: the reactionary journalist writing for a Catholic newspaper and the communist agent launched in revolutionary activities. These novels are examined in the next chapter, together with *Beloukia*, published in 1936. We shall see how the lone wolf changes his Don Juan costume for others, but maintains always his contempt for a society based on money and his solitary defiance of conventional values.

six

THE THIRST FOR THE ABSOLUTE

Gide, comparing the various potentialities of a man to the buds of a plant, observes that if all the buds are destroyed except one, it will grow and develop much more than it would have under normal conditions. He derives from this botanical observation a literary recipe for authors using a subjective method:

> In order to create a hero ... take one of these buds, put it in a pot, by itself ... choose preferably the bud that bothers you most. You get rid of it at the same time. This is perhaps what Aristotle meant by his "purgation of passions."[1]

It seems that Drieu followed the method recommended by Gide in creating the protagonists of the three novels to be examined in this chapter. For each represents one of the antagonistic potentialities of the author's personality: the conservative, the revolutionary, the degraded Don Juan, the

---
[1] André Gide, *Œuvres Complètes* (Paris, Gallimard, 1932–1939), IV, 616–617.

intellectual haunted by a sense of betrayal when he commits himself to political action. In each of the three novels, the efforts of the hero to establish a successful relationship with a woman result, or will result, in his betraying his most deeply held ideas. In each case, the woman is the temptress and the cause of the hero's failure in the quest of absolute values by which to live or die.

Although the three novels develop basically the same theme—the dilemma facing the intellectual who wants to be sincere and to participate in the great movements of his time—they offer a remarkable variety of form. Each explores different possibilities of the novel. *Blèche* (1928), which externally adopts the framework of a detective story, consists chiefly of minute psychological analyses and its implications are metaphysical. *Une Femme à sa fenêtre* (1929) is in complete contrast with the previous novel. *Blèche* is set in the heart of Paris, in the island of St. Louis, and most of the action takes place in a single room, *Une Femme à sa fenêtre* is set in Greece; action and dialogue replace lengthy, introverted meditations and a skillful plot takes the characters from one place to another. *Beloukia* (1936) is Drieu's first attempt at a form of philosophical tale, more, however, in the tradition of Barrès' *Jardin sur l'Oronte* than of Voltaire's *Candide*. Drieu later developed this original formula and produced some of his best fiction in that form: *L'Homme à cheval* (1943) and *Les Chiens de paille* (1944).

I

In *Blèche*, Drieu isolates in himself the bourgeois, the intellectual engrossed in political speculations, the conservative attached to tradition, the journalist who squanders his talent in political articles, and the result is Blaquans. The hero, however, has inherited some of the lucidity of the author and the treatment of the character is not consistently ironical. For instance in Gide's *La Symphonie pastorale*, the minister is never aware of his self-deceit, but in Drieu's *Blèche*, Blaquans

the thirst for the absolute

denounces his own hypocrisy and is uneasy about his insincerity.

Blaquans has organized his life in such a way as to avoid the petty worries of daily life. Blèche is his secretary. He works in a kind of hermitage far from the cries of his children. In this sober but comfortable setting, by contemplation and writing he strives for nobility in his life. He is highly respectable, and respected by the 200,000 readers of the *Catholique*. He is neither rich nor poor and his needs are limited. He is deeply secure in his married life: Marie-Laure, his wife, has all the virtues he could desire and respects his need of solitude. He has known a period of license and rebellion in his religious and political, as well as in his private life, but he has chosen to take sides with the forces of order. He is officially a Catholic writer. Rather than a deep conviction, pragmatic reasons have led him into this attitude. He is also aware that there is no firm religious belief around him, but his thoughts fall irresistibly into a Catholic pattern; he feels that he would be lost if he ventured outside it.

Blaquans lives in the shadow of the Catholic Church and uses it as protection, because his views on the points of dogma are most latitudinarian. On Sunday, for instance, he reads the mass at home and does not enter a church, disgusted by the social comedy played there by the attendants. He gives a description of the Sunday mass in the cities which prefigures Sartre's famous satire of the Bouville bourgeoisie at the same ceremony:

> In city churches there still gathers a bourgeoisie which has been, for a century, at this one hour of the week the prey of its weakest and silliest feelings. The bourgeois attend mass first to establish their rank in society while ranks are crumbling; secondly to set an example. But the commoners do not pay any attention, they know what this example is worth (p. 161).

Blaquans has no illusions about his boss, the chief editor, Vannier; the Catholic "cause" is for the latter just another business to exploit.

This inner contradiction in what should be the axis of

Blaquans' thought—his faith—is accompanied by various disorders in a man who is supposed to be a supporter of order. The disappearance of valuable earrings (given to him by his wife to pay for a trip to Russia and the United States), an unimportant incident in itself, takes on tremendous proportions in his life because of his ever present anxiety and his overwhelming feeling of guilt. The tragic element of life insistently disturbs the atmosphere of peace and quiet that Blaquans has tried so hard to create around him. He has deliberately tried to separate himself from the common herd and he is caught in his own trap; he cannot feel any ties of brotherhood with his fellowmen. The intellectual in him is lost in the small details of the practical world and in the simplest human relationship. Nothing can be simple for him; and sometimes he seems even to enjoy the complexity of the dilemmas which surround him. He is a *délicat* who loathes any contact with the coarser side of life. He is weak, and not beyond thoughts of vengeance, but at the same time is ashamed to use authority: he feels that his suspiciousness justifies crimes in advance. The distrust he experiences renders him despicable in his own eyes. He considers himself *un salaud*, "an ignoble, disgusting creature." "I am unmasked, I am nothing, I am disintegrating" (p. 22). He is reluctant to call on the institutions which maintain order in society: justice and policemen; he is a *bourgeois désaffecté*, a bourgeois ashamed of being one and unable to be anything else.

The same contradiction reigns in his sexual and sentimental life. Blaquans betrays his ideal of unity and nobility. His need for solitude seems to be a pretext to get away from his rather plain wife and his noisy children. The ease with which he succumbs to the temptation of Blèche's body after a rather formal relationship reveals the artificiality of his stiff attitude toward her during the previous year. His recourse to eroticism implies a failure to reach her heart: "this ephemeral union spoiled our relationship without uniting us" (p. 170).

It is in vain that Blaquans tries to organize a quiet life for himself. The "ivory tower" turns out to be an impossibility for him: "All of a sudden life is tragic; all of a sudden after months and years during which life had been closing its eyes to the daily cheating behind which you escaped its grip, it puts you back in the movement of its truth" (p. 180).

The incident of the earrings is only a pretext: the whole novel is the study of a state of anxiety born from the impossibility of communicating with another human being: "Anxiety had taken hold of me and would not let go from the moment I realized my complete ignorance about Blèche and this impression of ignorance had immediately become an impression of vertigo" (p. 213). Blaquans seeks and hates solitude. Unable to penetrate into another soul or, as he says himself, "to introduce in me anything but myself, to welcome the soul of my neighbour," he is condemned to analyze himself endlessly. The description of the single room of his apartment is symbolic in that respect.

The only true opening in these walls, because it was a purely intellectual opening, was the high mirror above the black marble mantlepiece, window of the soul, into which went deeper and deeper the perspectives of psychology overabundant and infinitely suggestive to the point of becoming metaphysical (p. 100).

Blaquans is the negative version of a Malraux hero. He has known during the war a moment of revolt against man's fate. "I have blasphemed, I cursed God in a moment of furor when all the passion of man, enemy of his gods, uplifted me in the bottom of a trench." He has shared then with many the rebellion against the order of the universe: "All of them, like me, had been possessed by that diabolical cry of anger against the atrocious order of the universe." But he has not faced the consequences of that moment of revolt. He has chosen instead the way of conformism. Too aware, however, of the contradictions and the artificiality of his situation, he is already a prefiguration of the Sartrean hero tormented by the consciousness of his "bad faith."

Blèche is another case of failure. She fails to be a woman, she fails to be loved, she misses death in a dramatic attempt at suicide after being wrongly suspected of stealing the earrings. She secretly loves Blaquans and welcomes any kind of attention from him, even cruelty. She has chosen to associate herself with men in their work, but there is something monstrous in the contrast of the supposedly intellectual activity of Blèche with her sensuous, almost animal nature. She has no confidence as a woman: "In her work with me, Blèche was like a writer who has admitted to himself his complete failure and has limited himself to harmless journalistic or scholarly works" (p. 121). Even her suicide cannot be sincere.

Suicide is the only way she knows to hold Blaquans' attention. She is still playing a role, not even with much conviction. This constitutes Blaquans' last disillusionment. In a world of appearances and make-believe, he at first thought, after hearing about Blèche's attempt at suicide, that only death has some reality, that only death can lend authenticity to human feelings: "Life cannot do anything decisive for love; death alone insures its passage to eternity" (p. 186). Death has the quality of certainty and he cannot live without this quality. Since he cannot find it in himself, he has to find it in someone else. The example of Blèche shows him that one is not necessarily engaged, in the sense of participation, even in the gesture of death: "She forced me to realize that for certain people suicide can be as false and as ineffective a gesture as their other gestures" (p. 229).

Blèche marks a step in the development of Drieu's personality and in the solution of what was for him a central problem of life: participation. The novel shows, by implication, that sincerity, both in private life and in political thinking, demands participation. It is impossible to lead a contemplative life of the ivory-tower type. In private life, the destinies of other people affect one intensely and their demands cannot be ignored. On the political plane, tradition and conservatism are not adequate; one must find one's own individual solution.

Aesthetically, the novel is not altogether satisfying, because the framework is traditional while the hero is modern. The author carefully indicates that the theft, which is the pivotal element of the plot, is only a pretext. Why not do away with it and depict frankly the drama of a man in search of sincerity while entangled in personal and social insincerity? *Blèche* is a novel of transition. It announces, in a way, the metaphysical novel of the absurd in which the hero is *l'étranger*. In spite of defects, Blaquans provides an interesting example of failure and consciousness of strangeness in a universe that lacks a common measure with him. The whole novel shows the impossibility of repeating the novel of psychological analysis in the tradition of the nineteenth century continued by Paul Bourget and his epigoni. In a climate of accepted and established values, the author, and the reader, can become interested in the description of human relationships on a psychological plane. The interplay of love, ambition, success, in their infinite variations, can then constitute the subject matter of the literary work. When all the accepted values are questioned, when the hero feels foreign or at least ill at ease in the existing order, the novel becomes metaphysical. The hero is in search of a reason to live, and his basic anxiety becomes the subject of the novel. Drieu has not dared to get rid entirely of the old form as Sartre was to do ten years later in *La Nausée*, but he has prepared the new climate of sensibility for the existentialist hero, the hero of the absurd.

II

Externally, *Une Femme à sa fenêtre* is quite different from *Blèche*. It constitutes, however, in the work of Drieu, another attempt to answer the same question that was at the root of *Blèche:* "How can the bourgeois intellectual be sincere with himself today? How can he harmonize his private life with his faith (or his absence of faith)?" Blaquans, in *Blèche*, had chosen to perpetuate an old civilization, and to be a Catholic journalist: Michel Boutros, the hero of this novel, is a Communist agent. The very locale of Blaquans' "cell," "at the flank of Notre Dame, in the shadow of a shadow," was symbolic of the renunciation of life to which he had condemned himself. Boutros, pursued by the police for an act of sabotage in which he risked his life, brings some fresh air into a stagnant milieu of diplomats in Athens. Blaquans' meager love affair with Blèche ended in a failure to communicate, because their relationship had been "a kind of dubious complicity, based on the affinity between the less good in Blèche and the worst in Blaquans." The passion between Boutros and Margot Santorini grows in a climate of generosity and admiration. The background of an empty Paris in September which smelled of decadence is replaced by a radiant Greece in May with orchards in blossom and choruses of young men and women singing at night in Delphi. After the defeat of his contemplative self, the failure to build an ivory tower, to partition off his life and to keep anxiety out, what will be the fate of the "adventurer," of the bourgeois intellectual seen now as a "man of action"?

Une Femme à sa fenêtre analyzes the psychology of a revolutionary—but in a period of forced inaction, in hiding after a dangerous coup. In the novels of Malraux, the adventurer is presented while engaged in action, in a period of highest tension. Michel Boutros offers a negative aspect of the adventurer when, in a state of enforced passivity, he is tempted to fall back into the bourgeois world he has fled. The temptress is the enticing person who gives the title to the novel. It is quite by chance that they are brought face to face.

The technique of narration owes much to the cinema. It would be easy to write a scenario following the novel closely. The gestures and external appearance of the characters are described with a richness of detail which reminds one of the searching eye of the camera. The time of the novel coincides with the actual duration of the narrated events. The different scenes could be transposed into film sequences with but little adaptation. For instance, the book opens with a vivid picture of the bored and vain clientele of a great cosmopolitan hotel in Athens at which Margot Santorini is staying. The gratuitousness of her milieu, the puppets who move aimlessly around her, constitute a background against which the figure

the thirst for the absolute

of the revolutionary will stand out all the better by contrast.

The visual quality of the next silent scene is effective. This sequence depicts a woman still young, disdained by her husband, who drops her social mask in the solitude of her boudoir and looks out the window before going to bed. A few hours later comes the passage of the lonely silhouette of the fugitive in the empty street, the miraculous apparition of a woman standing within the framework of an open window after a succession of unbroken walls. We have "shots" of the hesitation of Margot, the insistence of the stranger, his entrance into the room as the pursuers approach, the suspense while they pass by. These "shots" are treated with a visual imagination which must be emphasized because they show that Drieu is capable of concrete visual representation as well as of the most minute psychological analysis.

The action takes place in about eight days, and follows a chronological order with a few brief flash backs. The characters are not numerous. Besides Margot, her husband, Rico, and Michel Boutros, Malfosse plays a rather important role and is used constantly to provide relief by contrast to the three protagonists. Among the diplomats, the German, Pahlen, is the only one who has individuality. Not only is this milieu international, in contrast with *Blèche*, but the individual ancestry of many of the characters is mixed: Margot's father was an Austrian banker who became a naturalized Frenchman; her mother was a Frenchwoman of Irish ancestry; she herself is married to an Italian; but Rico is not tied by nationalistic prejudices and he talks lightly of his compatriots, including Mussolini; Boutros is French, but his mother is a Greek living in Egypt; he speaks English as well as French and has not lived in France since the end of World War I.

Malfosse is the only one who is a true Frenchman, and one senses with what bitter pleasure the author has detailed the pettiness of this archbourgeois. He may have become a powerful businessman; he has remained timid and ungenerous in his private life. A civil engineer from the Polytechnique, he has spent his whole life in worldly "success" and he is a lamentable failure as a man. Abandoned by his wife, he is now a ridiculous admirer of Margot. Even when he does what she wants, he does not do it gracefully; he lacks "class." He reflects the opinions of his milieu and he summarizes rather well the attitude of the average bourgeois toward communists in the 'twenties. They could not take communists seriously because they were unable to imagine any motivation other than their own. The values he defends no longer live in him. He blindly reveres everything that is part of Western culture and accepts the classic tradition and Christianity even if he does not know or understand old Greece and does not practice Christian virtues.

All Malfosse can offer to a woman like Margot is "peace, dignity, majesty," and he realizes then that it is rather dull compared to the romantic appeal of adventurers like Pahlen or Boutros: "These men had ideas about the world and it was with the whole world that they could entice Margot." The contact with Boutros has awakened some combativeness in him: "Now that I have known you, I will spend the rest of my life fighting against you." And Boutros rejoices at this sign of life which marks the evolution of the character: "Congratulations! I leave you in much better shape than I found you, Monsieur Malfosse" (p. 281).

Rico has a much more sympathetic attitude toward the Communist. He senses in Boutros an adventurer, rather than an orthodox "militant." Rico himself is not a bourgeois. He is a count, and nobility has no place in a bourgeois society. He is, in his own way, an outlaw: "I belong to a world, exiled by definition from modern life."[2] He is a cynic, a melancholy Don Juan, who feels lost and useless: "strange boy, not low, but insistent on negating himself, on destroying himself... soberly engaged in his métier of a man popular with women" (p. 89). A vain man, he has developed only the most superficial part of his personality, and he suffers from the neglect of all his other potentialities. He has been through the war, in

---

[2] If Boutros is a negative version of a Malraux hero, Rico is the degraded version of the Don Juan hero, as outlined by Montherlant in the Costals of *Les Jeunes filles*.

the thirst for the absolute

which he had a revelation that there was more in him than his mediocre accomplishments indicated. He enjoyed the manly comradeship of war; with the return of peace, he was unable to maintain this frank comradeship. To him, politics does not seem to be too different from war, but it is not so pure or so violent. He despises it and at the same time regrets not having engaged in it. He is admired by women and he enjoys being popular with them. He has followed the line of least resistance and he has become a "man covered with women." He plays the role with a passion beneath which it is easy to detect resentment: "To lose women and to lose himself through women had become the meaning of his strange destiny in which the most petty vanities filled the vacuum caused by the absence of grandeur" (p. 149).

"The vacuum caused by the absence of grandeur" is a striking formula which applies surprisingly well to most of Drieu's fictional characters and to the author himself. They are characters *en creux*, suggesting always the idea of the lack of something. The intense consciousness they have of what they are lacking constitutes their pathetic grandeur. An absence assumes, so to speak, a positive value.

The study of Rico's character throws an interesting light on the basic misogyny or even sadism of the twentieth-century type Don Juan, as described by Montherlant or Drieu. Women are for them only poor substitutes for a grandeur absent from their lives, but of which they have had an intimation. Whether they blame this absence on the mediocrity of the times in which they live, and on the decadence of the society around them, or on the limitations of their own personality, they use women as objects. Women, in a way, serve the same purpose for them as drugs for others: to forget their failures in life. Women have become for them a form of self-destruction. They cannot conceive of "love" (reduced actually to sensuousness) except as a form of destruction. Rico says: "For me, sensuousness is cruelty" (p. 255). If he responded to the tenderness of his wife, he would lose the aura of the hero pursued by a tragic fatality: the "wolf" is ashamed to turn into a lamb. Rico clings to his satanic role. The author points out the secret weakness of his hero in one of those general statements which are reminiscent of La Rochefoucauld in their lucid pessimism: "Weak men who have had a glimpse of the idea of grandeur cling desperately to the most somber aspect of their destiny which gives them the illusion of a resemblance with what they were not able to achieve" (p. 150). Boutros labels Rico a "boudoir stoic." But this stoic wants to punish himself; his cruelty toward women is coupled with an equivalent cruelty directed at himself: "Rico wanted to suffer; it consoled him for having been able only to enjoy, for not having been able to submit himself to discipline and effort" (p. 150).

In order to sustain the possibility of despising everything, he takes refuge in what he calls irony, but which might be described more accurately as cynicism. He admits that an intelligent person like Boutros may believe in an idea, but only as a drug. At most, politics is for him a "pretext," a form of self-destruction. He says to Michel: "I understand that one launches oneself in politics or big business as in anything else, to forget, to destroy oneself" (p. 142). He respects Boutros only so far as he feels that the Communist is not the dupe of his political convictions, that he is an outlaw like himself who had the courage to rebel frankly against society. He senses in Boutros a brother who has followed another way: "Boutros is a man who has perhaps great weaknesses like himself, but who has known how to make strong weapons out of them" (p. 155).

Rico's feelings toward both his wife and Boutros are ambivalent. He is amused to watch their mutual passion grow. He even favors it by suggesting the "surprise party" during which Margot has another opportunity to meet Boutros and, later, by sending the letter in which he encourages her to leave with the Communist. He acts as an accomplice but feels a secret envy for their happiness, even if the latter is not to last. For Boutros as well as for Margot, Rico is the image of the past they are trying to leave behind them.

the thirst for the absolute

The Communist agent has indeed tried to forget or even to destroy in himself that superficial aspect which the diplomat has developed to the exclusion of everything else: "to be liked by women." He has known love affairs in the past; he has been almost destroyed by one of them. Now he is afraid of women and at the same time fascinated by them. They represent all the things that he has tried to tear himself from: "Women for me mean money, luxury, softness, peace." He identifies women with society and its most unpleasant duties. Poverty can be suffered alone, but not with a woman. It is necessary to feed a wife and "her" children: "Well! food is something to be bought or bartered; one must give something in exchange for it" (p. 212). The man who can offer protection to a woman is the one who has permitted himself to become a cog in the capitalistic machine, like Malfosse. If women have money, they use its enervating effect to "tame" the male and he loses his independence if not his self-respect. In any case, they force the man to settle down, to stop, to rest.

We recognize in all this Drieu's habitual misogynistic arguments against women as a hindrance to the "voyage," the restless quest of a solitary hero. The originality of Boutros among the characters of Drieu's fiction is that he first meets Margot in circumstances which exclude sexual desire; the situation caught both of them "in the highest expression of their personality" (p. 103); in the midst of action for him, in an access of generosity for her: "Being both preoccupied by the risk they shared, they had not thought of anything else." The rare qualities of Margot's happy nature nourished an atmosphere of confidence between them. She has reached a sentimental maturity which makes her realize her past mistakes and appreciate all the more the chance of rupture that Boutros represents for her. He enjoys his role of awakener with a woman who has also had a bitter love experience in the past. The lesson of Delphi and its oracle is that he must integrate the woman into his system of life as an essential element of the cosmos. The physical aspect of love is part of the mystery of life and a step in its exploration: "Souls have hands and feet to be used; exercising one's members can contribute greatly to a healthy knowledge" (p. 260).

The scene of love-making in the sacred city of Greece is handled as a religious experience, putting the participants in contact with the elementary forces of the universe but at the same time giving them an intimation of vaster spiritual forces.

In spite of this exalted mysticism, Boutros keeps a lucid view of the future chances of his adventure with Margot. He foresees the destructive effect of satiety, "the first nasty bitch to bite at their legs." He is also curious to see what will be the result of the experiment—both for the bourgeois woman, stripped of the prestige and the graces of money, and for himself—how will he react to real poverty? They do not exchange promises when they depart. They will measure their love only in deeds.

A real metamorphosis will be necessary in both of them if they want to start anew. Love, in the Western tradition, is so closely interwoven in the whole fabric of the culture that it would be necessary to break the limitations imposed by the particular form of civilization. By placing the problem of love in the foreground of his study of the psychology of a revolutionary, Drieu has shown his desire to handle the problem realistically.[3] Michel analyzes the dilemma he is facing in a conversation with Margot:

> There are social boundaries, there is a social fatality. Neither a man nor a woman can cover freely the whole gamut. I have tried to love a working girl; I could not. If I were a worker, you would not love me. I must flee from you! With you I become a bourgeois again or I remain one ... It is easier to make a revolution in the street than in the heart" (p. 216).

The answer to the question, "Can a bourgeois love in any other way than as a bourgeois?" remains uncertain. But the problem whether a bourgeois can become a communist is examined in great detail, although the reader is left to draw his own conclusion.

Drieu must have meditated often on this question, since he

---

[3] Sartre had recourse to a "fantasy" in *Les Jeux sont faits* to explore the possibility of love between a worker and a bourgeoise.

the thirst for the absolute

was tempted to become a communist himself and since he had the opportunity of studying concrete examples of communist conversion among his friends. The dedication of *Une Femme à sa fenêtre* to Jean Bernier is indicative. Jean Bernier belonged to the same generation (he was a year younger than Drieu). He had not only witnessed but lived the renascence of "sports" just before the war and had been himself a distinguished rugby man around 1912–1914. During World War I, he had spent thirteen months in the front line in an infantry regiment.[4] He joined the Communist party in 1925 and remained in it until 1929. He was to be associated later with several leftist organizations, including the "Front Commun" of Gaston Bergery. In an essay of August, 1934, in which Drieu pointed out that his friends were all leftists, he says of Bernier: "One friendship dominates my whole life, that of Jean Bernier—a young bourgeois who remained for a long time on the borderline of communism, both before entering the party and after leaving it." Even though the novel is dedicated to Jean Bernier alone, it is likely that Drieu, when he drew the portrait of the adventurer, had also in mind his other friends:

Previously, there had been Raymond Lefebvre, another young bourgeois, one of the leaders and founders of the Communist party in 1920. I knew Aragon only at a time when literary politics alone occupied him and did not suffice to distract him from a certain deepening search for himself. There was also Emmanuel Berl, a liberal Jew, Gaston Bergery, a great orator, and finally Malraux, the archangel of permanent revolution."[5]

Faithful to his subjective method, Drieu gave to his hero many of his own traits and ideas also, so that his Communist is much more an adventurer than a "militant" or a man of action.[6]

---

[4] He published a novel in 1920, *La Percée*, based on his war memories. The 117th Infantry Regiment in which he served was the same as Gaston Bergery's, another close friend of Drieu's (a year older).

[5] "Itinéraire," in *Socialisme fasciste*, p. 242.

[6] I am using the terms *militant, aventurier,* and *homme d'action* with the same meaning they have in Sartre's introduction to Roger Stéphane's *Le Portrait de l'aventurier (T. E. Lawrence, Malraux, von Salomon)* (Paris, Editions du Sagittaire, 1950).

Boutros' connection with communism is almost accidental. The communist movement happens to represent, *at the time he lives,* "a great surge of life." Boutros has deserted France in 1918 and the petty "quarrel of the Rhine." On both sides, the herds of soldiers were too tired to continue the war by a revolution. But the Russians, in 1924, after Lenin's death, are still in full revolution, and Boutros says: "It will last as it will last. But I will have devoted myself to the strongest movement in the world, in *my own time*" (p. 144). In almost identical terms, in *La Condition humaine,* Malraux says that Kyo "had fought for what, *in his time,* had been charged with the strongest meaning and the greatest hope." With a prophetic sense, Boutros realizes that the drama of his age lies in the conflict between the two rival myths: "Lenin's Kremlin, crammed with statistics, and Wall Street, equally striped with crazy figures" (p. 168). His attachment to a political party springs mainly from negative sources: "I cannot, I simply cannot abandon myself to the nostalgia for what is finished" (p. 168). His engagement in violent action is mainly a means of fleeing from himself—of purifying himself from his past: "He had thrown himself into the action which purified him of all those sordid memories" (p. 54). Since he tries to escape the prison of his individualistic ego, Boutros tends to become a "militant." He insists: "You think that I have a personality . . . but I want you to realize that such is not the case . . . I am nothing, I am not interesting. What is interesting is what passes through me, what uses me as an instrument" (p. 202).

This need to sacrifice one's ego could find its satisfaction in other movements than the Communist party. National Socialism may appear just as good an antidote to the "civilization of solitude," as Malraux described the bourgeois Western civilization. In spite of his efforts to annihilate himself in favor of the party, Boutros has not renounced his freedom of judgment, and it is doubtful that such an adept would be welcome in any totalitarian party. Never would a true "militant" think and, still less, say: "I think that the communists are just as rotten in their hearts and their minds as the capitalists" (p. 279).

The same reasons that have won him over to communism make it impossible for him to be orthodox: "I do not care about the doctrine and all its pretentious details—it is a movement, something which defies death, which risks death and that's the only thing I love in the world" (p. 280).

The theme of the flight from the past finds a perfect setting in the décor of Greece, where historical associations are aroused by the name of every city. There is a new poetry of the ruins in this fear of being seduced by them. They represent the dead values which are part of the bourgeois inheritance of Western man. It is hard for a bourgeois to throw them away; Drieu had shown that a Blaquans had found it easier instead to defend a tradition in which he did not actually believe. The temptation of the past is powerful in Boutros and it is only by a strong act of will that he looks for salvation in new directions: ". . . he fled history as he fled the police, he was afraid of remaining a prisoner of dead values as well as of their guardians" (p. 169). For Boutros, nostalgia for the past is a crime against nature by which he is often tempted:

Where is life now? This is the feeling which prods me and wakes me up when I feel I let myself go to sleep, lie down on a dead beauty, in order to attempt an impossible love, which is a crime against Nature, against time (p. 175).

Courage, when confronted with temptation, tells him to flee. When he is asked to admit that he is perfectly indifferent to the Parthenon, he protests passionately, that "he has the courage to tear his thought away from it."

It is only by pretense or self-deceit that one can say that the Greek tradition is still alive in us. The lesson of the Greeks may be admirable, but it is the lesson of youth; one must turn one's back to it and do as well in *one's own time*. Drieu develops here, through the character of Boutros, a theme which can be traced to Barrès. In his *Voyage à Sparte*, the man from Lorraine had already asked:

Where is Athens? Has this goddess taken refuge in your souls? It was a moment of the divine in the world. Well! For us *today* the divine consists in a very strong and very distinct feeling of the evolution and the flow of things.[7]

Barrès experienced the impossibility of adopting a philosophy of life evolved for other times and other needs by men of another race:

How can I utilize this famous Athens where I wander? It would be necessary for me to find in my soul moral truths, needs, and emotions analogous to those expressed by these statues, this architecture and by this Greek scenery. It would be necessary ... let me be frank, it would be necessary for me to have the blood of these Hellenes.[8]

In a more concrete fashion, Boutros asks Margot:

Can you derive from the Acropolis the thoughts you need everyday? Can your idea of love, for instance, rest on this system of lines converging toward a point, forever lost to us? (p. 174).

More logical than Barrès, the creator of Boutros goes further and considers that the civilizaiton which built the cathedrals is equally unable to give us "the thoughts we need every day." The contrast with Blaquans comes to mind again. Boutros has felt, for instance, that in a place like Vezelay lay the secret of what Europe has been, but what is the use of such a discovery for us today? "Yes, I, too, felt life there; I felt that life had passed there, but it had passed."

It is in Delphi that Boutros becomes aware that only a Dionysian conception of the cosmos can suit his contradictions, his appetite for life, and the confusion of the time in which he lives. The answer of the oracle must be ambiguous since life is made up of contradictions. What has always counted for Boutros is the passion for life and the ability to detect the movements of energy—and the forces of triumph—in the time in which he lives: "Spirituality surged for him from those facts which talked so clearly to his senses: the sweat, the blood, the shouts, the smell of crowds marching behind their haggard leaders" (p. 249).

---
[7] Maurice Barrès, *Le Voyage à Sparte* (Paris, Plon, 1922), p. 59.
[8] *Ibid.*, p. 49.

the thirst for the absolute

The lesson of Greece for Boutros is not the traditional lesson of humanism—an abstract notion of the permanent traits of human nature. Every generation must find its own truth: "If I do not get along by myself, of what use can be the words of the dead to me?" (p. 169). Because Boutros is communing with what is alive in his day, he is able to understand the gift of divination of the Pythia: "He auscultated, with palpitating anxiety, the rhythm of crowds just as here the Pythia had lent her ear to the foreboding breath of destinies" (p. 249). In this conception of life and of nature, broader than in a rationalistic view which has become the caricature of Greek thought in Western civilization, the body and the senses are not separated from spirituality and, far from being neglected, are given their place. Woman becomes an essential link between men and nature; hence Boutros' reconciliation, toward the end of the novel, with the place of woman in his life and the ritual, almost religious character of the love-making scene with Margot. Physical love is a spiritual exercise. It is certainly not, as between Blèche and Blaquans, a surrender to the lower appetites of their personalities. "They were not making love in order to get rid of an itch of their skins, they were making love because their souls could no longer resist the longing for knowledge" (p. 263).

Margot is the worthy counterpart of Boutros. She is more vital than the society around her. She has often been disillusioned but she has never given up hope. Dreaming at her window, she is vaguely aspiring toward a fuller life. Michel Boutros will justify her hopes and her expectations where Rico, her husband, had disappointed them. Michel had the courage to do all the things she should have done and his example is contagious. Through him, she realizes how difficult and sometimes how cruel it is to be one's self: "It seems to me that I am afraid of being myself . . . In order to exist, one must be the enemy of one's own family" (p. 99). Her own reactions toward Boutros make her realize how deep the gulf already was between herself and her husband. The intensity of life she senses in the communist kindles a "fervor" in her.

She is no longer satisfied by the pale social comedy of her little world. She begins to understand better the perfect indifference of Pahlen, the German diplomat, who hides a far-reaching ambition. His notion of "sincerity" must not be different from that of her communist friend:

> Most men are not sincere even when they want to be so, because they are not strong enough. Only the very great, those who are also the shrewdest and most hypocritical in little things, are sincere: Napoleon, Bismarck. That sincerity is the only real one, it is frightening (p. 84).

But she knows Michel Boutros is not only a fanatic. She feels in him the conflict of a man torn between contradictory tendencies. The fact that he has dominated these contradictions is a guarantee of his strength; the fact that he has not stifled them shows that he has remained human. The equilibrium he has reached is threatened and, therefore, all the more appealing to her.

The coquettish woman whose insipid conversation with empty diplomats was recorded in the first chapter, is transformed by her nascent love for a man she can admire. The example of the "authenticity" of Michel, who has had the courage to adapt his life to his ideals, awakens in her an ardent desire to be sincere and to prove it by deeds rather than by theatrical tirades.

It is hard to imagine the marchioness giving up the luxury to which she is accustomed. But, after all, Boutros had given up everything and if he is not happy, at least he lives. Drieu has avoided the facile developments that could have been expected from the situation: a marchioness falling in love with a communist agent. Michel Boutros is much more an adventurer than a "militant"; he is the twentieth-century version of the romantic outlaw. It is understandable that his defiance of the existing order would be more appealing to Margot than the dull conformism of a Malfosse or the frivolous dilettantism of a Rico. Margot, like a Mathilde de la Mole, has plumbed the emptiness of a polite, refined, and weakened society. She is ready to appreciate what was called *energie* by Stendhal, *ferveur* by Gide, and was soon going to be termed "authenticity" by the existentialists.

Michel Boutros may be accused of being a "man of action" who talks too much. He is remarkably articulate and exposes his ideas in long conversations with Margot, with Rico, with Malfosse, but why is he spending so much time justifying himself in the eyes of decadent bourgeois? Why does he not act instead of explaining himself? His revolutionary ideal is a little too marked by an urge to destroy: he has a tender contempt for his Russian chiefs who are so anxious to rebuild their house. He thinks that they have more vitality than Western Europeans, and, therefore, will destroy them. He explains this obsession with destruction by his war experience. "Dream of a youth born among the fulgurating trees of war, exploding from the ground faster than in a nightmare and darkening the sky with their ink-black foliage" (p. 244).

This novel, on the whole, is a remarkable analysis of a state of sensibility characteristic of the time, perhaps because Drieu remained faithful to what he observed in himself and around him. His hero is very human; his weaknesses and the negative side of the revolutionary in him may have been overemphasized; it reveals the author's deliberate decision to be sincere in a novel in which sincerity is the key problem.

III

Beloukia was published in the spring of 1936. Drieu had already taken a political position in the struggle following the riots of February, 1934, and he was on the eve of joining Doriot's Parti Populaire Français. The novel does not seem, at first sight, to be closely connected with the events of the author's life. The artistic transposition is more elaborate than in the Gille novels. But under the form of a fable or an exemplary tale, Drieu develops familiar themes: the unavoidable limitations in the love relationship between two human beings, as in *L'Homme couvert de femmes*, complicated this time by the conflict of love and political passions, as in *Une Femme à sa fenêtre,* and solved finally by a recourse to death. Under the traits of the poet, Hassib, one can recognize an aspect of the author in his early forties.

The choice of the oriental setting and costume lends a quality of timelessness to a situation which might otherwise have appeared too marked by the times. It is not the only classical element in this new form of the novel of testimony. The tone is uniformly tragic. Beloukia is a princess. Love, fate, and death are always present in the action and the dialogue. The composition resembles that of classic tragedy: it opens shortly before the climax, here a revolution, and the denouement promises only despair, destruction, and death to the protagonists. The author has picked for an epigraph a line from Racine.

In each of the twenty sections of the book, the recurrence of certain symbolic objects and images, even of certain key words gives the novel a musical quality. One of those key words is *déchirer.* Hassib, more than any other character in the novel, is torn between contradictory tendencies and loyalties. This conflict finally puts him in a situation where he cannot avoid betraying everybody and everything. The only way out is death. The tragedy of his life comes from a thirst for the absolute which he cannot satisfy: he cannot entirely love Beloukia; he cannot give himself entirely to his political passion. In every direction, he finds insufferable limitations. In Beloukia he finds the limitation of her past, in which he had no part, as well as of the present, in which he shares her affections with her husband and her sons; she cannot give up her glory to follow him. He is detached from everything; she is passionately attached to precarious treasures. Hassib has found in the princess' love the unifying element of his life. But this love can bring him only torments by the contrast between the ecstasy of her short presence and the terrible loneliness of the greater part of his life, "without friends, without family, without children." The description of adulterous love would not be complete without the analysis of what threatens it from within, an all-absorbing jealousy and the self-destruction of love by jealousy. The result of three years of love (a thousand nights) falls to pieces when distrust enters Hassib's heart. He cannot believe that this life was only an illusion: he has to prove that he has given Beloukia the best of himself and she the best of herself to him.

The proof would be soon given, he could sense it. He would separate himself from Beloukia, he would even do her as much harm as he could. But he would die from it.

Always this proof, this unique, absurd divine proof, death (p. 100).

The greatest crime Hassib has committed, that for which he is apparently punished, is to have compromised with his thirst for the absolute. At his very first meeting with Beloukia, his pride gave way to his love: he decided to be satisfied with what this woman would give him instead of demanding her entire heart, as he had until then always done with other women. A metamorphosis immediately took place in him; he became: "A man who no longer refused, but accepted the ambiguity of fate . . . a man who gave himself away and withdrew himself again, who took and let go again" (p. 81).

This compromise affects his attitude toward politics, so that his political actions can always be interpreted as betrayals by ill-intentioned people. Instead of fighting for a great cause, he risks his life and sacrifices his soldiers to save Hassan, the adversary's son. He is anxious to save the life of Hassan because he realizes that his intentions were not entirely pure when he suggested the kidnaping of the son as a stratagem to hold the father. After he is wounded, in his delirium, he expresses regret at not having a son. In the same access of delirium he says that he prefers the sword which penetrates his heart to Beloukia's love. It is the disillusioned conclusion of one who has been unable to make life fulfill the promises of his youth: "Decidedly it was necessary to renounce the absolute in life and seek it in death. God finally won. He obliged His creature to prefer Him to His creation" (p. 212).

Who is the woman to whom Hassib sacrificed his political passion and who finally led him to destruction? Beloukia is the epitome of womanhood. She has the body of a courtesan, the strength of a huntress, the head of a princess. Night is her element and violence her climate. When she was fifteen she had been raped by a young chief plundering in the fire of a city in revolt. Before Hassib, she had had another love affair with an officer, Yacoub. He died in the Persian war.

If he had been killed in extraordinary circumstances of temerity and of defiance to death, it was because Beloukia had not been able to give him all her heart... One day, Yacoub had felt his manly nature awake again in him with its demand and since he could not conquer in life, he had sought the fatal victory over death (p. 33).

Hassib will be destroyed by the same torment of not possessing her entirely; he will admit also that he has been "less strong than life" and that he feels the need to take flight into death.

The humiliation of Hassib by Beloukia is symbolized by a situation which occurs twice in the novel: a first time, during a summer vacation, Beloukia manages to hide Hassib and to smuggle him into her apartment in the summer residence. He has to sleep uncomfortably in a cupboard. He is imprisoned, at her mercy, and he makes the bitter remark: "What difference is there between a man like me and a eunuch? The latter lives in a harem, the former wishes to live there" (p. 52). Again, when he is wounded and plagued by fever, she installs him in a little cabinet adjoining her room. From the tower he can see his friends fighting in the moat. He can even recognize some who are wounded or dead. Beloukia, from the ramparts, watches the same tower "in which Hassib was lying, annihilated by the gift he had made her of himself" (p. 209).

The last scene of love-making between Hassib and Beloukia is treated as a symbol of the eternal war of the sexes. It resumes the image already suggested in the novel and especially at the beginning, after Beloukia has been raped by the young soldier. The latter says, before taking his life: "I was only a saber and I struck you" (p. 22). Again, later, Hassib recognizes that part of Beloukia's attraction is that their embrace reminds him of war: "In Hassib's arms, Beloukia gave cries which recalled to him and foretold the fatal *élan* of battle" (p. 156).

The last scene is even more specific in its symbolism: "Finally, he came to her. His desire was first like the restrained and short movement of a wild animal. The princess was opening with delight to this promise which was not yet a threat" (p. 217).

Beloukia's last words, just before Hassib's departure, as she gives him a dagger, announced the end of the "man covered with women" and the birth of the man of action: "This is the dagger you need and of which women have deprived you for years" (p. 218).

Thus, *Beloukia,* apparently so different from Drieu's other novels, marks another step in the spiritual odyssey of the author. It represents his farewell to women and his first experiments in political action.

In 1936, Drieu had already written many articles in which he was obliged to sacrifice to the necessities of political journalism any fine distinctions of thought, a particularly difficult sacrifice for a writer whose thought was rich in nuance and who was always prone to understand, even to espouse, the position of the adversary. The artist in him, who remained alive, transposed in this poetic tale, the sense of conflict, of contradiction, of betrayal in which the political partisan must live. Hassib is, par excellence, "the torn-apart hero." The symbol of this fatal "tearing apart" is his love for Beloukia: she represents all the things he has renounced and his love for her is bound to bring him despair and death. In spite of his awareness of this impossible situation, Hassib is unable to love any other woman. He retorts to Balek, the eunuch, who had pointed out to him that his jealousy of Beloukia was unavoidable because everyone desired a woman "so powerful, so rich, so beautiful, and so ardent." "Would you then like me to love a petty-bourgeoise or a slave?" Balek's reply sums up the wisdom of the whole tale, a wisdom from which Hassib is, of course, unable to benefit at all: "No, but then suffer without convulsions. Your suffering is in proportion to your joy: it is the law" (p. 139).

In a similar way, Hassib's situation in relation to the cause of the revolution is untenable. In his youth, when he had not yet given up his quest for the absolute, he had written theoretical works on politics in which, in his wild idealism, "he confused the duties of the poets with those of the masters of the world" (p. 84). He has learned since to make allowances for the faults of the masters of the world, provided that their central aspiration is toward greatness. In the domain of action, he has also passed from the role of the observer to that of an active participant. He would prefer to see his intervention limited to the role of adviser or, as he says himself, of "exhorter."

But here, again, he is contradicting himself, for when he sees his ideas embodied in an actual plot he does not recognize them; they look now "incredibly frivolous and specious." To reveal the difference between idea and action, he uses the vocabulary of sex, just as he used war images to describe the sexual act: "Between an idea and a saber there is the same distance as between a virgin who thinks she likes her status and a mature woman who loves hers" (p. 174).

He despises many of his companions of action. Felsan is the prototype of the revolutionary whose reasons for engaging in action are obviously impure: he is one of those mediocre people who seek compensation for a life of failure in political fanaticism. The fanaticism of such men springs from their secret envy of those who are in power. Hassib suffers in their company because his "pure and rigorous sense of aristocracy" makes him recognize superior men even in the opposite camp. Hassib is also a *délicat*, extremely vulnerable, obsessed by a feeling of inadequacy, of weakness, and ultimately of guilt. He finds temporary relief in action. But the final refuge, the decisive remedy, can only be death.

The prefiguration in Hassib's destiny of what was to be the author's fate ten years later makes of *Beloukia* a rather unusual novel, more truly autobiographical than a retrospec-

the thirst for the absolute

tively autobiographical novel: Hassib was, in 1936, a portrait of the author truer than life, and the novel could be called a prophetically autobiographical novel.⁹

In *Beloukia*, as in the two other novels examined in this chapter, the author is intensely concerned with the idea of sincerity connected with participation. This time, he looks at it from a slightly different point of view and shows how sincerity leads inevitably to playing the role of traitor.¹⁰ The man who is at all times sincere in his words and thoughts and actions is faithful to no one. The scene in *Beloukia* which best dramatizes this theme is the one where Hassib, powerless in the tower, is forced to watch his friends fight and die in the moat below.¹¹

The three novels are studies of "bad conscience" which insist on the weaker aspects of the psychology of the adventurer. *Blèche* shows how the choice of any role in life is impossible for the bourgeois intellectual; *Une Femme à sa fenêtre* and *Beloukia* show the impossible situation in which the choice of another role places him. To be most efficient in the party of the revolution, he must become an instrument, a "militant," and his whole personality rebels against this role. His fate is as tragic as that of a Racinean hero; it is no wonder that the adventurer as a type has taken such an important place in contemporary literature. His is certainly a more interesting literary figure than that of the militant. Sartre says that he would choose to follow the adventurer in his solitude. It is easy to recognize Hassib's or Boutros' contradictions in the following portrait of the adventurer as Sartre sees him:

He lived until the end in an impossible condition: avoiding and seeking solitude, living in order to die and dying in order to

---

⁹ The character of Hassib, the poet, who loves horses and women, foreshadows the character of the guitarist Felipe of *L'Homme à cheval* (1943). Hassib also has a guitar (*Beloukia*, p. 11). In the later novel, the separation between the man who dreams and the man who acts is accomplished physically: Don Jaime leads cavalry charges and Filipe sings inspiring songs.

¹⁰ The parallel of Constant in *Les Chiens de paille* with the image of the archtraitor, Judas, reveals the continuity of the theme in Drieu's fiction.

¹¹ A similar scene seems to express the same theme in *L'Homme à cheval*. See chap. ix.

live, convinced of the vanity as well as of the necessity of action, attempting to justify his undertaking by assigning it an aim in which he did not believe, seeking the absolute objectivity of the result in order to dilute it in an absolute subjectivity, desiring the failure he refused and refusing the victory he desired, wanting to build his life like a destiny and enjoying only the infinitesimal moments which separate life from death."[12]

[12] Stéphane, *op. cit.*, p. 26 (Sartre's preface).

seven

THE WORLD OF PRETENSE AND ILLUSIONS

In 1936, "Les Editions Populaires Françaises" in Saint-Denis published a thirty-page pamphlet, *Doriot ou la vie d'un ouvrier français,* under the signature of Drieu La Rochelle. Its price was only one franc, since it was intended for wide distribution. In the preface Drieu wrote: "When one knows well this life, when one understands it well, when one draws from it all the lessons it contains, one is another man." The transformation, however, did not obliterate the novelist in Drieu. The same year, the *Nouvelle Revue Française* in its December issue began publication of part of *Rêveuse bourgeoisie,* a novel free of politics, which appeared in book form in 1937. The author had found a more direct outlet for his political views; at the same time, and for two years until October, 1938, Drieu contributed political articles to the Doriot party's paper *L'Emancipation nationale.*

Some critics judging this new turn of his career, accused Drieu, along with other artists like Malraux, of betraying their art and raised the question of the betrayal of the intellectuals (*la trahison des clercs*). The point of view of those critics can be summed up in what J. N. Faure-Biguet wrote in the weekly *Marianne:*

> May those who have the immense happiness, the immense value of being artists understand that their duty, their mission is not to push us towards a party or a man, to entice us to such and such a banner but to cleanse our minds clogged by the more or less slanted news with a little dream, a little beauty, a little of that joy which comes from dream and beauty.[1]

Ramon Fernandez answered this criticism by showing that politics had replaced religion for the writers of the time: "I mean, as Thibaudet said, that political anxiety today has replaced and corresponds in concrete terms to the problem of salvation and destiny."[2] According to Fernandez, engagement in political activities had become for certain writers a way of renewing themselves, of finding themselves, and of enriching their personality. He even argued that, in the particular case of Drieu, *Rêveuse bourgeoisie*, far from showing the loss of the author's subtlest qualities, would not have been so good without Doriot or what Doriot represented for Drieu.

It is an interesting hypothesis and one can indeed observe that henceforth the publication of each one of Drieu's novels will follow an active political campaign involving journalistic activity.

It should be noted, however, that Drieu had interspersed the publication of his fiction with political essays even before he took sides in the political arena and that the progress in his fiction may just as likely be ascribed to the fact that the author had reached his maturity as a writer and as a man. *Drôle de voyage* (1933) and *La Comédie de Charleroi* (1934) had already shown unquestionable mastery both in form and content. Drieu did not write anything better afterward although he wrote on a larger scale.

The chief characteristics of *Rêveuse bourgeoisie* and *Gilles*

---
[1] Quoted by Ramon Fernandez in his article, "Est-ce une trahison?," *NRF*, No. 284 (May, 1937), 769.
[2] *Ibid.*, p. 771.

is that they are *romans bilans,* a summing-up of a man's life, of a man's philosophy and also of a novelist's themes previously developed in individual novels. *Rêveuse bourgeoisie* resumes the subject of *Etat-Civil* by introducing the childhood and youth of Yves Le Pesnel, but broadens and deepens this subject by going much further into the origins of the boy, by varying the points of view and multiplying the characters over three generations. Finally, *Rêveuse bourgeoisie* is the novel of a family (Drieu first intended to entitle his novel *La Famille Le Pesnel*) and even of a class, as the present title indicates. The novel of the person born into such a family and such a class will be *Gilles* (although Gilles is presented as a foundling, he is distinctly a bourgeois).

In spite of great differences in form and content, the two novels should not be considered separately. They are complementary. To use the words of Marcel Arland: "... the novel of this family and the novel of this individual complete each other like a tree and its fruit."[3] Gilles Gambier in *Gilles* is the product of the declining bourgeoisie described in the first novel. The two books have a similar structure: *Rêveuse bourgeoisie* is divided into five parts, connected but easily separable; the four episodes of *Gilles* even bear distinct titles. From the "Mariage d'argent" uniting Camille Le Pesnel and Agnès Ligneul in *Rêveuse bourgeoisie* to the "Epilogue" in which Gilles ends up fighting in the Spanish Civil War, Drieu paints a vast historical picture of three generations of a French family.

In contrast with Drieu's previous novels which, for the most part, described a crisis and were built on the pattern of a French classic tragedy, *Rêveuse bourgeoisie* adopts the form of a narration unfolding over long periods of time. Under this marked difference of form, however, the all-pervading theme of decadence is easily recognizable: this novel is the story of the decomposition of an individual, the decomposition of a family, the decomposition of a class. In order to alleviate the danger of monotony, Drieu has picked for the subject of

---

[3] Marcel Arland, "Drieu La Rochelle," *NNRF*, No. 13 (January, 1954), 112.

each part of the novel a salient crisis marking a new phase in the story of this decline.

At first sight, *Rêveuse bourgeoisie* seems to be a return, on Drieu's part, to a more conventional or traditional form of novel. Its length, its realistic, painstaking portrayal of the small details of middle-class daily life brings to mind the naturalistic novels of the 1880's and 1890's in France. In that respect, *Rêveuse bourgeoisie* constitutes one example among many of a return to a kind of neonaturalistic technique in France, in the 1930's. Drieu's former friend, Louis Aragon, who was better known until then for his surrealistic experiments in poetry and in fiction, also returned to a novel form reminiscent of Zola. In 1934, he had published *Les Cloches de Bâle*, presenting it as the first novel in a series under the general title of *Le Monde réel*. In 1936, the second lengthy volume, *Les Beaux quartiers,* appeared. This revival of the long, naturalistic novel may be traced back to Roger Martin du Gard who had begun publishing in 1920 the panoramic novel, *Les Thibault,* also the novel of a family. In 1936 he had brought the chronicle of that family up to World War I with *Eté 1914.* The first volumes of Jules Romains' cyclical series of *Les Hommes de bonne volonté* appeared in quick succession after *Le 6 Octobre,* published in 1932. All these novels shared a common trait; they described French society before World War I.

Drieu may have been tempted to emulate them. But his motivation sprang from deeper sources, for he returns to the subject of his very first novel, *Etat-Civil*, published sixteen years before. In spite of its neonaturalistic appearance, the novel is subjective. The story of the previous generations of Ligneuls and Le Pesnels is presented only to help understand the present generation, that of Yves and Geneviève, the author's own generation.

The whole narration of the first three parts is a reconstruction of the past by Geneviève. She is anxious to tell the story in her own name and the opening lines of the fourth part indicate very clearly the author's intention. "Somehow, I have

the world of pretense and illusions

been able, so far, to tell about my life through this indirect device. But now I talk openly in my own name. It is myself, the daughter of Camille and Agnès, who speaks directly. All that has gone before was in order to come to the point of talking about myself and about Yves" (p. 240).

This sudden change of tone three-quarters of the way along in the novel might have proved a fatal error in hands less skillful than Drieu's. But he succeeds in making us accept this shift, and the painstakingly detailed description of the engagement, wedding, and stormy married life of Camille and Agnès now assumes its full significance. For it is seen as the reconstruction by an imaginative child of the dramas which have preceded and accompanied her childhood and irretrievably conditioned her personality.

Certain critics, baffled by this sudden change of rhythm at the end of the book, accused Drieu of having written this latter part very hastily.[4] It is true that the narration in the last two parts moves much faster, but this seems to constitute a deliberate artistic device on the author's part. The difference in literary treatment corresponds to and expresses the difference between the two periods described. World War I brought about the destruction of the old order of things. This change was not a political one only: it affected the social structure and the mores as well. *Rêveuse bourgeoisie* in its two main divisions, life before 1914 and the life of the generation which was twenty in 1913, reflects this transformation through a change of rhythm.

Drieu had very definite views about the new structural form of the novel describing contemporary urban life in contrast with the traditional novels of the nineteenth century describing nineteenth-century life. For him the change of content demanded new form. He had expressed this view in an essay on Aldous Huxley's *Point Counter Point*.[5] He thought

---
[4] See, for example, Robert Poulet, *Parti-Pris*, p. 90. But the critic seems to have read the novel rather hastily himself, for example, he confuses the names and writes "Ligneul" when he means "Le Pesnel."

[5] "A Propos d'un roman anglais, *NRF*, No. 208 (November, 1930), 721–731.

that the contemporary novel was bound—since it intended to be a faithful picture of contemporary society—to be the novel of the individual: "Our epoch offers us only individuals, who, isolated in cities, cannot lift their depressed imagination toward any figure in the crowd. There cannot be any intrigue and conflict among human beings when they no longer live in coherent little groups, animated by common illusions."[6] He ascribed the so-called crisis of the contemporary novel to this sociological factor: "The same thing happens in the novel as on the stage: the drama, the conflict of passions is no longer possible. There is a similar evolution in both cases: the drama becomes a series of tableaux; the novel—when it aims at being vast—is a sheaf of unilinear tales."[7]

Rêveuse bourgeoisie appears at first glance to correspond much more to the definition Drieu gives in the same article of the novel in its traditional nineteenth-century form:

> A novel is a work which ties together several lives, involves them and carries them in a reciprocal action, modifies their daily mood and, after this common action has been exhausted, leaves them transformed—annihilated or exalted.

This definition applies well to *Rêveuse bourgeoisie* which may explain why the literary critics, accustomed to admire what is familiar, greeted this novel as Drieu's masterpiece, especially in its first three parts. Those first three parts have another traditional aspect; they introduce scenes of provincial life mixed with scenes of Parisian life. Drieu saw in the "province" an essential element of the "old novel:" "The element which introduces so much dramatic virulence in the old English, Russian, and French novels, is family life, often reinforced by country life." The stock of the Le Pesnel family is distinctly Norman. The provincial background of the Ligneul family is more mixed but not distant: "Whichever way Mme Ligneul looked (in her ancestry) she found the province. Her mother had lived in Saint-Malo and in Caen, her father, born in Caen, had transplanted his quiet life to

---
[6] *Ibid.*
[7] *Ibid.*

the world of pretense and illusions

Neuilly, which, in 1870, was still provincial. And on M. Ligneul's side it was the Valois from father to son in an unbroken line" (p. 58). The first and the third part of the novel are set in Normandy and Brittany. For many characters in the novel, Paris is seen from a provincial perspective: it represents the mythical city of perdition, a modern Babylon. The trip to Paris of Camille's parents for their son's engagement assumes a symbolic meaning and almost epic proportions. One of the factors in Camille's failure and decadence is that he is what Barrès would have called a *déraciné*, he is uprooted in Paris. He never entirely adapts to Paris; his family is only "camping" in the metropolis. His children will suffer from this social isolation.

It seems that Drieu has deliberately maintained an old-fashioned literary atmosphere for two-thirds of his novel in order better to emphasize by contrast the distinct character of twentieth-century life and the maladjustment of the bourgeoisie encumbered by too many vestiges of the previous period. He does not hesitate to make a direct reference to Balzac within the novel and he establishes a parallel between his characters and those of Balzac.

We were in Grandfather's room where the furniture of a country Empire style brought from Valois impassively gazed on the bankruptcy of his Parisian dreams. This simple old man in his cap had had his own hallucinations just like any other madman of Paris. A little like Goriot—if he had not found a Rastignac for his daughter, he had at least equipped his grandson to be one. In this beginning of the twentieth century, we were repeating the stories of the previous century (p. 264).

There are indeed in *Rêveuse bourgeoisie* many similarities with Balzacian novels. It is a story in which ambition, marriage, and money are inextricably mixed. In Balzac's novels, the young man from the provinces trying to make a place for himself in Paris also usually needs a big dowry to make things easier. He usually marries a girl from a good family, although his heart is elsewhere and Rose, Camille's mistress, is in the romantic tradition of the good-hearted prostitute. The bourgeois triangle also has a historical basis: it is an imitation of a situation then accepted in higher society: "It was the time, in higher spheres, of solidly established *ménage à trois*" (p. 236).

Episodic characters like the calculating priest, here the abbé Maurois, or like the meddlesome old maid, here Mademoiselle Receveur, seem to come directly from Balzac's scenes of provincial life. Their petty calculations influence the development of the plot. The village priest, by his shrewd determination, makes the marriage of Camille and Agnès possible, just as, later, the jealous spinster is instrumental in preventing Agnès' remarriage to Le Loreur and in preparing her reconciliation with Camille.

The opposition of province and Paris is eminently Balzacian. To all the country people, Paris looks like a dangerous jungle full of devilish snares and yet at the same time a fascinating dreamland. They are proud to see their children risk themselves in it, but if they fail, they are quick to blame them for their attempt: "If Camille had not been spoiled by Paris! The priests are right; Paris is Babylon" (p. 196). The theme of the corrupting effect of Paris reappears all through the novel, Camille's aunt, Mademoiselle Rozelle, the embodiment of the virtues of the provinces, hard, strong, outspoken, is the first one to sound the alarm: "Camille and his brothers have left for Paris; it would have been better for them to stay here" (p. 61). Toward the end of the novel, Yves' failure at his examination, and the decline of the Ligneuls, provoked by the ever threatening bankruptcy of Camille, their son-in-law, are signs that the province has not stood successfully the test of Paris. Yves' grief over his failure takes on a wider meaning:

This grief was taking a decisive significance: the Ligneul family had failed in its ascension. It had chosen poorly its allies. The Le Pesnels, more brilliant than the Ligneuls, had also less consistency and stood less well the test of Paris (p. 264).

All those traits, important for the external appearance of the novel, do not, however, affect its substance. The protagonists are not Balzacian. Their story is, in one way or another, the story of Camille, *un homme qui se défait,* "a man who falls to pieces" to use the phraseology of Barrès. In that respect, *Rêveuse bourgeoisie,* when it succeeds in being impassive, reminds one of *L'Education sentimentale.* But it is Flaubertian only in the same way that Flaubert could say of Madame Bovary: "It is myself." If Yves is obviously an image of Drieu, or of what he might have been, the delicate bourgeois killed at the beginning of the war; if Geneviève is, transposed, another potential development of the author's personality, Camille Le Pesnel is unquestionably a certain aspect of himself that he is always afraid to recognize in the mirror: the weak person, the braggart, the liar, the man obsessed by lust, who can never carry out anything, the talker who satisfies himself with the sound of his words, the victim of a perpetual illusion, the product of a "dreamy bourgeoisie."

The obsessive fear of resembling his father plunges Yves into self-destruction. The reader sees Camille through the eyes of his children and the extremely personal distortion of Geneviève and Yves makes of him a monster. Skillfully, the author utilizes this childish distortion to give fantastic dimensions to the character of Camille. Only at the very end of the novel is Geneviève, after the death of her father, able to consider his life and his character with some perspective. *Rêveuse bourgeoisie* offers thus a penetrating analysis of the feelings of a child toward his parents and more especially toward the father: little by little the monster is brought down to the dimensions of a man. The child, in this case Geneviève, has to be grown up to be able to judge her father fairly. Into the forming of her own opinion of Camille have gone the views of her mother, her grandparents, family friends like Le Loreur and Gustave Ganche, as well as those she acquired in the company of Yves in childhood and adolescence. But all these views are necessarily prejudiced; Geneviève is able to form a mature judgment only after she has found herself and can trust herself. The children's psychology is neither Balzacian nor Flaubertian but decidedly post-Proustian or even post-

Freudian. The ambivalent attitude of Yves toward his father, for instance, is delicately analyzed:

> He was a monster for whom Yves felt an equally violent attraction and repulsion. And when in his thought he brought together his mother and his father, she, also, appeared to him as a monster provoking in him feelings of a painful ambiguity (p. 179).

The story of the sentimental life of the three women, Blanche Ligneul, Agnès, Geneviève, makes an interesting historical picture of the attitude of women toward love and marriage over three generations. It is one of the surprises reserved for the reader of *Rêveuse bourgeoisie* to find in Drieu the misogynist an attentive observer of the status of women in modern society and, in a way, an apostle of their liberation. The grandmother is puzzled by her daughter's boldness in paying a visit to a man without the knowledge and consent of her husband. She is absolutely unable even to imagine what might have taken place:

> Although she had read a few novels and she went to the theater to see rather bold plays she had not the faintest idea of the emotions and violent movements which can throw a woman into the arms of a man. What she knew of love was exclusively limited to the husband-wife relationship (p. 114).

The author analyzes what the relationship between M. and Mme Ligneul has been with a mixture of irony and emotion. The passage shows that Drieu's skill in evoking physical love is not limited to passion or voluptuousness:

> During the first nights, around 1870, she had undergone M. Ligneul's ministry with a great amazement which she had tried to overcome and transcend little by little, by dint of patience, good will and good humor; she was keeping for herself her amazement at the ways of nature.... Besides, M. Ligneul himself seemed very embarrassed. So, they shared the difficulty of the experience which united them just as if it were work, grief or sickness (pp. 114–115).

The awakening of the senses is complete in Agnès. She is immediately attracted by Camille and the physical character

the world of pretense and illusions

of that attraction is violent, almost irresistible. Camille realizes that he can put an end to the most violent scenes from his wife by resorting to sex. Agnès, however, knows the temptations of adulterous love. They arise from a desire to take revenge on her husband, and those attempts at liberating herself show all the more the strength of her attachment to him. For she remains faithful. Even though she attacks her husband in front of the children, she does not allow them to judge him.

Geneviève's youth is not protected as strictly as her mother's had been. For her brother she has a passionate affection which is not always too different from the passion of Amélie for René. Yves and herself constitute a "couple" in revolt against the older couple of the parents. She lives vicariously Yves' love for Emmy Maindron, so that Antoine Maindron, in love with Geneviève, feels half excluded from the "trio." Antoine is, however, the first man who makes her realize that she will be irresistible to men. She experiences with him the romantic exaltation of adolescent love in that summer of 1913, full of promises: "It was the same complicity between handsome, sensitive rich people and handsome, sensitive poor people which delighted Yves and myself in Balzac and in Stendhal" (p. 246). The war marks the great turmoil in which all the social barriers are destroyed: Geneviève surrenders to a young pilot on the day of his departure for the air corps. He is killed. As an army nurse she has love affairs with her patients. She marries Antoine Maindron, whose sensuousness destroys their love. She leaves him to follow an adventurer, Edouard Nicorps. With him she spends the money she had inherited. They travel around the world going to the countries of the old gods he adores: Bolivia, Peru, Mexico, Egypt, and upon their return Nicorps decides that they should separate. She becomes an actress. At the end of the story, she is pregnant by Viremont, a journalist.

Geneviève has not hesitated to divorce Antoine Maindron, whereas the possibility of her mother's divorce had caused such heated discussions in the little world of the Ligneuls.

Apparently, the author does not take a position on the question of divorce. In the second part, divorce is suggested by Mme Rabier, who is intelligent but is considered by the timid bourgeois surrounding the Ligneuls as a dangerous, corrupted person (her daughters are married and have lovers; her son has followed the unusual profession of *couturier*). The defender of the old order is Mme Vettard, whom the author does not make very attractive: "Mme Vettard, a distant cousin of M. Ligneul's, had married a rich landowner in Valois. She lived in a gross nothingness of which she used to say: 'There is one thing of which we can't complain—my husband, myself and the children—we are happy'" (p. 152).

Rêveuse bourgeoisie is not a *roman à thèse*. On most issues, Drieu tries to describe the facts and transcribe what people of different opinions think. Politics is remarkably absent. The Ligneuls and the Le Pesnels are, in principle, against the government of the Third Republic: "Still imbued with the sense of hierarchy of the old regime, these petty bourgeois who had hardly left their province, were surprised and shocked at seeing their equals or their inferiors in power" (p. 191). Camille Le Pesnel's opinions in politics reflect only what he reads in his paper, *L'Intransigeant:* the violent articles by Rochefort. This detail completes the portrait of Camille, but politics is never examined as such. One might be surprised that there is no mention of the Dreyfus case, for instance. But here again, it is a trait of the "dreamy" bourgeoisie. Drieu always denounced as one of the major weaknesses of the bourgeoisie its systematic political "absence."[8]

If Drieu, in *Rêveuse bourgeoisie,* does not pay much attention to politics, he gives us nonetheless an idea of the currents of thought of the time by his intellectual portraits of a few types and by indicating their relationship with the traditional heroes of the French novel. The gap which separates the generation of Camille from that of the Balzacean heroes is marked in the portraits of the pseudo realists of the type of Le Loreur

---

[8] "The essential, unforgivable failure of the bourgeoisie has been its political 'absenteeism'" (in the article: "Si la bourgeoisie veut encore être quelque chose," *Avec Doriot,* p. 164).

the world of pretense and illusions

and Gustave Ganche, conscious imitators of the ambitious young men from Balzac's and Stendhal's novels. In spite of their airs of cynicism, they are just as dreamy and ineffectual as the bourgeoisie they condemn but from which they come. Gustave Ganche has found in books his dreams of glory:

> This generation was nourished on books in which its predecessors had shown that for a century the young French bourgeois would not sleep because of the memory a young Corsican had left; it was still interrogating Julien Sorel and Rastignac (p. 189).

This articulate free thinker and leftist (at the time the Parti Radical was really "radical") whose opinions inspire fear in the timid Ligneuls and Le Pesnels, is actually quite harmless.

> A member of the Executive Committee of the Radical Socialist party and a Freemason, he was rereading his history handbooks, *Le Rouge et Noir*, the adventures of Rastignac and of Rubempré, and waiting. His mother, after coming into her fortune, had finally been able to make up for the father's strictness and gave him almost luxurious monthly allowances. This is what enabled him to wait (p. 191).

These two men, solidly established in the bourgeois order, consider love as part of their philosophy of action; in order to get acquainted with the subtleties of the heart, they lay siege to Agnès, in a grotesque manner with ridiculous results.

Yves, who had been awakened to intellectual awareness by people like Gustave Ganche, represents another generation, anxious to break away from bookish dreamers. He has read Balzac and Stendhal, too, but he has also drunk at the source of *Les Fleurs du mal*. The masters of his generation were Barrès, Gide, and Nietzsche. His grandparents had hoped he would have a leisurely, aristocratic life and had earned as much money as they could to make this possible. But his father had squandered the money. Emmy, the first girl with whom he falls in love, is rich. The memory of his father makes him wonder how much unconscious calculation has entered into his infatuation for an heiress. He reads too much, and prefers dreaming to action: "Since I had met her, I was only dreaming of the future instead of earning it day by day" (p.

265). He is perfectly lucid and refuses to dupe himself by waiting and dreaming like a Gustave Ganche, but he recognizes in himself, with horror, the decadence of a worn-out bourgeois. After his failure at the examination, he tells his sister:

> Can't you see what a perfect failure I am. I'll never be able to do anything but that: to chatter. At sixteen, I was keeping an intimate journal. I adored Amiel: I don't reach up to the ankle of that dwarf. Grandpa and Grandma brought me up to be a man of private means and to write my intimate journal like André Gide. I counted on Emmy's dowry as Papa had on Mother's. There are families in which people get tired very quickly (p. 270).

Yves, in order to escape the kind of life he hates, which seems to take shape with the ineluctability of fate, decides to tear himself away from it by joining the colonial troops in Africa in which life will be particularly hard for this delicate and sensitive young bourgeois. War is the great experience which reveals to Yves his true self. After he is fatally wounded, he can tell his sister that he was right in leaving Paris. He may die now, because he has lived:

> I got used to that life . . . I was born for it but unfortunately not prepared for it by my education. The training has been atrocious. I almost gave up, but the fear of resembling *him*. . . . Now I am all right. I love to be in command, to risk (p. 307).

He can also reassure her about the frightening inheritance from their father. The latter is a coward but cowardice can be conquered. Yves dies two days after his family's visit.

Death in action, in a period of extreme tension, must have been one of the secret wishes of Drieu, for he has described this situation in his war poems as well as in his fiction. Geneviève follows a different way to escape the Le Pesnel destiny. Instead of expressing a passionate refusal, like Yves, she utilizes her weaknesses and transforms them into virtues for the art she has chosen. Here, the subjective personal character of *Rêveuse bourgeoisie* appears clearly and the reader can measure the progress made by Drieu the man in the solution of the problem of his origins and of what he considers a terrifying heredity. In *Etat-Civil* the author had wanted to portray "one he had been" in an effort to get rid of the individual features determined by his family and his class. But in *Rêveuse bourgeoisie* he does not hesitate to face reality and to make of Camille Le Pesnel, the father whom he feared to resemble, who appeared so fleetingly in the sketchy *Etat-Civil*, the central character. Now, like his heroine, Geneviève, the author seems to be convinced of one thing: "One never gets out of one's family." It is vain therefore to vow hatred to one's family or to condemn the family as an institution. It is equally impossible to put into practice the Biblical commandment: "Thou shalt honor thy father and thy mother." Geneviève sums up the philosophy of the novel by revealing the secret of her own liberation from the inheritance of a terrible father. She is just as far from the religious precept of honoring one's parents as from Gide's outbursts of hatred against families:

> One must fight Camille; otherwise one would die. Because one is upon earth to be something else than Camille even though one may be burdened by his particular gifts and overwhelmed by his terrible presence. The question is not: do I or don't I have his vices? but: will his vices be my virtues? The children have the advantage of knowing more than their own parents because they had a chance to observe them (p. 323).

Whereas Yves had violently rejected the inheritance or at least had fled from the source of infection and had proved to his satisfaction that he could be different from his father, Geneviève exploits her weaknesses in the service of the dramatic arts. When she describes her talent for acting it is easy to make the transposition with the author's talent because she gives a valid definition of the art of "fiction" applicable also to literature. Addressing her dead father, she says:

> Was not your worst defect, your worst weakness, transmitted to us so that we might make out of it our virtue? You lied and people said that for you it was a profession to lie. Well for me, to say that is not a metaphor. My trade is to lie and to be sincere as you were

in the moment of each lie. All the rage of my profession is in that: with what fervor I live each role that I play. With what desperate effort I flee the lie of my whole life by giving reality to each one of my lies (p. 326).

Thus, one of the remedies for combatting the inescapable inheritance of the *rêveuse bourgeoisie* is lucidity—a lucidity which, if it does not bring happiness, at least prevents Geneviève from belonging to the immense herd of the *comédiens sans le savoir*, the actors who are not aware that they are acting a role instead of living their lives, a lucidity which allows her to utilize the very defects of her dreamy family.

The author has himself known both Yves' and Geneviève's experiences. His effort to become integrated in the outside world through war marked his emancipation from family and class; later he tried to prolong this experience by his political, revolutionary actions. At the same time, he tried to cultivate his lucidity. As a writer, he denounced the world of the *comédiens sans le savoir*, the world of pretense and illusions. Caught by his own preaching in favor of action and authenticity, he refused, when the time of final commitments came, to retire into the role of the irresponsible writer. He thought he had to take sides or he, too, would be only an incorrigible dreamer.

eight

THE REAL WORLD

The publisher's statement on the cover of the *Nouvelle Revue Française* announcing the publication of *Gilles* in 1939 presented the novel as the first attempt by a French novelist at a panoramic view of the twenty years just passed: 1917–1937. The timing of the novel was propitious; France was entering World War II and everyone felt that an era was drawing to a close. Drieu was in many ways well qualified to write the novel of his generation—the generation that came of age in 1914. His political essays showed that he had meditated on the great problems facing his country and his time and that he had applied to their solution a penetrating intelligence. As a writer of fiction, two works at least, *La Comédie de Charleroi* and *Drôle de voyage*, had already won him a prominent place among his contemporaries; his recent *Rêveuse bourgeoisie* had just proved that he could write successfully a long, ambitious novel. The expectations of the critics and the public were all the greater because Drieu, in spite of his forty-six years and the long list of his published work, was viewed more as an author of promise than of accomplishment.

The very title of the new novel, *Gilles*, was likely to arouse curiosity. Gilles and Gille Gambier had been appearing in Drieu's fiction since 1925.[1] The fictional hero was universally recognized as the counterpart of the author. People were entitled to expect in the summing up of Gille's memoirs a *roman à clef*, with easily recognizable contemporaries. The author's personality was controversial and puzzling, but even his political enemies knew that they could count on Drieu's sincerity. And since he had been associated with important literary and political movements, his testimony was bound to reveal unsuspected aspects of famous men and a backstage view of cliques and movements. An added guarantee of Drieu's independence of judgment was the fact that he had broken with Doriot and his party a year before, in November, 1938.

These considerations affected the book's success; it sold well. Of all Drieu's novels it is certainly the most widely read and the best known. It was greeted with a slight disappointment by some critics and with enthusiasm by others. The existentialists have used it as a case history to show how a nihilist can turn into a fascist.[2] This "golden and dirty" novel, as Sartre calls it[3] has remained as controversial as the author himself. There is no doubt that it is one of the important French novels of the first half of this century.

Gilles Gambier is the soldier—(especially in the first, "La Permission," and the last part, "Epilogue," of the novel); he is the Don Juan "covered with women," destroying some women and destroyed by others, the decadent enveloped in the ambient decadence, denouncing it and being part of it, the artist who has known Dada and the surrealist movements—their group is called "Revolte" in the novel—the

---

[1] Possibly the "s" of this Gilles indicates that he is the sum of all the previous Gille's.

[2] For example, Simone de Beauvoir in *Pour une morale de l'ambiguité* (Paris, Gallimard, 1947), p. 80.

[3] J. P. Sartre, *Situations II* (Paris, Gallimard, 1948), p. 228.

political journalist who attends political meetings and analyzes party intrigues, the contemplative mystic who wants to invent his own way of praying and his own God, the adventurer fighting in Spain in the ranks of Franco in order to find finally in the atmosphere of impending death and of virile comradeship the only way for him to live intensely.

Gilles is first of all an *Entwicklungsroman*, the *Wanderjahre* of Gilles Gambier before he finds his way. It is a picture of the times only so far as Gilles is a child of the times; a product of World War I, educated by the Paris of the surrealists and of a declining Third Republic. It is a picture of only that part of the generation with which Gilles associates: most of the characters exist only in relationship to Gilles, including the women who are part of his *éducation sentimentale* and the friends who are in some way his "harmonics" or, on the contrary, enable him to define himself by contrast.

I

Gilles is above all, the child of World War I. *La Comédie de Charleroi* gives a picture of the front; "La Permission" paints a picture of war only as seen from Paris, from the *arrière*. Characteristically, Gilles Gambier is without known parents and he is introduced to the reader emerging at the Gare de l'Est, on leave from the "kingdom of men," the front, to which men have withdrawn. He will never feel quite at home in Paris, which he calls by contrast "the realm of women." Although he has a voracious appetite for all the things of which war has deprived him—women, gaiety, luxury, leisure—the shadow of war is always present for him. Gilles feels guilty at being in Paris while young men are dying at the front and his nostalgia finally takes him back to war. In a way, war has unfitted him for civilian life; war has given him an intuition of what he conceived to be the noblest part of himself and has thus revealed to him what he considers the highest ideals of mankind.

But war has also been a school of skepticism which has

taught him always to distrust the so called *beaux sentiments* of the *arrière*. In the trenches and through the violent contrast between life at the front and in Paris, he has acquired a sense of the essential absurdity of man's fate as well as of the hypocrisy of the human comedy. One of the incidents in the opening pages is particularly revealing from that point of view. Gilles has just met Benedict, a war companion who, after courageous conduct, has obtained a less exposed assignment. They go together to the Comédie Française to see a play by Henry Bernstein, *L'Elévation*. The two soldiers shock the audience by their behavior: they boo the conventional sentimentality of the drama which exalts the sacrifice of the fighting soldier. The very title of the play, indicates one of the central motifs of the novel, that is, the idea of sacrifice, of death, and redemption. But the play is only a parody of genuine experience: "On the stage the suffering body of the soldier was offered like a soiled host to the avid pity of the audience" (p. 10).[4] For soldiers like Gilles and Benedict, this unauthentic performance is a "disgustingly heroic play" (*saloperie de pièce héroïque*). But the audience is ecstatic.

Later in the novel, the French audience at political conventions will show the same blindness or play the same "comedy" of accepting empty words and abstractions, of taking the pseudo for the authentic. The Comédie Française offers thus, in a microcosm, an image of the tragic French comedy of pretense and make-believe. Political men, such as the leaders of the Parti Radical Socialiste, constitute later the "troop" of actors for the French public. Would-be literary men, also deprived of all authenticity, will play for themselves similar "comedies" by staging fictitious trials of their famous contemporaries.

For Gilles, the laws of life are derived from his war experience: "He had found in war an unforgettable revelation which had inscribed in a luminous picture the first articles of his faith: man exists only through struggle; man lives only if he

---

[4] All page references are to the definitive edition of *Gilles*, published in 1942 with a preface. In the 1939 edition many passages had been suppressed by the war censorship.

risks death" (p. 75). Gilles' agonistic conception of life finds its justification in the spectacle of nature, in the sea waging its eternal war against the coastal cliffs of Normandy (p. 88), or in what the microscope reveals in an apparently peaceful laboratory (p. 159). Drieu, the author, indicating that he does not consider Gilles as representing himself, points out that this extreme attitude of his fictional hero is a repercussion of war. He makes Debrye, a pacifist, denounce to Gilles the psychological origin of his metaphysical views: "You are too much afraid of being afraid. It happens that for your generation war is the first experience in your life. You are afraid of not responding generously to it. So there you are, building a whole philosophy of life on resistance to diarrhea" (p. 75).

This outlook on life, so strongly marked by war, makes all traditional activities of peace seem ridiculously limited. What will Gilles do after the war is over? He is equally dissatisfied by the three guesses of Myriam, his fiancée: enter politics, write, influence other people. His answer to her question about his plans reflects both his uncertainty and his ambition: "Do something which transcends all the labels. How can you classify me so quickly?" (p. 32). He will never accept the neat partitions established in more peaceful periods among the activities of the "intellectual," the athlete, the priest, the warrior, the lawgiver. Later, when in the desert Gilles dreams of a Utopia not too different from the aristocratic society of Plato's *Laws*, the role he assigns to the "contemplator" in it is violently contrasted with that of the traditional writer or intellectual.

Here, there was no question of the inertia of the last century "intellectuals"—lolling in their libraries, dominated by physical weakness, abandoned because of their political incompetence to the dictatorship of a crowd yearning for mediocre needs and mediocre satisfactions, lost in the rising tide of ugliness in articles of everyday use, in clothes, in houses, and retiring into a subjective, idle dream more and more poorly nourished and meager (p. 351).

Gilles brings back from war the new concept of the intellectual who can no longer be satisfied with exercising his function gratuitously and irresponsibly: "No thought, no feeling has any reality unless it is put to the test by the risk of death" (p. 75). Gilles' spiritual guide, Carentan, has a similar notion of literature and, judging the young men of the literary movement Révolte according to the standards of past centuries, he explains their decadence in military terms: "... in former times, men thought because thinking, for them, was a real gesture. Thinking was, in the last analysis, giving or receiving a sword thrust... But nowadays men no longer have any sword" (p. 338). He has taught his disciple a virile liberalism which despises the "cowards of the spirit" who never take a firm position and his motto is *tranche toujours* (always decide).

But Gilles cannot so easily decide or take sides, because the alternatives which are offered to him appear equally unworthy of any commitment. The "real world" is so disappointing that he is thrown back to a contemplative position and he remains an outsider. For instance, when Révolte causes a scandal at the literary meeting in honor of Boniface Saint-Boniface, Gilles is ashamed of his friends of Révolte and yet on many points he shares their opinions. The result is that he remains an exasperated but passive spectator: "Gilles watched all this without saying anything. Everything looked hideous to him and made it impossible to take sides. Gilles was furious at not having found some way of taking a more active position in the debate" (pp. 211–212).

He knows the bitterness of living in a time he condemns and hates. His contemporaries have lost the sense of balance between body and soul. Their debates are gratuitous and limited to words. Carentan, Gilles' guardian and spiritual father, who has witnessed his irritation and shared his contempt for the Révolte group explains to a foreigner: "You see, what ruins the French is that they no longer feel their body: they are all brains nowadays. One can say anything, but since it has apparently no consequence, nobody says anything" (p. 212).

the real world

Gilles learns how difficult, if not impossible, it is to dissociate himself from his contemporaries. The tragic fate of Paul Morel, a victim of Révolte, who finally commits suicide, makes him reflect on his own decadence. He is trapped by the world in which he lives. "I have let myself be caught in a terrible trap these past few years. I have lived in the world of the weakest crime ... I let them steal my soul" (p. 325). He is able to satirize them, to see through them, but is nonetheless in danger of becoming one of them:

> Yes, when I was with them, I seemed to have some defense, I did not lack irony, I could see through their ruse, their weakness, because these criminals are nothing more than weak men. But I was denouncing them only with words and my thought was surrendered to them (p. 325).

They brandished promises of action but all their threats ended only in Paul Morel's self-destruction. Rather than break away from them, one must oppose them:

> My thought was paralyzed by their thought. Even while distrusting them, moving away from them, I could only make fruitless gestures without strength. This is why I failed in my adventure with Dora, but at least this terrible failure has opened my eyes; now I am their enemy (p. 325).

When those helpless dreamers talk of joining the Communist party, there is no possible hesitation left for Gilles: "These grotesque (funambulatory) petty bourgeois talking of communism, that was too much" (p. 338). Révolte has been for him an alibi.

He is entirely aware of the indelible mark of the corruption of the times on his body and his soul. A striking symbol of the duality which results from this situation is offered in the description of Gilles' naked body:

> This body was disconcerting; it was bipartite like an anatomy diagram. On one side it was the body of a well-set up man, with a full and straight shoulder, an ample chest, a narrow hip, a well-fixed knee; on the other side, it was a lightning-stricken carcass, tormented, warped, dried out, puny. This was the side of war, of slaughter, of torture, of death (p. 349).

Gilles has been physically wounded during the war. But the moral sickness of the nation is worse and the contagion unavoidable. As Carentan says, there is syphilis in France. It is impossible to be a Frenchman and not to contract the disease. Gilles realizes that he lives in a dying country and that he is dying himself. The visible sign of France's death is the demographic situation: the country is dying from avarice. Gilles has no child and he is dying of a miserly sense of himself: "What was it that he called solitude except a miserly complacency of his ego?"

Yet Gilles possesses a sense of life within a dying country, a sense of strength in the midst of weakness. He seeks in vain the forces he could join to help rejuvenate the old order. Since he failed to find in the literary and spiritual movement of Révolte any promise of renewal, he is tempted to join the party of revolution. But he finds that he cannot adhere to the Communist party in spite of a strong temptation to join those forces pitted against capitalist society. He does not believe in the Marxist materialistic and deterministic explanation of history. He dismisses the Communist doctrine as the journalistic vulgarization of Hegel's philosophy. He considers that the Christian dogmas of trinity, fall, redemption constitute a dialectic of an infinitely higher caliber than the Hegelian triad. Moreover, Gilles is permeated by Nietzsche's pragmatic skepticism. With the insight of a moralist, he recognizes beneath the would-be scientific dogma of the triumph of the proletariat, the will to power.

The cases of Communist "conversions" among his friends are not convincing. When, for instance, he sees his ex-friend Galant become a Communist, Gilles realizes that for Galant it is like "entering religion" after too many disappointments. Moreover, Gilles is persuaded that eventually the Communists will become the worst reactionaries and will destroy forever the illusions of the rationalist philosophy of enlightenment based on the ideas of equality and progress.

On the contrary, Gilles is likely to be attracted by a metaphysical system which emphasizes the infinite importance

the real world

and the irreplaceable character of each being. He remembers the flower he has seen blossoming all by itself on a March morning in the trenches below Amiens, in the midst of destruction and horror:

> Then he had felt that this infinitesimal palpitation was an image of his soul. Revelation, in this trying place, of the truth that each moment and each being is irreplaceably unique; a petal in a cluster is assured of its infinite importance in the eyes of the creator by the delicate perfection of its shape (p. 373).

Gilles is thus led to look for salvation in the opposite direction to the one which his country and the civilization in which he lives seem to follow. He gives up all his material belongings: his books, his furniture, his paintings. He rejoices at no longer having any money and realizes that he had been misled by his first wife's money. What should have brought him freedom had entailed heavier chains. Life has taught him renunciation. He is free from love and friendship. He cuts his last ties with society. He resigns from a precarious position at the Quai d'Orsay, which he was using mainly as a vantage point for viewing the international scene. He lives in perfect solitude. But he feels that he must mark by a physical separation his dissociation from this country and this form of civilization. He retires into the desert.

Gilles' retreat in the desert at the beginning of the section entitled "L'Apocalypse" is clearly symbolical. He is following the pattern of a prophet's life. Meditation in the solitude of the desert reveals to him the meaning of his past life and his destiny. He will preach to his corrupt countrymen virtues they have forgotten. He will predict the scourge of heaven unless they do penance and reform (heaven being here identified with the eternal laws of a tragic nature engaged in ceaseless battle). He rediscovers elementary values, the incorruptible riches of man: "True solitude is plenitude. Here, solitude is man with his riches, with his sky, his earth, his soul, with the hardness of the only things that belong to him: his hunger, his thirst, his prayer like a lost cry" (p. 350). Islam gives him an image of the ideals of contemplation, asceticism, and what he calls *paresse*. He has had enough of progress. He wishes that the march of European civilization would halt.

Even in the desert, Gilles cannot help meditating about society. He realizes that he is not meant to decipher the secrets of religion, philosophy, or poetry. Politics is for him the substitute for those higher activities. But he will infuse mysticism into politics. Politics will be his form of prayer, of *oraison* as in a spiritual exercise. The political myths of his age will provide the pretexts for those prayers: "Country, Class, Revolution, Machine, Party" (p. 358). He knows that his "prayer" is a lost prayer. The only means at his disposal to transmit his thoughts is journalism:

> He regretted ... that his intimate discourse had to condescend to so mediocre a vocabulary as that of the newspapers. But while blaming his time for it, since it was unable to nourish a vaster discourse, he intended not to disdain any longer this means of intervention, in the absence of any other (p. 358).

The articles of *Apocalypse*—the political magazine he has founded after his return to Paris—are not narrowly political. Gilles has a broader perspective in mind than his country, continent, or even planet; daily events furnish only the pretexts for his meditations on history. He takes his place in the tradition of the antimodern current of thought. He deviates, however, from this purely disinterested course when he is lured by his friend Clérences into direct action. *Apocalypse* is used to prepare the way for Clérences' accession to power. New contributors are accepted who corrupt the original spirit of the founder. French readers cannot accept satire, still less prophecy. Gilles' satire becomes correspondingly more inexpiable; his pen creaks and he runs down everything in France.

At the beginning of 1934, Gilles at forty feels that his Parisian life has come to an end. He has fallen back into the old rut: he has a sordid affair while Pauline, his second wife, is dying of cancer. Ironically, Gilles is now a successful journalist. His articles are published in the main newspapers but nobody pays any attention to his prophetic views.

the real world

The revolutionary days in Paris following February 6, 1934, evoke hopes in Gilles: here is what seems to him a last chance of renewal. But the inertia of the French political leaders is complete. When Gilles exhorts Clérences to do something; to abandon at all cost the routine of the old parties, of the manifestoes, of the meetings, of the articles, of the speeches, Clérences only answers that he has to go now to the Chamber of Deputies. Gilles is so outraged that he declares that he is now ready to go along with anyone who is prepared to overthrow the regime—no matter who it is and what the conditions are. Gilles has become a fascist. He cannot forgive himself for having used Clérences such a long time as an alibi. As Gilles tries a last time to stir Clérences to direct action, the latter replies that there is no longer any ambition left in France and that he cannot be ambitious all by himself. He accuses Gilles of always carefully avoiding commitments himself. The death of Gilles' second wife coincides with the death of France. He wants to go away, to plunge into a different universe. Once more, Gilles retires from the world after selling all he has to pay his debts.

His last incarnation, in the "Epilogue" as Walter, an agent of international fascism in Spain at the outbreak of the Civil War, indicates implicitly the way he has chosen.[5]

Walter (even his name, his *état-civil* has been changed) has regressed, but this time by his own choice, to the solution

---

[5] Although no mention is made of Doriot or his party in the novel, a friend of Drieu's, Alfred Fabre-Luce, quite rightly invites us to read *Gilles* with the politcial circumstances of the period 1934–1938 in mind: "Drieu... between the neo-boulangism of 1934 and Franco's victory lived at Doriot's side through the aborted tragedy of French fascism. His book must be read with this cipher." (Alfred Fabre-Luce, *Journal de la France, Mars 1939–Juillet 1940*, Paris, Imprimerie S.E.R., 1940, p. 215.)

Drieu's silence in *Gilles* over the Doriot interlude is eloquent. In the absence of any evidence concerning the chronology of *Gilles*' composition, it is reasonable to assume that, roughly, Drieu wrote it between 1937 (date of the publication of *Rêveuse bourgeoisie*) and October, 1939, date of the publication of *Gilles*. He had joined Doriot's party in June, 1936, and left it in November, 1938, after the Munich crisis. The period of the composition of *Gilles* must therefore have coincided for Drieu with a great disillusionment over French fascism.

offered by war twenty years before: only a life of dangerous action can bring him peace.

Twenty years had passed like a flash and he was back at his starting point. The heavy, firm, physical yoke of danger, the implacable bar over all the quivering of the individual, and at the same time, this peace of the soul. He was on the right way (p. 464).

He has finally taken sides. This choice corresponds to his passionate preferences.

But he is aware that his ideal must suffer from the necessary compromises of action. He loathes the massacres which follow the victory of his side, even though he knows that the enemy does likewise. He thinks also of all the concentration camps in Germany, in Italy—but then there are some in Russia, too. Is he an accomplice to all that? He cannot refuse this unavoidable consequence of taking sides: does he not want passionately something that others refuse just as passionately? He feels that it would be hypocritical to claim that he wants something only if certain conditions are fulfilled. For too long he has been paralyzed by moral distinctions. He does not want to be an "amateur."

When Gilles reappears in Extremadura around Christmas, 1937, he is satisfied with the obscure role of a journalist. He accepts the sacrifices that this implies:

I am a type of man that has always existed. Dreamer and man of action, solitary and pilgrim, initiated and in the ranks ... I am one of those modest men who help action and thought to renew always their threatened union (p. 479).

In the last incident of the novel, the attack on the village by superior enemy forces, Gilles' role presents a reduced image of his whole life. He had foreseen the "surprise" attack. As everyone rushes to action, he tears to pieces the report he was preparing with the comment: "Lost prayer." He decides to stay even though there is still time for him to escape. He feels old. When the enemy artillery makes the place untenable he is tempted to leave. He is not fighting in his own country to defend his own soil. But he soon regains his lucidity, his irony. In this extreme danger he is again himself. "He found himself alone. He found himself again. For the last twenty years what had he been? Not much. Before, there had been moments like this one which he remembered as moments during which he had existed" (p. 483).

He has no regrets for what he leaves behind: the audiences in the movie theaters of the Champs-Elysées watching the newsreels about the Spanish Civil War, give themselves the illusion of experiencing what he is actually living. He is no longer the same Gilles. He does not desire women any longer. His love affairs have been delusions anyway. His desire to see Chartres or Florence again is dead: after all their images are engraved in his soul. As for the divine, his only way to approach it is through his body, by projecting himself against "a savage death." As he hears a wounded Spaniard invoke "Santa Maria" his thoughts are recalled to the idea of sacrifice and redemption:

Yes, the mother of God, the mother of God made man, who suffers in his creation, who dies and is born again. . . . Gods who die and are reborn, Dionysos, Christ. Nothing is ever accomplished but in blood. One must always die in order always to be born again (p. 484).

Gilles is the victim of his times. In a period of decadence, the only way to shape one's destiny is by taking one's life at a chosen time in order to give some meaning at least to one's death. The form of death may be suicide or the seeking out of dangerous situations.

II

One of the reasons—perhaps, the main one—why Drieu makes of Gilles a foundling who does not know anything about his parents is that he wants to demonstrate that his hero is a victim of the times. If Gilles' failures in life could be explained—even partly—by family or hereditary reasons, the demonstration would be weakened. Gilles has been brought up by Carentan as "a free man" (p. 95), not a rootless man, but one attached only to the essential values. He is supposed to be as free as possible from prejudices—a modern Emile, Carentan remarks.

It should be noted, however, that Gilles' reactions are much more understandable if the reader sees in him the Le Pesnel–Ligneul ancestry of *Rêveuse bourgeoisie*. Gilles Gambier is no abstract figure of *l'homme libre*. The novel would have been too didactic if the author had consistently maintained that fiction. Fortunately, Drieu has not succeeded in dissociating Gilles from his background. Gilles has deep roots in the French middle class and his efforts to become *un homme libre* began only in adolescence, as was the case with young Cogle of *Etat-Civil* and Yves Le Pesnel of *Rêveuse bourgeoisie* both in reaction against their milieu. He suffered from lack of money as a student. The mirage of money—represented by his marriage with Myriam Falkenberg, a rich Jewish heiress—would not have provoked so strong a reaction in a detached, unprejudiced *homme libre*. "The apparition of money in certain lives can be a miracle similar to that of love: it agitates powerfully the imagination and sensitiveness, at least in the first moments" (p. 33). Gilles seems to be the victim of the "Le Pesnel fatality." Geneviève in *Rêveuse bourgeoisie* remarks: "Between marrying for money and begging there is no middle way for the Le Pesnel" (p. 302). The author writes about Gilles: "Was it an effect of war? The idea of earning money never occurred to him. For him there was only one alternative: Myriam or poverty" (p. 150). His idea of being "liberated" from worries about money resembles that of Balzac's young men. He justifies his marrying for money on the basis of rather naïve views about society, reminiscent of Vautrin exhorting Rastignac. He wants to start in life with the same advantages as the rich in a capitalist society in which money represents power.

But the difference is that to Gilles, money offers mainly the possibility of leading a leisurely life, devoted to disinterested study: "I want to think quietly. Oh! to think quietly, in a pure, noble, isolated place, like this library. Give me your books; your money is your books" (p. 39). Like a *bourgeois délicat*, he hates the humiliations he would have to suffer in order to make money. He is convinced that he cannot create his fortune by himself: he prefers to owe his entrance into the region of ambition to a sensitive and intelligent person like Myriam rather than to a humiliating protector. This assumption that one cannot satisfy one's ambition without outside help is based on the idea that society around him is corrupt and based on injustice:

> At a time of saturated civilization, there are many people like that, who claim to keep white as ermine the fraudulent illusion of their egotism, only because it is subtle. But ermines are intact only in fairy tales (p. 67).

This child of the twentieth century does not share the robust vitality of a Rastignac or a Julien Sorel. The latter was a true *homme libre:* he had no class loyalties; he was patient, stubborn; he believed in his own destiny. Gilles has a taste for disaster. He refuses the world as it is. He wants to leave it: "War is my homeland." He is basically afraid of the outside world. As soon as he thinks that he may lose Myriam and the refuge against the world that her fortune represents, he shivers: "He no longer saw anything, but cruelties, threats, inexorable condemnations everywhere" (p. 20). He is unable to enjoy a life of luxury, either. He has a bad conscience. He comes to the conclusion that he is capable only of one act: self-destruction (p. 37).

After Dora—the American mistress with whom he has an adulterous affair—has abandoned him because she finds him weak, Gilles does everything to alienate her by appearing weaker than before. He is seeking failure. He says to himself:

> You are alone and that is what you have always wanted, with all your weakness. Somewhere, within you, an imperceptible little devil rejoices at finding himself free, free to be nothing, abandoned forever to weakness, inefficiency, failure. This little devil will grow and will become the demon of self-complacency (p. 276).

Gilles the egocentric, individualistic bourgeois is too much absorbed in himself to be really interested in the person he loves. In each of his love affairs, he shows a remarkable lack of insight into the character of his partner. The person he seems to come closest to understanding is Myriam, his first wife. She comes to life as a character in the novel; he has "recreated" her. Gilles always picks his women in such a way that his loves are bound to end in failure: Mabel—the nurse he meets in a war hospital—because of her emptiness; Alice—the army nurse at the front—because of her age; Dora—the American diplomat's wife—because of her stupidity, her family, and her obvious attachment to her social status; Pauline—his second wife—because of her past and her background. As for the last love, Berthe Santon, Gilles starts the affair with full awareness that it is a dead end. His constant concern with himself is illustrated by an incident of the Dora episode. At the most acute point of his despair over the loss of Dora, he undertakes a written study of his first experience with Myriam.*

Incapable of seeing quite clearly his present state of mind, agitated as he was by the whirling winds of passion, he was looking for a firm point in the exact knowledge of another moment of his life, of another aspect of his soul (p. 263).

It is clear that Gilles is more interested in himself than in Dora or Myriam. None of the women in his life has ever been necessary to his existence.

III

One of the fascinations of *Gilles* is that it contains a rather unique portrait: the self-portrait of a fascist. It seems clear that Gilles is or has become a fascist for emotional rather than intellectual reasons and mainly as a reaction against the bourgeois world to which he belongs. Gilles' ideological uncertainty is shown in a discussion among Gilles, an Irishman, and a Pole during the Spanish Civil War. Their posi-

---

* Since we can admit that Gilles is a fictional transposition of the author, this indication of Drieu's method of work is interesting and seems to be confirmed by the publication of his novels concerning certain crucial events of his life within an interval of a few years after they actually took place.

tion is full of contradictions because they are nationalists fighting for both Catholicism and fascism, which are at odds with each other. They agree that, if necessary, they would sacrifice their allegiance to the Church in favor of fascism because the Church is "indestructible." They would fight fascism, however, if their respective countries were at war with fascist countries. Gilles explains why he puts nationalism above international fascism.

If you cannot manage to make fascism triumph in your respective countries, you will meet the atrocious consequences of your inefficiency and you will defend, if necessary, your country against fascist powers even at the risk of contributing to the triumph of antifascist forces (p. 474).

Gilles adds, showing an almost carnal love for his country as he points out the impossibility of the concept of an "international" fascism:

"Fascism, like the Church, can afford to wait, but one cannot sacrifice the body of one's homeland to the powers which are utilizing fascism."

In the event of a fascist victory, however, Gilles does not see how German hegemony could be avoided in Europe. His prediction is particularly interesting in view of what the author's position was going to be later: "Against the invasion of Europe by the Russian army, a spirit of European patriotism will have to be born. This spirit will come to life only if Germany has first given full moral guarantees of the integrity of all the countries of Europe. Only then will she efficiently fulfill the role assigned to her by the tradition of the Holy Roman Empire to lead the European line of tomorrow" (p. 475).

Gilles' effort to reconcile Roman Catholicism with fascism is only one illustration of his love of contradictions: on most fundamental Christian doctrines, he differs not only from Roman Catholic orthodoxy, but even from any specific form of heresy. He is not a heretic; he is a heresiarch. It is one of his last remarks in the novel. "I'll always be a heresiarch..." (p. 484). He shares Carentan's anti-intellectualist stand: there are no "ideas" in religions, but only facts of human experience.

Christianity is a collection of all religions. There is in it the most primitive and the most developed. Because of that very fact, it is indestructible. Under the Greek, the Jewish words, there is the experience of the races, the unavoidable experience. Sin is the story of Oedipus ... (p. 102).

Gilles' "heretic" position toward fascism is just as obvious. He seems to be on Franco's side mainly for the negative reason that he cannot be a communist. He cannot be an obedient Marxist; it would require too much hypocrisy to pretend that he adheres to this Jesuitic organization directed from Moscow. He feels too strongly his "Europeanism" to accept an extra-European leadership. But his own "secret, delicate, and complex doctrine" seems to have little in common with the international fascism involved in the war in Spain. To use a word dear to Gilles—and to Drieu—fascism is only a "pretext." What Gilles accepts of fascism is much more a general attitude than any specific ideas:

At bottom my tastes were passions. This taste for solitude was a taste for a secret, delicate, complex doctrine to be attached like a precious captive to the back of some horse of the Apocalypse (p. 476).

The intellectual in him is so curious that he is always fascinated in watching the deviations and metamorphoses of an idea as it is "lived." "What delights! He lived an idea. He followed with a battered but always voluptuous curiosity its turns and its twists caused by the resistance of the human material on which it tried to put its imprint" (p. 476). The use of the two adjectives "battered" (*meurtrie*) and "voluptuous" (*voluptueuse*) reveals a general trait of Gilles' psychology. He finds pleasure in what makes him suffer; he experiences a sense of life whenever he is involved in a contradiction. The very elusiveness of his thought becomes for this antirationalist a guarantee of its "authenticity." "Is it possible to seize on a thought which, put to the test of diverse circumstances and facing contradictory difficulties, finally turns against itself?" (p. 479).

Gilles' capacity for self-analysis is one of his most striking features. It is closely connected with his propensity to contemplation. He is more interested in what action teaches him than in the action itself. And this passionate interest paralyzes his activity: "A contemplator, Gilles, at a given moment, always thought of abandoning the struggle in order to consider the new element of knowledge that it had brought him" (p. 76). On the other hand, he is led to act because of his basic contempt for pure thought cut off from all contact with reality. He acts even when he disapproves of the aims or the methods of his action. The fear of being an "amateur" is thus at the source of this almost compulsive urge to act, or at least to participate in a collective action. When Gilles, during the Spanish Civil War, sees a young Communist led by the men of his side to the firing squad, he silences the instinctive protestation of his humanity, turns around, closes his eyes and says "I am not an amateur" (p. 471). Almost anything is better than being a dreamy bourgeois.

The overrefined Parisian, the *civilisé nerveux* in Gilles finds relief and, it seems, further evidence that he has chosen the right way, in the fact that his comrades in Spain are not Frenchmen. Frenchmen have all become bourgeois. But Spaniards are still primitive. Spain is for Gilles the symbol of what is very old in Europe and therefore, in his reactionary view, young.

Almost all the troop was very young and came from the neighbouring Old Castile. Robust young peasants of an impregnable simplicity, they were of that eternally primitive race which still fills the depths of Europe and from which comes now this great irresistible movement which astonishes the delicate minds in the cities of the Western world (p. 477).

Gilles is afraid of himself and of the big cities; he takes flight into the strong discipline of the army and makes a conscious effort to restore the "primitive."

The corollary of this infatuation of the over-refined decadent with primitivism is Gilles' anti-Semitism, another fascistic trait. It may not be accurate to talk of anti-Semitism since the author rejects this term through the character of Carentan as "an oversimplified, messy notion, like all 'isms.'" But the same Carentan seems to state the author's position which was already apparent in previous works: "There remains the experience, what the actual contact with persons teaches us. Well! I cannot stand the Jews because they are, par excellence, the modern world which I loathe" (p. 99). Gilles is in contact with many Jews. His marriage with one represents, symbolically, Gilles' marriage with the "modern world." For Myriam is a scientist and studies in a Sorbonne laboratory. Benedict, the Jew from Algiers, has shared the war experience with Gilles: a real comradeship can therefore exist between them. Myriam's father represents the important place occupied in France by the Jews in finance, industry, and, indirectly if not directly, in politics. M. Falkenberg is the friend and adviser of Morel, the minister who eventually becomes president of the Republic. His cousin is the young Léon Blum. Falkenberg is of Alsatian origins and he loves France. He gives his two sons for the country. His children have been baptized in the Roman Catholic Church. He is a democrat: "for a Jew to be a democrat has a carnal meaning" (p. 106). For Gilles this is M. Falkenberg's main fault. Gilles had already remarked when Myriam introduced him triumphantly to the Morels, "The Jews get ahead, mixed in the ranks of democracy" (p. 68). About Preuss, his collaborator on *Apocalypse*, whose thought derives always from the most narrow conservatism of the Parti Radical Socialiste, Gilles remarks: "The Jews remain sterilely faithful to 1789 which took them out of the Ghetto" (p. 401). Gilles seems to identify the triumph of the thought of Jews with a decadent society. For instance, he says to Lorin, his Marxist friend, who does not like Preuss:

And yet Preuss is of the same race as your Marx and your Freud. Isn't it ludicrous that you, an anticlerical, should have replaced Jesus and Saint Paul by Marx and Freud. There must be a biologic necessity in the role of the Jews which explains that their words are always to be found in the saliva of decadences (p. 387).

Gilles, as a nationalist, considers that the Jews have been decadent ever since the disappearance of the Hebrew nation because of what he terms "their fall from any kind of authenticity" (p. 455).[7] In the same way that Gilles admires people as different as possible from himself, such as the simple, primitive peasants of Old Castile, he is afraid of his friends the Jews of the big cities, because he thinks he recognizes in them his own "defects": over-intellectualism, abstraction, hatred of violence and blood, liberalism, and faith in democracy.

A further component of the fascist personality appears clearly in the misogyny of Gilles. Gilles comes from the front at the beginning of the novel and goes back to the front at the end, when he has become "dead to women." His first remark on arriving in Paris is that it is the "kingdom of women." The "kingdom of women" means peace. During the period of peace between the two wars (here World War I and the Spanish Civil War), women have a prominent role, and it is a nightmarish period for Gilles. When he first visits Mme Morel, the wife of the future president of the Republic, to obtain a favor, Gilles remarks: "One does not consider history enough from the angle of women. Women arrange everything. Gilles saw immediately the history of the Third Republic from the angle of Mme Morel" (p. 68). The "kingdom of men," whether it is the forest of Argonne, the desert of Champagne, the marshes of Picardy, the mountains of the Vosges, or the front of Extremadura, is the only place where Gilles lives: "There, men had retired in their strength, their joy, their pain. They had left their factories, their offices, their homes, their humdrum lives, money, women, especially women" (p. 61).

Like his prototypes in the other novels, he hates all the things which belong to the world of women: "peace, enjoyment, ease, luxury." All these things come to him from women and corrupt him. He has to "bathe" again in war to become

---

[7] As could be expected, Drieu himself favored Zionism to restore the "authenticity" of the Jews. See *Le Français d'Europe*, p. 134. His position was not always consistent in this question. In 1926, when he advocated the end of all nationalism in order to create a unified Europe, he said: "The French must become the Jews of the United States of Europe" (*Genève ou Moscou*, p. 235).

clean. The deep contempt he has for women is connected with his war experience. For instance, after his disappointment over Mabel, a war nurse, who was not a virgin as he had expected her to be, he tortures her with a sadistic contempt: "You are mediocre. But you don't have the least idea of what there is in me. You don't know what depths I have reached in myself, at war" (p. 57). When he goes back to her a few days later, he humiliates her by treating her like a prostitute, and notes: "Perhaps the soldier, who is not very strong needs to see a feminine body humiliated and pained in the same way as his own body" (p. 59). His "hunger for women" is actually the quest for a form of death: "He hungered for women, for this infinite sweetness of the spasm they give. Another aspect, which he hardly knew, of death" (p. 7).

The feeling of perfect solitude which he is sure to experience with a prostitute is what he seeks. He has no desire to have a woman of his own: "He loved those who belonged to everybody, and thus not at all to him" (p. 45). Gilles has an instinctive aversion to girls (*les jeunes filles*). Even before he marries Myriam he is always tempted by mature women. After the lamentable failure of their physical union, Gilles decides that he cannot love a *jeune fille*.

He had decided that he was right in loathing Myriam. He did not like this frail flesh, this shy soul, that was all, and he refused to lie. Toward women, his sensitiveness had taken on a certain aspect in Paris; there was no denying it. He was a man of pleasure, a man born for pleasure. And he was tied to women of pleasure (p. 130).

Femmes de plaisir does not necessarily apply to prostitutes only. Gilles looks for a type of woman who is physically strong, ample, evokes an image of force, and who has had a long and varied love experience. Gilles himself recognizes that there is some childishness in this taste for mature women. He notes about his love for Alice, an older woman:

He first had toward her the elementary impulse of the young boy, because he had not had a mother. Besides, young men, especially those who have been absorbed in a great tumult, a great virile test like war or revolution, are always like children with their first mistress (p. 137).

He consciously takes advantage of the fact that Alice is so much older (he is twenty-three, she is more than forty; it is his first real love and most likely her last one): "She loved Gilles with a mother's resignation. The love of mature beings for young ones is willy-nilly confused with kindness" (p. 147).

Gilles has no interest in the personality of the woman he loves. He pays little attention to Dora's face, which he considers ugly. He is in love with her body, which represents for him, among other things, such abstract notions as "the Nordic race," which arouse Gilles' most violent emotions. A woman is for him a "pretext" to evoke certain ideas: "When he took this big body in his arms, he held an idea of life which was dear to him. A certain idea of strength and nobility he had missed since Alice" (p. 182). A woman can be a substitute for a crowd which, dominated, can also give him this idea of strength: "Why look for it elsewhere? Why look for it in the masculine world, in the charms of ambition? A woman is a reality as much as a crowd" (p. 182). Gilles has the feeling that this form of passion for a woman is inferior, however, to that which would exist in a "virile society." The vocation of Don Juan is, therefore, for Gilles as for all of Drieu's Don Juan characters, a substitute for a *grandeur absente*.

There are many traits in Gilles' character which point to misogyny. One is tempted to look also for signs of homosexuality, especially since he expresses himself so violently on the subject, like other heroes of Drieu: "Along with drugs, homosexuality was the sickness by which his heart had been most torn in Paris. A hundred sicknesses made this huge sickness of which his people were dying, of which he had almost died" (p. 455). The author has clearly indicated some of those signs, but since he has not chosen to emphasize them nor to draw final conclusions from them, it seems pointless to read more into Gilles' character than the author has put.

The testimony of the women he has loved is uniform and

indicative: Myriam says: "You never loved me" (p. 143). Antoinette has warned Dora: "She says that you don't love women" (p. 217). Pauline generalizes: "I know that you no longer love me. I was not the woman you needed. But no woman can touch you. You certainly wasted your time with women. You don't love them" (p. 413). Berthe Santon joins the chorus: "You don't love me, you never loved me" (p. 427). Gilles himself recognizes in his love for Dora an androgynous element:

All this flesh, all this life which is similar to me, which is mine. Here is this woman, it is myself, myself finally met, recognized, greeted. Joy: the joy of being at last at ease with myself. "And he made him male and female say the Scriptures" (p. 182).

In a scene with his friend Cyrille Galant, Gilles makes this revealing remark: "You envy me because of women. And because you are a little inverted, it is also inverted love" (p. 315). In a scene with Clérences, Gilles confesses feelings of inversion: "I have just made a woman's scene with you. Take me, hurt me. An invert's scene. We are worse than fairies" (p. 424).

François Mauriac has detected in Drieu "a female nature." He cannot explain otherwise the attraction for Drieu—"this young nobleman, Oxonian in his manners and his bearing,"—of Jacques Doriot, the chief of the Parti Populaire Français. Mauriac quotes the brochure in which Drieu describes Doriot.

Doriot is tall and strong, everything in him expresses health and plenitude: his thick hair, his powerful shoulders, his broad stomach. Behind his glasses there is an observing glance. He is a calm, slow, reserved man with unexpected reactions which can be extremely violent and can suddenly seek the total and rapid destruction of the adversary.[8]

And Mauriac comments on Drieu's "crime":

... he adored force, and he hated weakness. It is the crime of female natures: I don't mean that the nature of our Drieu "covered with women" was such in an abject meaning; but you understand

---

[8] François Mauriac, "Drieu La Rochelle," *La Table Ronde*, No. 18 (June, 1949), 914–915.

clearly what I mean: his fault, his sin, was committed from the beginning when he took the measure of that France for which he had just fought and suffered so much and despaired of her."

The close examination of Drieu's testimony about Gilles as a fascist hero seems to confirm in this respect Mauriac's psychological insight. Drieu's portrait of Gilles constitutes one of the most damning documents about French fascism of our time—and it is probably a valuable contribution to the study of the "fascist personality" of all times. Here the merits of Drieu's concept of testimony in fiction emerge clearly: all the elements for judgment are placed in the reader's hands.

IV

A noticeable consequence of Drieu's method is that the substance and individual fictional existence of the other characters in the novel corresponds to the closeness of their relationship to Gilles: those with whom he identifies, like M. Falkenberg and Paul Morel, have greater reality. It is characteristic that their inner thoughts are revealed by themselves in passages narrated from their own point of view instead of from Gilles' or the omniscient author's. To a smaller degree, characters like Cyrille Galant and Gilbert de Clérences have the sympathy of Gilles because they represent some of his own traits; they are engaged in the two fields of activity that interest him most: Clérences is an up-and-coming deputy in the Parti Radical Socialiste, and Cyrille is second in command in the would-be revolutionary literary movement Révolte under the despotic leadership of Cael. Besides, their mutual resemblance is symbolically represented by the fact that they are half brothers. Finally, some characters are represented mainly from the outside and are frankly treated as caricatures: Lorin, Preuss, and Chanteau, for instance, belong to that category. The women are mere reflections of Gilles and they vanish as soon as they are sent out of his life, except for Myriam Falkenberg, who has a certain fictional existence and

⁹ *Ibid.*

reappears in the novel both physically and as the haunting figure of remorse in the mind of Gilles.

M. Falkenberg and Paul Morel are touching figures. They have a common trait which must have aroused the interest and the sympathy of the author of *Le Feu follet:* they both commit suicide. Myriam's father is characterized by his solitude. He never loved his wife and does not like women. He has only contempt for his daughter. His secretary, who is also his mistress, is unable to persuade him to live. His superior intelligence is annoyed by the folly of men; he cannot accept the loss of his two sons. One has the feeling, however, that his decision is motivated more by his detachment than by grief. Powerful and solitary, like Vigny's Moses, he aspires to rest and nothingness. His haughty pessimism is not without grandeur. He represents overtones of Gilles' character. Paul Morel might be said to represent undertones of the same character. He is Gilles' "sunken image." His suicide is the last refuge of the weak and the delicate who have been hurt by the outside world because they have never been able to adapt to it. His weakness of character has made him the victim of Révolte. The analysis of his impotent hatred toward his father compensates for the absence of Gilles' father in the novel. One feels that Paul is there "in order to satisfy the secret and unspeakable needs of the author."[10]

Cyrille Galant is Gilles' friend and becomes Gilles' enemy: he is the enemy brother. The scene of their final quarrel is one of the most vivid in the novel. Gilles' last word is characteristic of their relationship: "And remember that I will never hate you, I will always despise you" (p. 316). Later, when Gilles learns that Galant is entering the Communist party, he does not laugh at him like Lorin. He and Clérences are able to measure what this decision means for their unfortunate ex-friend after his disappointment in love with Antoinette.

The character of Antoinette establishes a strange bond between Gilles, Galant, and Clérences. She has been the mistress

---

[10] *Gilles*, preface, p. vii. In *Rêveuse bourgeoisie*, the relationship between father and son was also one of hatred.

of Gilles while still Clérences' wife, and she has left her husband to follow Galant, whom she eventually abandons to marry a rich man. Conversely, when Dora leaves Gilles, Galant feels it as a failure of his own.

The friendship of Gilles and Cyrille Galant fails because they are too much alike, too egocentric. No common cause, no common work has obliged them to raise themselves above their jealous individualism. Even though in politics they follow directions which apparently diverge completely, Gilles' analysis of Galant's motivation is revelatory of the psychology of both extremists.

Gilles was beginning to understand how the deception of an absolute could be necessary for a mind as vacant as that of Galant who, very poor in temperament like all his contemporaries, detached from all traditions like all of them, because of the infinite crosscurrents of culture, could not adhere to anything except by study (p. 370).

Gilbert de Clérences is one of the few characters who appear in all of the first three parts of *Gilles*. He remains in the background in the first two, but plays a predominant role in "L'Apocalypse." Like Gilles, he is good looking, has been courageous in war, where he won the Croix de Guerre, and was also an interpreter. He is intelligent, and the tone of his friendship with Gilles is one of half cynicism: Clérences approves Gilles' marriage; later, Gilles is understanding about the disorders and orgies of Clérences' conjugal and sentimental life. He knows that Clérences has married Antoinette partly from ambition because she is the daughter of an influential minister who shortly afterwards becomes president of the Republic. Clérences seems to be sure of himself. He is ambitious and plans to enter politics from the time he is in the army. When we find him again in "L'Elysée," he has partly fulfilled the promises of his youth: still very young, at least for the French political world, he is the favorite of Chanteau who is head of the Parti Radical and a potential premier. He is not a politician according to the usual mold: he is full of fantasy, dresses like a "dandy," spends lavishly, has a pretty wife, and loose morals. His reputation in political circles is bad, but he surprises and attracts people, and maneuvers with great skill. He enjoys Gilles' unconventional conversation. Gilles, half-amused, half-indignant, admires the ease with which Clérences adapts to the left-wing "look."

He had composed for himself a marvellously deceptive costume: "Democracy has replaced the good Lord but Tartuffe is still dressed in black" had exclaimed a veteran journalist at a congress of the Parti Radical. And indeed, at a distance of fifty yards, Clérences seemed to be dressed like the beadle of a poor parish: heavy shoes, tightly fitted black suit, soft-collared white shirt, narrow tie ... crewcut. On closer examination, one could see that the black material was a thick English woolen, the shirt made of the rarest shantung and the shoes handmade and sewn by a shoemaker for millionaires. Finally, Gilles had discovered to his great delight that the model for the tie had been provided by one of the Fratellini clowns (p. 321).

This portrait is in the best tradition of the political novel and reminds one of the bishop of Agde as Stendhal makes him appear in *Le Rouge et Le Noir* to the dumbfounded but amused Julien Sorel. The actors of the French "comedy" are now engaged in circus acts.

When Gilles starts his own political magazine, he resumes his relationship with Clérences and the idea dawns on him that this ambitious young man, in spite of shortcomings of which Gilles is aware, might become the embodiment of the dreams of a generation. Gilles is ready to give him his full support. There is something mystic in his vision of the teamwork which may bring a man to the crest of his generation.

This is the first appearance in Drieu's fiction of one of his fondest dreams: the ideal pair—the man of action and the man of contemplation. He could accept the role of "seated man" (*un homme assis*) so long as there was a "standing man" (*un homme debout*) who would be more or less his creation, whom he would inspire and in whom he could rejoice because the man of action would satisfy his dreams of glory.

The description of Gilles' gradual disappointment in Clérences is effective. It is a justification of Gilles' pessimistic

the real world

views about French decadence: Clérences is the most promising young man of France's most powerful party at the time, and he is unable to accomplish anything. Clérences' failure is due partly to the party's organization, and especially to its chairman, Jules Chanteau, an eloquent demagogue, but it is also due to the French public and to his own shortcomings. Gilles is seeking something new. His favorite words are "rupture," "renaissance," "passion." The French public is "intelligent," curious, polite, and extremely distrustful of anything and anybody that might disturb the neat and narrow vision of a world in which France holds the first place and of a France where a degenerate form of the rationalism of Descartes reigns supreme.

Clérences' inaction in February, 1934, arouses the most violent anger in Gilles. The latter's attack is unjust: Clérences' main fault in the eyes of Gilles is not to be what Gilles wanted him to be: a leader who upsets the old order and brings about a new one. Gilles must give up his wishful thinking and look at the situation with Clérences' eyes, those of a realist, of the intelligent cynic that Gilles himself is in his less exalted moments:

> No, Gilles Gambier, you are as cowardly as I am. You had better tell yourself what you have just told me ... There is nothing to be done in this country because there is nothing to be done with us; you know it as well as I do ... We are meticulously enjoying our bourgeois destinies (p. 424).

Gilles is obliged to recognize his own portrait in his friend, whom he now despises so much.

The character of Clérences is among the most effective in the novel. It is perfectly integrated in the intrigue and brings out another aspect of Gilles' character while preserving a marked individuality. It provides a picture from the inside of French political impotency. The fact that many people have seen in Clérences the literary transposition of Drieu's political friend, Gaston Bergery, only adds to the value of *Gilles* as a document. The same is true of Cyrille Galant, in whom one could recognize a certain aspect of Louis Aragon.

It would be erroneous, however, to see in *Gilles un roman à clef*. The characters of Galant or Clérences are composite, and correspond to the artistic vision of Drieu. Moreover, they are affected by the general tone of the novel and participate in an action which, even in its broad lines, is not faithful to reality. Drieu's extensive experience both in literary and political circles has allowed him to draw profusely on the documentary richness of life. His view is disillusioned but this is his literary privilege. His characters stand out as types; after reading *Gilles*, one would hardly be able to look at the photographs of the cabinet members of the Third Republic without thinking of Gilbert de Clérences or Jules Chanteau. Révolte is a personal and partial view of Dada and surrealism. This view is strongly marked by the disillusions of Gilles about French literature in the 'twenties and more particularly about a movement which advocated direct action and violence in the quest of the absolute. Gilles' interest in action and politics makes him emphasize the complete failure of that movement in that particular domain. The portrait of Cael, the chief of Révolte, may appear to some a valid representation of André Breton. It is also a more general description of a certain type of contemporary intellectual and might apply to many besides Breton.

It seems, however, that in creating characters Drieu needed the starting point of concrete reality. The character of Carentan, representing the ideal father Drieu wished for himself and gave to his hero as guardian, is never convincing and is decidedly one of the weak points in the novel. In spite of certain concrete details meant to obviate the danger of extreme idealization, he is idealized and marred by sentimentality.

The criticism of the characters of *Gilles* formulated by Marcel Arland seems to us, fifteen years later, entirely unfounded:

Evoking persons he has known very well, on whom we are sometimes tempted to put a name, Drieu, as a novelist could not give us, nakedly, his testimony; he transposes, therefore, enough to deprive himself of the advantage of a direct testimony, but not enough to create fictional characters. In the same way, he invents an intrigue, some elements of which are borrowed from reality but which leave an impression of ingenious artifice, of a game of allusions.[11]

It may be that for those like Arland who knew the original protagonists, the particular image they had of them interfered with the fictional characters. For us, with a little perspective, the fact that contemporaries were tempted to give real names to the characters is only an added guarantee that the novel is documentary, in the best sense of the term.

V

As for the plot, it is aimed mainly at showing the downfall of a particular man and French decadence, as seen in Paris. It serves this purpose and it should not be criticized merely because one does not agree with the purpose. Drieu himself was aware of the limitations imposed on the novel by its very subject:

> To talk ... of *Gilles*, I must go back to the idea of decadence. This idea alone can explain the terrible insufficiency which is at the core of this book.
> This novel seems insufficient because it treats the subject of the terrible insufficiency of the French and it treats it honestly, without dodging the issue or seeking alibis. To show insufficiency, the artist must bring himself to being insufficient ... One has hardly noticed that almost nobody has taken the risk of depicting Paris society in its reality of the last twenty years. There is a good reason for it; because one had to denounce a terrible absence of humanity, a terrible deficiency of blood. That would be inconsiderate.[12]

Drieu, in the same preface, admits that there was not in his subject material for heroic transposition. He points out that to write the epic of our time, Malraux had to choose his heroes from Chinese or Spaniards. Drieu's plight is strangely similar

---

[11] Marcel Arland, " 'Gilles,' par Drieu La Rochelle," *NRF*, No. 318 (March, 1940), 405.
[12] *Gilles*, preface, p. viii.

to that of Flaubert when the latter undertook to write a novel describing contemporary life and taking place in Paris:

> I want to write the moral history of the men of my generation; "sentimental" history would be more accurate. It is a book of love, of passion; but of a passion such as can exist today, that is to say inactive. The subject, such as I conceived it is, I believe, profoundly true, but, because of that very fact, probably not very amusing. Deeds, drama, are lacking a little, and then the action is extending over too considerable a period of time.[13]

Many among Flaubert's contemporaries refused also to see in *l'Education sentimentale*, a valid and representative picture of their generation. It is the fate of most undertakings of that kind. Only the perspective of time allows the critic to appreciate their true value as documents. Frédéric Lefèvre was prompt in immediately recognizing this merit in *Gilles*.

> Reading *Gilles* will not be useless later to anyone desiring to penetrate the psychological secrets of the period between the two world wars, to understand the turmoils of those disturbed, convulsed years, rich in germs and abortions.
>
> In this novel of nearly five hundred pages, some are admirable, none is indifferent...[14]

To write a novel on the scale of *Gilles*, it would seem that many years' work would be necessary. There are evidences of hastiness, mainly in the integration of incidents. But the style is of a high order, even when the subject offers a temptation to be merely facile. The speeches at the convention of the Parti Radical are neither a caricature nor a stenographic reproduction. The hilarious description of the "literary" meeting in honor of the poet Boniface Saint-Boniface maintains a rare balance between the pitiful and the grandiose. The pen of the pamphleteer appears here and there but scorn usually remains witty. The dialogue is excellent, and in a novel in which so many ideas are discussed, long ideological conversations are carefully avoided. One feels, reading *Gilles*, that

---
[13] Gustave Flaubert, *Correspondance* (Paris, Bibliothèque-Charpentier, Fasquelle, 1924), V, 158.
[14] Frédéric Lefèvre, "Le Livre de la semaine," *Les Nouvelle Littéraires* (January 6, 1940).

the real world

Drieu, at forty-five, with more than twenty books and innumerable articles behind him, can finally afford to write rapidly and to improvise, in other words, to be himself. The reward of this long apprenticeship and achieved maturity, is that the style is really the whole man. Ramon Fernandez found the right words to describe this style—and behind it the true and intimate Drieu.

... a kind of spoken style transposed in the written one, which allows the repetitions, the suspenses, the changes in register, and in speed of the spoken word. But this spoken style is the contrary of eloquence. Let us rather call it murmured style, that of a low-tone conversation, in a simple tone, with the hesitations and the meanderings of familiar conversation.[15]

Drieu had recaptured in *Gilles* with greater variety and on a larger scale the tone which seemed best suited to him, the tone of *Drôle de voyage* and of *La Comédie de Charleroi*. Even in *Rêveuse bourgeoisie*, one senses at times the effort and the tediousness experienced by the author, in writing a "novel" with all the formal qualities of the genre. This may explain why certain critics prefer *Rêveuse bourgeoisie* to *Gilles:* "Among all Drieu's novels," writes, for instance, Marcel Arland, "*Rêveuse bourgeoisie* is the most amply articulated, the most dramatic and the most faithful to the spirit of the genre. It is Drieu's masterpiece as a novelist."[16] To apply the standards of the "spirit of the genre"—assuming that such a spirit exists—particularly to a novel written in the period between the two wars, is a little arbitrary. The great merit of the major novels written during that period is their contempt for formulas and their exploration of all the possibilities of the genre.

In a more recent article, Marcel Arland himself has shown more consideration for the "audacity" and the value of "compulsion" so noticeable in the fictional production of the between-the-wars period. By contrast with the too-neat tech-

---

[15] Ramon Fernandez, " 'Gilles,' par Drieu La Rochelle," *Marianne* (January 10, 1940).

[16] Arland, "Drieu La Rochelle, II: Les Réponses," *NNRF*, No. 13 (January, 1954), 112.

nique characterizing current French fiction, he expresses regret for what now appears as a great generation:

> Between the two wars, we saw the dislocation of the entire framework of the novel. Critics grumbled. In their opinion, we were witnessing the death throes of a literary form—just as though this form had not renewed itself in the very measure in which it had proved faithless to its traditions (witness the works of Malraux, Bernanos, Céline, Jouhandeau, Montherlant, Drieu La Rochelle, or Sartre).[17]

Drieu himself, according to his friend and biographer, Pierre Andreu, preferred *Gilles* to all his other novels. This preference is justified, and we agree with Gaëtan Picon, who, in his survey of the new French literature expresses the belief that if posterity had to retain only one book by Drieu, it would be *Gilles*:

> ... *Gilles* (1939) is, without any doubt, one of the greatest novels of the century—and one of those books in which the disarming sincerity of a man rises to the grandeur usually reserved to literary transpositions.[18]

There is no doubt that sincerity is the author's chief virtue in *Gilles*. The honesty of his self-analysis, however familiar it may have become to the reader, always comes as a surprise, the author managing to be one step ahead of the reader in analyzing his own faults and weaknesses. The quality of surprise renders bearable the confessions which might otherwise become somewhat monotonous. As Drieu points out in his Preface to *Gilles*: "I was not less severe for myself taken as a pretext, than for any other contemporary. I flogged mercilessly the times in myself" (p. v). This may explain why, in spite of the violent tone of Drieu's attacks against democracy and his unrestrained expression of opinions bound to be objectionable to most readers, such as his anti-Semitic stand, the general purport of the novel is not offensive. For the tone of bitter sincerity that permeates the book maintains the interest

---

[17] *Idem*, "A Literary Letter from Paris," *New York Times Book Review*, January 1, 1956, p. 18.
[18] Picon, *Panorama de la nouvelle littérature française*, p. 89.

the real world

of the reader, even when the ideas irritate him. Gilles may be weak, and at times sordid, but the tone of authenticity never fails.

In *Gilles*, Drieu has finally achieved the aim he had set himself from the beginning of his career:[19] to give a picture of his time which would be modified and qualified by a pitiless portrait of the man who draws it. He had been groping for a suitable form. The novel of testimony was the answer. It was the end result of two apparently conflicting tendencies: the distrust for pure ideas and the scruples of an overly critical mind. It is a romantic outsider's view of the real world of his time. Its dimensions, its psychology, its vocabulary, and its hero are romantic; only the hero's intellectual views—like those of the author—are antiromantic.

---

[19] *Genève ou Moscou*, p. 15. In 1928 Drieu had already outlined his method: "... the judgments of a man of letters on the whole of society can be accepted only if they are accompanied by a pitiless analysis of the individual conditions which determine them."

nine

THE MAN ON HORSEBACK

In *L'Homme à cheval*, published in 1943, Drieu, aware of the danger of writing about recent events, has avoided a too literal transposition of the real. He places his action in Bolivia, in 1868. He indicates, however, at the end of the novel, that the manuscript belonged to the papers of a mysterious political refugee, most likely from Spain, who lived a miserable, solitary life in Paris. He hints that the tale was written by someone who "never set foot in Bolivia, at most dreamt of it" as the many material inaccuracies would suggest. This uncertainty about the locale in terms of time and space is a favorable atmosphere for a philosophical tale of universal application.

The author's disdain for the details of plot sets the tone of a certain form of *roman pur*. The characters, all representative of a group or symbolizing an idea or attitude, move in a rarefied atmosphere. The altitude of the country with its high mountains is constantly emphasized. The last part of the novel is set on the shores of Lake Titicaca an "extreme point of this extremist land which can be compared only to Tibet." "Man here can be concerned only with the divine" (p. 221). The intrigues of love and politics are viewed from a high vantage point in this grandiose setting. The destructions of war are quickly hidden by a nature indifferent to man and his agitations.

The whole story is told in the perspective of past time by Felipe, the guitarist, as though he were writing his memoirs. The full title of the manuscript found among Felipe's papers was: "Fragments of memoirs on Jaime Torrijos written by his brother." But the vagueness of certain passages, contrasted with the vividness of particular scenes puts the readers in an atmosphere of day-dreaming and fantasy. The final and quite unexpected note in the epilogue confirms that this effect was intended: "There has not existed a Jaime Torrijos according to history . . ." (p. 243).

By thus placing the reader beyond the limits of the possible by using the exoticism of place (there are enough picturesque details to maintain the pretense of Bolivian local color) and distance in time (the action takes place around 1868 at a time when cavalry charges were still possible), the author renders acceptable and even legitimate the melodramatic devices of a romantic adventure. The novel abounds in crimes, conspiracies, coups d'état, duels, spies and counterspies, tortures, and secret meetings. What gives the book its unique flavor is that the disillusioned experience of an aging man, the dramas of ambition, power, love, death, and renunciation are incorporated in the romance. It is the artistic transposition of the tragedy of a man who has been seduced by the romantic aspect of the rise of fascism, has become its victim, and has desired to be its martyr.[1]

The originality of the characters in this novel lies in the fact that they develop on two levels: on an intellectual plane, they are manipulated to illustrate the political conception of

---

[1] A "martyr," as its Greek etymology indicates, is essentially a "witness." One of Jaime's words to Felipe when they part is: "You shall write all you have loved here. You shall testify" (p. 240).

the author; on a more emotional and personal plane, they tend to present a partial solution of the enigma of the author's personality and summarize the experience of his life. As with his previous fictional characters, Drieu develops different tendencies of his own personality in separate characters. These characters illustrate at the same time one of his favorite ideas that in a man of thought there is always the embryo of a man of action and, conversely, he thinks that men of action have a remarkable capacity for assimilation of ideas. By a phenomenon frequent among writers, Jaime, the handsome cavalry lieutenant, is created to compensate for Drieu's inadequacies, failures, and disappointments in real life. He is the Drieu of the charge at Charleroi if the charge had not been halted by machine guns and if Drieu had become the military and revolutionary leader that for a moment he felt he could be. Jaime is also compensatory in that he represents the "man on horseback," the hero whom Drieu kept seeking after he realized that he himself was not able to be a man of thought and a man of action at the same time.

Felipe, the guitarist-theologian, is a recognizable transposition of the contemplative side of Drieu, ever interested in the study of religions. His three great sources of inspiration are war, women, and religion. Felipe at first is merely curious to see what the results of Jaime's ambition are going to be. But he becomes more and more committed to him until between them it is "forever, in life and death."

Drieu seems to have taken pleasure in ridiculing and humiliating the intellectual aspect of himself. Felipe is so ugly that women are unable to love him; he is reduced to the most abject prostitutes; he takes refuge in music and theology. His role during a crucial battle, in which he awkwardly rides a mule, is decidedly not brilliant. He is too intelligent not to see two sides of a question and he shows a remarkable ability to espouse the point of view of the enemy. When he meets Don Benito, the "protector" against whom he is plotting in favor of Jaime, he succumbs to his charm and is alarmed by the thought which suddenly occurs to him: "If I had known

Don Benito before Jaime ... wouldn't I have loved him very much?" (p. 61). At the last moment, he knows he would not have the courage to kill Don Benito. This Hamlet needs to be coupled with a man of action to accomplish what he has conceived.

The impossibility for a man of contemplation to be at the same time a man of action is dramatically symbolized during the battle between the rebels and the forces which have remained loyal to Don Benito by the presence of Felipe, who has been made a prisoner, in the enemy's very post of observation in a church tower: it gives him the impression he is a traitor to his own cause. Felipe is so curious that he cannot help enjoying the sight of the charge from the outside: "Fate had brought me back with ironical justice to my contemplative disposition" (p. 51). However, his role in inspiring Jaime to continue the fight is decisive and at this point he acts fast and efficiently.

He hesitates to estimate the nature of his role in the making of Jaime. Perhaps Jaime would have been the same without him. Perhaps he has even done Jaime more harm than good. Jaime must always reassure his companion who has a perpetual tendency to plead guilty. The guitarist recognizes that his role is limited to decisive but temporary interventions. At the end Jaime acknowledges his debt to the poet: "It is you, Felipe, who put all these words into my head. Who was I? A cavalry lieutenant, jumping on horses, handling the sabre and the carbine, wallowing in the love of soldiers and women. You have put words into me" (p. 266). The man of action even humiliates himself and admits that, in the end, he has accomplished no more than the dreamer, and at what cost! "Felipe, I hate you, you are me, I am only you. Look. I am only a dreamer like you and a gatherer of words. I have not been able to conquer Lake Titicaca. I am only a traveling dreamer like you ...," (p. 227). At the end—supreme fulfillment for the author—the equation is made between the man of action and the man of contemplation. Felipe no longer feels this "passionate subordination" toward Jaime which had tormented him for such a long time.

In the characters of Conception and Camilla, Drieu sums up the two great categories of women under which all his feminine characters can be classified: the prostitute and the *femme du monde*. His misogyny is even greater than in earlier novels and Jaime and Felipe are almost entirely "men without women." Jaime has found in his country and in war his real loves and Felipe has taken refuge in art and theology. Any sympathy there is for women goes, however, to the prostitute. Jaime admits: "I love women only so far as they are prostitutes and betray me" (p. 183). The hero must be a man without women. Conception's intimacies with Jaime's colonel in La Paz arouse Jaime's jealousy and he kills the colonel, thus upsetting all the plans for the revolt against Benito. The conspiracy nearly fails. Camilla's action in taking her cousin Manuelito as a lover also leads Jaime to kill Manuelito in a duel thus arousing the implacable hatred of the aristocrats. Women are traitors and troublemakers. During the Indian revolt, Camilla spies on Jaime for her brother-in-law, the Mason Belmez; Conchita does the same on behalf of Florida, the Jesuit father. Women are "frightening," says Felipe. Evoking the liaison of Camilla and Manuelito, Jaime does not hesitate to generalize; it illustrates a universal feminine weakness.

Turn your back on a woman, then look again. She will have put your caricature in your bed. Conception with her grooms is hardly better than Camilla with her Manuelitos (p. 193).

Conception has at least one advantage over her aristocratic rival. She does not pretend that she gives any more than her body. She is the blind instrument of elementary forces. Jaime has loved Camilla for three days and with such intensity that it is enough for their love to pass into eternity, but he rejoices that he was able to recover from it and to put an end to it.

Jaime's real and lasting passion can only be for his country.

Felipe has recourse to the image of the androgyne to explain Jaime's relationship to his country and in so doing he refers to his female nature:

"Bolivia is my wife," laughed Jaime.
"You are Bolivia's wife, too. The male genius of Bolivia has fecundated the flexible soul of the man of action in you. Bolivia and you are one. You constitute the perfect androgyne, having met because you were already united" (p. 204).

Jaime's political program in its broad outlines corresponds to ideas that Drieu had always advocated. Crushing the nobles (*briser les grands*) is a transposition of his distrust for the French Right which he considered obsolete in its allegiances, pessimistic, and decadent. He is afraid that the Right would always block any thoroughgoing social reform. The bourgeois element in it could not be integrated into a totalitarian state in which the sense of belonging to the national community would be supreme: the bourgeois are too individualistic. In the novel, Dona Camilla, the *femme du monde*, is representative of this whole class: "What is a *femme du monde?*" It is the daughter of a defeated, beheaded aristocracy.... This has been true since 1792. Aristocrats all over the world are beheaded people who walk on, out of habit" (p. 190). The fact that the Church supports them and leans on them indicates that the Church also, may represent merely the survival of an archaic institution. Dona Camilla is unable to love Jaime as the embodiment of Bolivia; she sees and loves in him only the individual. Felipe points this out to Jaime. "She inflicted on you her conception of life, their conception of life: they are individualists, as the English philosophers say. She has loved you as an individual" (p. 203).

She represents for Jaime the danger of seduction by the refinement of a decadent class. Felipe, the artist, is fascinated by her aristocratic milieu. He and Camilla both adore music and books. Camilla reads *Les Fleurs du mal:* "... which had arrived in Bolivia shortly before. It had come through a diplomat of our country in Rio de Janeiro, who had received it from the local French representative, M. de Gobineau" (p.

156). But Jaime is a "doer" and nothing must interfere with his deeds. He has come to power to destroy the delicate life of Dona Camilla and of her peers. Camilla cannot furnish a bond between Jaime's popular origins and the aristocracy. For, as Felipe tells her, she is unable to leave her caste, and therefore to accomplish the union of the people and the aristocracy within herself. Jaime is wedded to Bolivia and its people. The love of a Conchita does not interfere. "Conchita, with her body belonging to everyone, was the image of a soldier's and a leader's fate: Jaime belonging to Bolivia like Conchita to the Bolivians, could not be ashamed of Conchita's body" (p. 114).

No hope of renewal can come from the aristocracy. The aristocrats are unable to organize a revolution successfully. Their plot against Jaime ends in failure. They are easily subdued by Jaime and his men. They are only pitiful. But Jaime has risen from the people. He is half-Indian, and plans to base his power on the support of the Indians. However, he has first to emancipate them. One recalls that Doriot's party was called Populaire and the name of its paper was *L'Emancipation nationale.* Drieu seems to have seen in fascism mainly a short cut to what he called "socialism"; he feared, however, that its alliance with nationalistic elements would introduce reactionary principles. During the occupation, he expressed his disappointment at seeing that Germany was postponing the establishment of a European socialism. Drieu had disapproved of the alliance of French fascist groups with bourgeois and capitalistic elements. He had also denounced the hypocrisy of French deputies who labeled themselves socialist and received fat salaries as attorneys of international oil companies. Jaime is by contrast, a passionately simpleminded man:

> He was not a cold-blooded gentleman who affects good manners; he was not a dandy who mixes hypocrisy and cynicism; he was neither a gentleman, nor a *caballero;* he was a man as passionate as he was thoughtful and was not ashamed of his passion. He hated his enemies, and did not try to hide it from them or from himself (p. 198).

Jaime is not the kind of man to accept paralyzing compromises. His enemies see the threat he constitutes for the interests they represent. The Church defends the rights of the aristocracy. Freemasonry shares the fears of the bourgeoisie. The two form a coalition against the new order. If the spirit of the Christian religion were still alive in the Church, if Masonic ideals still inspired Masons, Jesuits and Masons would understand the meaning of Jaime's desire to revitalize the primitive Inca religion after he has restored the Inca empire. Jaime's intentions, as interpreted by Felipe, coincide with the Masonic dream.[2] But they are blind because the spirit is dead.

Jaime is prevented from achieving the emancipation of the Indians. Another great project, the restoration of the Inca empire, was the third in Jaime's program. "I am here to crush the nobles, awaken the Indians and restore the Inca empire" (p. 119). *L'Homme à cheval* is not a gratuitous exercise of imagination and we are justified in substituting the word European for Inca. European unity had been the dream of Drieu's life.

Jaime fails miserably in his effort to federate the countries of South America. He is defeated by a coalition of Peru and Chile. Others have failed before him: first of all, Bolivar; Lopez, in Paraguay encountered the coalition of Argentina, Uruguay, and Brazil; Rozas was unable to prevent the separation of Argentina and Uruguay: "The time has not come, perhaps it will never come" (p. 220). With the assurance of a prophet, Jaime announces, however, that his enterprise will not be forgotten: "The time will come for great actions, for imperial actions." Jaime is equally sure that his failure to emancipate the Indians is temporary: "I want to renovate the Indian people. Like a true statesman, I want the unavoidable... I am only a precursor, I'll have many successors" (p. 196).

The meaning of the pilgrimage to Lake Titicaca which forms the last part of the tale is clearly indicated: "Here,

---

[2] See *L'Homme à cheval* (1943), p. 197.

thank God, the frontier was invisible and there was no custom official or soldier to signify it. It was right, because it is here that Peru and Bolivia are one, as they were one at the time of the Incas" (p. 22). No customs officials, no soliders in Europe: such had been Drieu's dream for more than twenty years. The Europe of 1942 or 1943, France divided in several zones, nationalism more aggravated than ever, seemed to be as far as possible from that ideal.

The man who, as early as 1927, had called himself in the title of one of his books *Le Jeune Européen* and who in 1944 entitled a collection of essays *Le Français d'Europe,* made a pilgrimage to the only place in Europe which seemed to be sacred territory, untouched by war—Switzerland. Drieu, on the shores of Lake Geneva, like Jaime, on Lake Titicaca, rediscovered the spirit of what Europe had been at the time of the organic complexity of the Holy Roman Empire (called in French "Saint Empire Romain germanique"), and the present-day example of how a federation under a liberal but firm leadership could work:

Jaime came to the place where, for years, without actually being, he had lived. And he, who had been greatly defeated, came here to contemplate the victory he could not touch. He was here at home, much more than in La Paz (p. 224).

In the same way, Geneva had been for Drieu the only hope for a European federation. The title of his 1928 book was a warning: Geneva or Moscow. Now that Moscow was threatening Western Europe again, he went for reassurance to "the sacred territory of Europe, the last bastion against the Slavic invasion," in this Geneva from which one can see the highest point in Europe just as Titicaca dominates South America with its Cordillera Real of the Andes. An article published in March, 1943, "Notes sur La Suisse," indicates what Drieu saw in a "mythical Switzerland": the Swiss unity is a mystery, the mystery of a trinity in one body (German, French, Italian elements combined in one country), a complex soul incarnated in a single political body, a body as complex as a soul. "Switzerland is there to remind us first of all that Europe is not a juxtaposition of Germanism and Latinism but an inextricable interpenetration of these two mythical currents."[3] The Holy Roman Empire was a forerunner of this unavoidable integration. "Switzerland is, physically and spiritually, the European point, the point where so many things intersect and overlap."[4] Switzerland combines Catholicism and Protestantism. Paradoxically, the German cantons originally were Catholic, the French ones, Protestant. From the fourteenth to the sixteenth century, Switzerland had been a great military power. "Switzerland has been made of a federation and of an hegemony within the federation but the hegemony has always followed the methods of the federation."[5]

Jaime at Titicaca, Drieu at Geneva in 1943, gaze at the Promised Land which they know they will never reach. Their decision is taken: Drieu will go back to France and kill himself whenever he decides to do so and Jaime says: "We are of those who want to die with clear eyes" (p. 240). Jaime decides not to return to La Paz, but to renounce all his worldly power. He parts from Felipe: "It is time we die to each other, as to all we have loved" (p. 240). He feels he can do no more for Bolivia than what he has already done: "Whether I retire today or ten years from now, it will be the same ... My time is over" (p. 338).

The nakedness of the novel, the absence of direct references to the author's life, the tone of detachment mixed with a poetic and even musical atmosphere, are sufficient to explain the predilection of certain critics. Pierre-Henri Simon even sees in it Drieu's only achievement in the domain of fiction:

> In the field of pure fiction, I see in his work only one success: *L'Homme à cheval*, his last book (1943). In it, a relaxed Drieu, detached from himself and liberated from the anecdotal detail, has managed to imagine, in a Bolivia of dream, the symbol of the high destiny which he had missed: the life of a military and political hero devoted to glory and love. As the narrator is the Protector's guitarist, an obsession with music accompanies this

---

[3] *Le Français d'Europe*, p. 234.
[4] *Ibid.*, p. 236.
[5] *Ibid.*, p. 214.

tale of violent passion and great deeds in the midst of distant and sublime scenery.⁶

This exclusive preference seems excessive. Moreover, to emphasize too much the tone of detachment would also be misleading. In spite of appearances, *L'Homme à cheval*, more than any other of Drieu's novels, is a novel of testimony. The transposition in time and place allows the author to express his political, philosophical, and aesthetic testament in all its purity. Confronted by the foreseeable defeat of fascism and the end of his own life, the author persists in affirming his ideal of heroic life. The times may not be favorable, the message is still true: such seems to be the portent of the epigraph—a quotation from Balzac's *Séraphita:* "Woe to him who would remain silent in the desert believing he is not heard by anyone."

The general philosophy which underlies the action of *L'Homme à cheval* is the Nietzschean philosophy of *The Will to Power* as Drieu interpreted it: "Man is an accident in a world of accidents. The world has no general meaning. It has only the meaning we give it, for a moment, for the development of our passion, of our action"⁷

By contrast with the rationalistic, optimistic point of view of those who believe in progress, it is a pessimistic, tragic viewpoint which recognizes in the development of the history of mankind a pattern of "eternal return" in Nietzschean terms or of closed cycles in Spenglerian terminology.

Jaime's career presents, in a microcosm, the pattern of one of those cycles. Felipe translates it in terms of art in a melancholy melody that he plays on his guitar: ". . . it started in a very slow rhythm, rose by starts each time more surprising, climaxed in a frenzy in which my fingers would be torn and went down in a sudden and sad calm. This melancholy melody would be our story" (p. 20).

At the end of the dictator's career, not much has been ac-

⁶ Pierre-Henri Simon, *Procès du Héros* (Paris, Editions du Seuil, 1950), p. 114.
⁷ *Socialisme fasciste*, p. 70. This text has been quoted above, Chapter Three.

complished in terms of tangible results. Even the few results that Jaime has obtained will not survive him. The trials of his prospective successor look grim:

"I have designated Fernandez as my successor ... alas!"
"Yes, alas is right: he won't be accepted by the people ... He won't be obeyed when you are no longer here to command. He is boring, awkward, he will be overthrown" (p. 238).

It is clearly implied in the melancholy conclusion of the book that, notwithstanding his plans, Jaime Torrijos has acted mainly out of impulse or under the pressure of circumstance without always realizing what he was doing. As for Felipe, who has put "words" into the dictator's head, he has acted out of purely aesthetic reasons: he finds Jaime more beautiful than Benito; he is not personally interested in power at all; he hates and scorns it. He refuses any official position after Jaime has come to power and he is not even the "gray eminence" that his political enemies see in him. Jaime is at first for him "a stone" he throws "in the water of his dream" to watch the ripple it causes (p. 28). For him to replace a tyrant does not mean to overthrow tyranny: he has no system; he believes politics is a game, with its rules, and everybody cheats. To win in it, however, one must pay lip service to the rules: "A cheat does not perform his tricks openly or all the other cheats start howling" (p. 31). The guitarist knows in advance that Jaime will not find happiness in power. The dictator rises to power because he can no longer stand being humiliated by his hierarchical superiors: he must dominate the others to quench his "fury of contempt" (p. 14).

This contempt which is one of the springs of the will to power isolates the dictator from his fellow men and makes impossible any human happiness. Power, for Jaime means constant torture. It makes him *méchant* (wicked and malicious). Felipe had noted in Don Benito "this air of wickedness which cannot satisfy itself nor replace the impossible delights of a vanished kindness" (p. 22). Felipe too must humiliate others and the sight of humiliated people is the only relief to their torment. It is a very temporary relief because it arouses more hatred and eventually makes their isolation worse. One evening at the palace the nobles have been invited to see Conchita's dances. Jaime humiliates them by forcing them to pay homage to "the most beautiful whore in Bolivia." Felipe is then struck by Jaime's "hunted and tortured expression" (p. 94).

Jaime was no longer the same... Jaime had become old. I had never seen him with this distorted, deeply wrinkled face and in the eyes this flash of feverish, malicious consciousness. Something of Don Benito's glance had passed to him (p. 89).

The poet has no illusion about the influence of the man of thought on the man of action. The transmutation of ideas into acts makes these ideas utterly unrecognizable: "Did I find in what Jaime said what I had sometimes whispered to him? Thought which has become action, tempered in blood, forged into a steel weapon is foreign to the thinker" (p. 191).

But for the guitarist, who is a poet, Jaime's adventure is wholly justified on an aesthetic and spiritual level. In a world without apparent meaning or direction, man has to create his own values; or rather the man on horseback offers his countrymen a new reason to live. He gives shape to his life and to his people's destiny. He renews the arts and revitalizes religion. It is a fugitive victory over nothingness. Like Sisyphus' task, this apparent victory is actually a constant failure. But victory is not what counts; the struggle and the sacrifices it requires bring the few moments of intense life which constitute the only joy for man. Felipe has always regretted having once asked Jaime what he planned to do after his victory (p. 43). The privileged moment is the moment of the charge regardless of its outcome. The song of the Agreda cavalrymen is the expression of this spirit of gratuitous sacrifice. It is sung by the soldiers going to the battle: "the souls of the men, at the refrain, rose in a single *élan* above themselves swinging on their horses" and "the highest chorus upon earth composed the magnificent illusion of a song which reached the stars" (p. 42). It is in those moments that the beauty of man's fate can be fully appreciated: "If you have not heard, singing at the top of their lungs, men who, by the grace of war, know at last that they are going everyday toward death, you cannot know the fugitive beauty of being their brother" (p. 42). When the cavalry actually charges, Felipe, who, from the enemy position, knows that they are going to be slaughtered and defeated cannot repress his exaltation: "It was one of those rare moments when it is given to man to be himself by throwing himself entirely out of himself" (p. 51). There is literally something semidivine in this rush of horses and men at the highest point of animality—and in the gratuitousness of their action: "Mystery of mankind which gives itself for nothing, to nothing. O beauty frenetically self-sufficient. O minute forever lost, forever eternal in the heart" (p. 52).

What makes the beauty of such a moment for Felipe who is at the same time an artist, a theologian, and a "lover of horses" is that the charge is an image of sacrifice, an embodiment of the "cult of death in life." The narrator of *La Comédie de Charleroi*, after the charge, expressed the same belief: "What is the use of living if one does not use one's life to strike it against death as against a flint? . . . If death is not at the heart of life like a hard core, what a soft and soon rotten fruit."[8]

The gesture of sacrifice is the essential gesture of life, the one that gives it meaning: "Eternal gesture of all religions, the sacrifice, the gesture of sacrifice which only sums up and stylizes the gesture of life. Man is born only to die and is never so much alive as when he dies. But his life has meaning only if he gives it instead of waiting for it to be taken from him" (p. 232).

The "shape" of sacrifice in war is that of the charge. The religious sacrifice derives its own shape from that of war: Jaime, at Felipe's instigation, celebrates a rite by killing his battle charger, Brave, in the presence of his soldiers. They rediscover the spirit which is at the heart of all religions: a certain way of reaching God or at least a form of the absolute upon earth. After thus stylizing the essential gesture of war

---

[8] *La Comédie de Charleroi*, p. 70.

and of the military hero, Jaime, realizing that there is no other possible victory for him than over himself, renounces everything and retires to the jungle. He has combined the destiny of the saint with that of the hero by this final and complete detachment. The shape created by the warrior, which has found its expression in religion will also influence art. It is the aesthetic justification of the "man on horseback." "Give us great men and great actions so that we rediscover the sense of great things" (p. 228). Jaime's parting words to Felipe are *"Tu témoigneras"* (You'll bear witness). "The fragments of memoirs on Jaime Torrijos, written by his brother," that is to say *L'Homme à cheval*, is the testimony.

Jaime is thus the prototype of all "men on horseback." By his very presence he has provided a call to grandeur. He has helped men to rise above themselves. His countrymen have followed him out of enthusiasm; his call corresponded to a deep urge in them: "What we call revolutions, pronunciamentos, coups, protectors, is not all that in the blood of Spaniards and Indians the same ceaseless and inexhaustible quest for the absolute upon earth?" (p. 225).

The hero gives shape to history: Jaime has given a new meaning to the word Inca:

It seems to me that this word has lived again and meant something again. Anyone who will want to find its meaning again will have to decipher my annals. The sweat and the blood of men, the tears of women, the hooves of horses, and the moaning of the cannons' wheels will testify (p. 225).

Jaime has come to renew music as well as theology. He has given meaning to Felipe's life:

Who was I? A guitar player, a pale student of theology; and all of a sudden, you stood in front of me; you were the shape. The shape. As a lover of beauty, I rushed toward that shape which was living beauty. Suddenly, music, theology were a single figure walking in the world (p. 226).

Jaime verifies Felipe's theory that "each hero nourishes ten great artists": Beethoven would not have been Beethoven without Bonaparte; Shakespeare owes everything to Elizabeth; Goethe would not have written the second Faust if he had not seen the French Revolution.

Finally Jaime has shown that the blood shed by heroes brings new life to the ideas of religion and revivifies the ritual: "Gods, like poets, need to live the blood of sacrifices" (p. 231).

ten

THE TRAITOR

Drieu's two last novels are as poetic as the genre of the novel permits. In *L'Homme à cheval*, the ideas are presented in images and symbols rather than in philosophical discourse. *Les Chiens de paille* contains more material of a philosophical nature but it is still essentially symbolic. Both novels read like modern "fables." Beneath the characters of Felipe, the guitarist and Jaime Torrijos, the cavalry man, transported into a nineteenth-century Bolivia in *L'Homme à cheval*, and Constant, the Frenchman, in the occupied France of 1942 in *Les Chiens de paille*, it is easy to recognize the familiar anxious interrogation of Drieu the man and Drieu the political writer attempting to solve the riddle of his destiny.

More than in his journalistic production, it is in Drieu's fiction that is to be found the testimony of this nationalist who assumed the ignominious role of the traitor. The "reasons, the beautiful reasons," he refused at the cost of his life, to explain to policemen and judges[1] are dramatized in his two

---

[1] See *Récit secret*, p. 419. Speculating on the causes of his first attempt at suicide, Drieu considers the possibility that he may have simply been afraid:

last novels. As usual with Drieu, the message is presented in a mood more interrogative than dogmatic and it is not without ambiguity.

Two attitudes, embodied by two figures, fascinated him at the time these books were written—that of the prophet in the person of Isaiah and that of the traitor Judas. The reason he could identify himself with Isaiah, "this aristocrat... who could see beyond the border of his little country, who saw that the time of the empire had come,"[2] was that he recognized in him the impossible situation of the patriot preaching collaboration with the conquerors.[3] A meditation on Judas and a reëxamination of his role as a traitor are at the heart of *Les Chiens de paille*.

The paradox of creating a lasting work of art out of the most ephemeral reality—the political one—is the challenge that fascinated the artist in Drieu at the very moment when he was more involved—as a man—in daily political reality than he had ever been before in his life. To make the challenge more difficult, he did not resort to the transposition of time and place which he had recently used in *L'Homme à cheval*; he set the action of his last novel, *Les Chiens de paille*, in the occupied France of 1942.[4]

The author states in the preface that he had first intended to delay the publication of this "brief tale" which he wrote in the spring of 1943. He wanted to see whether the rapid changes in the political situation in France and in the world would make the novel seem dated before it was even published. But he decided to publish it in 1944, apparently without change, realizing that any book is tied to the time in

---

"... afraid of being beaten, torn to pieces by the crowd, afraid of being humiliated by policemen and judges, afraid of having to explain to vile men [his] reasons, [his] beautiful reasons."

[2] *Le Français d'Europe*, p. 121.
[3] *Ibid.*, p. 131.
[4] The book was published by Gallimard in the summer of 1944. It has not yet reached the public because Paris was liberated before the printed book reached the bookstores and it was suppressed. I am very much indebted to Professor Warren Ramsey and to Michel Mohrt who obtained permission from the publisher to lend me a copy of the novel.

which it has been written and can come to life only at the moment: "Later, it does not matter if some of its elements grow old; they grow old with the rest of life. And this short, imperceptible process of growing old permits the deepest substance—if there is any—to come to life." Read in the perspective of more than a decade the view of man's fate which underlies this novel appears indeed more important than its literary aspect.

As sheer narration, *Les Chiens de paille* is a satisfactory novel, illustrating Drieu's skill at telling a story. The interest of the reader is constantly maintained at a high pitch. We are at once plunged with Constant Trubert, a fifty-year-old veteran of World War I, who has escaped from a prison camp of World War II, into the mystery of his new situation at La Maison des Marais, in the coastal, "forbidden zone," in northwestern France. We piece together bit by bit the elements of that situation. Constant has been sent there by his "boss" Susini, the owner of La Maison des Marais on the vague mission of getting acquainted with the neighborhood pending more definite orders. We get acquainted with the different actors of the drama: Philippe Préault, an industrialist of the vicinity, a French patriot and an Anglophile de Gaullist; Salis, a Communist mechanic who used to operate the filling station; Dr. Bardy, a physician and a collaborationist, Liassov, a Russian painter who lives in a house hidden in the coastal dunes with his young wife, Roxane; Cormont, a young man in charge of an officer's school for the training of leaders of the youth camps in France.

Curiosity concerning Susini has been built up by the mystery that surrounds him and the allusions of the other characters so that his appearance at the end of the first part satisfies our expectations. Susini finally reveals to Constant that arms and ammunitions were hidden in his house after the defeat in 1940 by the previous owner of La Maison des Marais. Constant, retrospectively, understands the anxious interest of the different factions in him and their concern over the house.

the traitor

The second part of the novel explains how Constant met Susini and what the latter represents. Since he is, along with his half brother, one of the kings of the black market, we are initiated (always through the concrete adventures of Constant all over France) into the mechanism of black-market operations in France at that time—from the clandestine, unlawful slaughtering of cattle, to the intricacies of the channels of distribution.

In the two last parts, the different factions clash in their effort to get control of the weapons and the action moves as fast as that of a thriller until the final *coup de théâtre*. Although the novel follows outwardly the most frequent pattern of any novel of adventure: the quest for a "treasure" and the fight of different groups over it, it also develops on an entirely different level because of the symbolic value of the treasure. The cache of weapons and ammunition represents the potential active participation of France in the war with what is left of its resources. This political level gives the novel of adventure a much broader range of meaning, since it provides the opportunity for giving an ideological picture of France during the German occupation. This level is further transcended by the point of view of Constant who participates in the action while trying to maintain an absolute detachment and who seeks the eternal under the transient.

The dual attitude of Constant, the central character, allows the novel to develop simultaneously on the level of the world, that is to say, a more or less political level and on the level of the afterworld, a kind of mystical or religious level. Drieu has achieved in Constant the most satisfactory balance between fiction and reality of all his characters. He has put enough of himself in Constant to give him life and interest but he has sufficiently transposed the autobiographical element which characterizes most of his protagonists to avoid making him a new version of Gilles, or Hassib, or Felipe.

In the preface, the author stated his own position in order to point out that it does not coincide with that of Constant: "A writer, who is a European socialist, who denounced the invasion and the destruction of Europe, has written this brief tale at the same time as his polemic articles."[5] He points out that this position had not been taken without sacrificing many conflicting feelings. He has used the novel to give expression to those conflicting or contradictory positions. He specifically warns us against completely identifying him with Constant: "who represents rather well . . . one of the existing tendencies among intellectuals today in France. Constant is not the author. A character is never the author; a character can never be but a part of the author" (p. 12).

Drieu has been able to create a Constant who is really above the warring ideologies by embodying every aspiration of his own personality in the various protagonists who in their different ways of loving, despising, or holding a grudge against France play the tragedy of patriotism in a country which is no longer the master of its own fate. At one time or another he is behind Salis, the Communist, Bardy, the Germanophile, Préault, the Anglophile, and most of all, Cormont, the young, solitary hero who defies the rest of the world and his own compatriots in his passionate attachment to "France, France alone."

Constant embodies the mood Drieu describes in the preface as his own "when going beyond my opponents and myself and the world of opinions, in an effort to reach another world, I throw backward toward them as toward myself a glance which is more scornful than charitable."

This scorn, in Constant, is compensated by understanding and even a certain amount of sympathy for his fellow men: "His ultimate curiosity toward human beings was so acute and so supple that it somewhat resembled charity" (p. 30). With him, even indifference "takes necessarily the aspect of charity" (p. 53). Constant reads the Oriental mystics and the epigraph is taken from the Tao Tê Ching of Lao Tse. Like the wise man praised by the Tao Tê Ching, Constant is not self-seeking. Being perfectly disinterested and indifferent, all information comes to him. The men representing the different

---

[5] *Les Chiens de paille*, preface, p. xi.

the traitor

factions confide in him mainly because they interpret his silences according to their own wishes. After a few weeks in the region of the marshes, he knows them all well.

Of the three agents of foreign powers, Bardy, the Fascist, has been an ardent nationalist for a long time. Since World War I, he has felt and suffered from, the increasing weakness of France. For a long time he had thought of seeking support for French nationalism from British nationalism, but the interests of England were for the most part extra-European and the hypocritically liberal viewpoint of the British alienated Bardy. After 1934 he tried to lean on the Germans. In 1940 he became a collaborator, mainly because he no longer felt at home in his own country. He does not feel resentment toward the Germans for occuping France. He was humiliated by the defeat of his country because he felt partly responsible for it, like other Frenchmen, but the occupation was only a consequence of the defeat. Perhaps, he expected that his attitude was going to be that of the majority. Now his position is isolated; it is this solitude that arouses Constant's sympathy. Moreover, Bardy no longer has any illusions about the Germans; they are very weak themselves and Hitlerism is only the German equivalent of a middle way between capitalism and communism; their only justification would have been to make a truly socialist Europe—which they have not done. He foresees the defeat of Germany by Russia. The prospect does not displease him entirely: the Russians embody better than the Germans his ideal of authority and aristocracy. This does not prevent him from telling Préault violently that "he prefers to be German rather than English." He has obviously given up the idea that he could still be a Frenchman.

Because Philippe Préault cannot accept the presence of the Germans, he identifies himself with the British who are free of German occupation. He does not realize that by joining with the British he loses the special quality of a Frenchman which is the very thing he wants to preserve. Others identify themselves with the Germans so as not to feel "occupied." Préault belongs to the intellectual bourgeoisie and he "dreams" more than he knows about England. In his wishful thinking, and because he is, at heart, a nationalist, he hopes that after liberation by the Allies, the French will rid themselves easily of the Anglo-American influence and thus end all their troubles. In his physical appearance, he is a little ridiculous, as are all the bourgeois characters in Drieu's fiction. The Malfosse of *Une Femme à sa fenêtre* would probably behave like Préault if he were placed in the same situation.

One of the surprising results of the occupation is the new friendship of the archbourgeois Préault with the Communist Salis. Préault is naïvely pleased to have established a relationship of complicity with a man of the working class instead of being the object of Salis' hatred as an employer. He reports everything faithfully to the Communist as Constant detects from the conversation of Salis, but as soon as the situation becomes serious, Salis assumes the initiative without consulting Préault. It is indicated that eventually Préault will be the dupe of his alliance with the Communists. In spite of all his defects, or, perhaps, because of his defects, Préault is represented as the true image of France, better than the others who are trying to imitate foreign attitudes or assume foreign masks:

The true French visage, after all, was Préault's, not at all imitative, in spite of awkward and childish allusions—but completely obsolete, antediluvian, as narrow-minded and scrupulous in his individualism as in his nationalism; as ignorant of the British and the Americans whom he thought he loved as of the Germans whom he hated, as much astray in his love for the Communist as he was not so long ago in his hatred for them (p. 213).

Constant has more sympathy for Salis than for Préault because he has always felt out of place with the bourgeois and he instinctively sympathizes with outsiders. The feeling is mutual and Gabriel Salis trusts Constant enough to tell him the story of his life and of his grudge against his father, who had early abandoned his mother, and of his bitterness against life in general. After being an anarchist during the Spanish Civil War (his father was a Spanish painter and Gabriel had spent

the traitor

part of his youth in Spain), he has become a Communist. The case of Salis shows how an oversimplified idea replaces God in the life of a fanatical Communist and justifies a form of asceticism. In spite of his efforts to suppress his personal feelings, Salis has not become an orthodox automaton, the ideal "militant." One senses the violent reaction of his individualistic personality against the very order he is trying to establish. In spite of this contradiction which, after all, shows that he has remained a human being, Constant considers Salis' position toward France much more logical than Préault's or Bardy's:

> Salis showed a much more vivid awareness, a much more active hypocrisy, a much harder cynicism. At least he knew that he was no longer a Frenchman and he did not pretend to be one. At least he knew that his patriotism was nothing but the party line (p. 31).

The time of *patriotism* is over. Salis, at least, has understood that lesson: they are all engaged in a civil war on a world-wide scale, a war of religions. The resemblance to sixteenth-century France is striking: "Then in a very similar way the French Protestants would hand over France to their allies the Germans and the British while the French Catholics were guilty of the same betrayal in favor of the Spaniards." France is no longer self-sufficient. Its power is negligible compared to that of the great Empires at war.

One man, however, symbolizes the persistence of the pure ideal of France, France alone. It is the young Cormont. While the others are trying to avoid the shame, the insignificance, the embarrassment of being French by identifying with the present victor as with Bardy, or the potential victors as with Préault and Salis, Cormont assumes the full responsibility of being a defeated Frenchman. He is attached to an idea of the eternal mythical France which cannot be affected by what he considers contingencies: "France was an entity, a goddess definitively installed in the Pantheon or the Olympia of History" (p. 122). He fanatically refuses to be the agent of any foreign power or, as he puts it, of any "Roi de Prusse." "I am against the millionaires, against the people's commissars, against the S.S., against the Pope, against Masonry, against the Jews" (p. 116). He has been disfigured during the war in 1940. He is only twenty-five, talks and acts rashly, stiffens his uncompromising attitude to the point of irritating Constant but wins his sympathy by his idealistic disinterestedness. He has no selfish motives and serves his idea of France passionately. He is the only one who is able to make Constant abandon his detachment.

Although he is capable of understanding all these characters, Constant refuses to talk their language and even less to take sides. In a country disintegrating under his eyes, Constant has chosen to adhere to the attitude which an absurd fate imposes on him, the attitude of the adventurer. In a world where all values are upset, where the lucid observer cannot find a cause worth committing himself to, least of all his country, Constant finds the only constancy possible in his loyalty to Susini: "I am an adventurer and Susini is another one. Adventurers hold to each other" (p. 127). He refuses to be the dupe of the so called *intérêts supérieurs*. When Préault protests that Constant is not of Susini's breed, that he has a sense of altruistic aims, Constant replies that "Superior interests" are "only gloves that gentlemen put on, but their hands are dirty just the same." He generalizes: "A statesman has dirty hands just as the least of his policemen or his valets" (p. 127). And Constant who is rereading the Gospels with a passionate interest, adds: "It was also the opinion of Jesus Christ when he insisted on involving Sir Pontius Pilate as much as the poor Judas" (p. 127).

Constant is also, in a way, the victim of circumstances. He is getting old and he is tired. He is a veteran of World War I and he has just come back from a prisoners' camp in Germany. He has escaped and he has illegal papers. He returns to a country where everything has become illegal, where illegality is praised as a form of fighting against those who impose their order, the German occupants. Is is "normal" that he should accept employment from a Susini, this Corsican who is the degraded Napoleon of the period. Susini tries to be on good

the traitor

terms with all camps and creates deliberate uncertainty as to whom he supports. He is an expert at the *double-jeu*. Constant is obliged to admit to Cormont that Susini is only a black-market operator and as the action develops he cannot help being disappointed about his "boss." He had previously made a conscious effort not to face the question of Susini's ultimate ends: "He had remained in the world under protest but he had remained there. In the most sordid part of the worldly affairs: as Susini's employee. (Who was Susini? It was of no importance to know it.)" (p. 208).

His indifference to the political comedy which goes on around him is symbolized by his attachment to Susini: "His loyalty to Susini . . . was the measure of his indifference toward all and toward Susini himself" (p. 199). Constant manages to act with absolute detachment toward the three or four men representing the conflicting ideologies because he is no longer of this world. He is thinking of death and above all of "what is beyond death." He reads only books which are concerned with the afterlife. He is initiating himself in Indian thought, the Buddhist and Taoist systems. He retires in the sand dunes, reads his favorite books and meditates: "He would read a sentence and in the sand, he would consider the infinite sign made by a tuft of dried and withered grass. In his mind the sentence and the tuft were tied. He was this tie and the world was this tie" (p. 25).

This identification with the world allows him to look on the humans still engaged in the comedy of love and politics with the detachment of cosmic powers. The detachment of the contemplator is not very different from that of the artist. It is made possible for Constant because of the proximity of death: "This fugitive scene of three civilized men, tired, nervous, worried, divided—between a machinery out of breath and the eternal marsh was soon going to disappear in the eyes of Constant who was himself going to disappear" (p. 40). The more fleeting the scene, the more tempting for the artist to fix it in its temporal uniqueness.

Whereas Constant is irritated by the veiled threats of men

like Préault and Salis who want him to take sides with them and make him wish he were in a Tibetan convent, he is in immediate sympathy with a man who is both an artist and a contemplative, Vladimir Liassov, the Russian painter whom he meets by chance at his house in the dunes. Before seeing him, Constant has admired one of Liassov's frescoes in the artist's garden. He feels drawn toward the artist who has painted this group because the painting reveals that its creator possesses the "secret of all religions": "a perfect atheism engendering the purest sense of the divine" (p. 49). The group represents the gods: Buddha having at his right Osiris and Dionysios, at his left Christ and Attis and, on the edge, Orpheus and Mohammed. They look at the same time very human and hieratically stylized. His still lifes inside the house express the same feeling: "The same furor of living perfectly vain and aware of its vanity, deliciously free between despair and joy which was apparent on the face of Buddha or of any of his acolytes" (p. 51). With Liassov, Constant can interpret freely the Christian myths.

He can also talk with Liassov about the three men they both recognize as the masters of modern man: Nietzsche, Dostoievsky, Van Gogh. The example of Liassov helps him to reconcile the cult of action with art and religion. Constant has been a Nietzschean ever since he was able to think. He realizes that his growing preoccupation with metaphysics, that is to say in this case the afterlife is not consistent with his early Nietzscheism. He begins to wonder whether the contradiction is not in Nietzsche himself. His ideal had been that of heroic life. Now the ideal of the saint has more and more appeal for him yet he cannot separate the two aspirations: "Life for him did not exist without religion nor religion without life, one extreme without the other extreme" (p. 53). Perhaps one way to escape the contradiction action-contemplation, life-religion is to adopt successively the two attitudes: devote oneself to contemplation after a full life: "After all Constant was not a degenerate who takes refuge in the afterworld but a man who had lived and who was slowly, progressively making his way toward the detachment and the transcendencies befitting his age" (p. 147). Perhaps also the decadence which doomed his country did not permit the full blossoming of all human potentialities in him: "And little by little he had entered that disincarnation which is proper for an aging man but which corresponded also to the destiny of the little, condemned world from which he came" (p. 157). Constant's consolation, however, is that he has first done all he could in the way of life recommended by Nietzsche: ". . . before undoing himself, he had made himself, before cultivating death, he had cultivated life. However complete was his acceptance of the mystic attitude, he conceived of it only as the flower on the tree of life" (p. 157).

But if one sees in the opposition of life and religion the two extremes of concreteness and abstraction, art offers the most satisfactory reconciliation of the two terms "the extreme in abstraction was possible only in the extreme of concreteness: one could speculate about the non-being only with a brush in hand and carrying on the tip of that brush one of those delightful colors which are the acme of the ephemeral and of the real" (p. 53). Constant envies the painter who "captures the infinite in a line" and shows a true heroism in trying "to make an inlay of the eternal in the daily:

> How he would have liked to be a painter! Yes, it would have been the best way to accept the ephemeral and to consecrate this ephemeral. Through this art while enjoying matter one destroys it better than through any other art because hypocritically one seems to obey it better (p. 97).

His experience has allowed him to understand religion, politics, art but conversely he must make of his life a work of art: by voluntary death he can give it a religious and political meaning: "He knew that everything he had thought was in preparation for a central realization which would truly confirm his life, would introduce into it this sacred and final element without which it seemed to him his life would not have been lived and would not have found its original character of eternity" (p. 46). But if Constant's death is to be the crowning of his life, the masterpiece giving it its full signification, the choice of this exemplary end is determined by his considerations on his country, on what has been his philosophy of life. Underlying the main subjects of Constant's meditation: Nietzsche, the gospels, the French situation, and Constant's own destiny, the unifying element is the notion of decadence. These subjects seem to develop in parallel directions until they converge in his death. Judas, like Constant, must have been a "Nietzschean" in his youth. The political situation of the Jews at the time of Christ is similar to that of the French in 1942. Constant's interpretation of Judas' personality and motives helps him realize the actual and symbolic acts he intends to carry out himself.

His present mysticism makes Constant realize how far he has deviated from the ideal of his youth. He had been a disciple of Nietzsche who passionately condemned the metaphysical thinkers. According to him, human destiny must find its accomplishment upon this earth without any transpositions.

The meditations on Judas develop in a parallel with the main events of the plot in *Les Chiens de paille*. It is clear that Constant identifies with the "traitor." Like the other disciples, Judas had thought for a long time that Jesus was going to become the King of the Jews, an earthly leader who would distribute favors to his followers. Judas was animated by the "will to power."

In his youth, in his ardor, in his pristine faith, which was confidence in himself, in his friends, in his leader, he had wanted conquest, victory, earthly triumph. He had wanted to realize in life itself the maximum power, the extreme limit of life conceived by life. He would have desired the total fulfillment of his ego, of the ego of his friends, of the ego of his country. He had wanted the triumph of the Jews over all other peoples and especially over themselves (p. 142).

Toward the end of Jesus' life, Judas realizes that none of those hopes are going to be realized, that from a purely worldly point of view Christ's adventure is a lamentable failure, that

the traitor

those in power are going to condemn Jesus—the priests, the Pharisees, the Sadducees among the Jews, as well as the occupying Romans. Judas begins to listen to John's mystical interpretation of the Kingdom of Heaven as opposed to an earthly one, a Kingdom of Heaven which is to be attained through suffering and sacrifice. But then someone must be the agent of Jesus' death which will represent the ultimate sacrifice. All the enemies of Jesus are too hypocritical to take the initiative. Judas assumes the responsibility of being instrumental in killing Jesus. The thirty pieces of silver are a mere pretext; Judas has much higher aims.

Judas has some amount of free choice however small it may be; he weighs the pros and cons and he chooses. He seems to choose the thirty pieces against his reputation. Who can stop at this trifle? Much more is at stake. He chooses that the world should move, that the world should breathe. This *deus ex machina* makes the machine move (p. 113).

Constant sees in Judas a Satanic and a Promethean figure. He establishes a parallel between him and the spirit of evil in other religions: Ahriman, almost equal to Ormazd, the other God of Manichaeism: "One can admit that Judas has done more than any man for the salvation of mankind since he not only accepted a temporary torture but an eternal torture" (p. 113). His role can also be interpreted in terms of Hegelian dialectic: "This Judas, was a fellow who understood dialectics and who, knowing the thesis, was bravely assuming the antithesis, in his desire to engender the synthesis" (p. 113).

In terms of Nietzscheism, Judas' decision is an expression of decadence and degeneracy. He gives up the only gift of which we are sure, life, for another gift which he can only imagine: "Judas was giving up making Jesus a King, he resigned himself to making a god of him: wasn't there a terrible degeneracy in that choice?" (p. 143).

Constant sees the reason for this degeneracy in the fact that Judas belongs to a nation weakened, conquered, and occupied. Its geographical position between powerful empires at war with each other makes of it a prey for invading armies:

The Chaldean, Assyrian, Egyptian, Persian, Greek, Roman armies had trampled over this little country and had remained for centuries on this corpse which became more and more cerebral as it was becoming less social, less political, less warlike, more incapable of affirmations supported by muscles and arms (p. 144).

The Jewish intellectuals and priests extol the supremacy of the Jewish genius, which by that time is a purely intellectual and spiritual supremacy. If Constant interprets the Gospels in this manner, it is because he identifies himself more and more with Judas and feels more and more clearly a similarity of situation between the French and the Jewish nations. In spite of his cosmopolitanism, Constant is a Frenchman. By traveling abroad, he has tried to escape the promiscuity of his fellow citizens, but in vain.

At bottom, he knew that, as a Frenchman, he was dead, that, no longer being able to be a Frenchman as one used to be at the time of Louis XIV, he could not longer be a man and that, condemned to degeneracy in life, in the world, he was doomed to the afterworld, to metaphysics, and to dream (p. 145).

Since France has become an empyrean goddess, Constant is justified in his retreat into mysticism. The gods of the different religions have become too particularized for him and he seeks now the sense of the divine through and beyond all religions: "The unspeakable which the Upanishads, the Buddhist Sutras, the Tao, the Zohar try to strip of all categories" (p. 123).

Constant has gone as far as possible from the ideal of Nietzsche, the master of his youth. Meditating on Nietzsche and his teaching, he discovers the inner contradiction of Nietzscheism: Nietzsche is the first conscious decadent of Europe. The cornerstone of his philosophy of despair is not sound: "Nietzsche was putting all his hope in will power, in the miracle of a will which, leaning on a corrupted instinct, becomes the most artificial thing in the world" (p. 145). The

the traitor

same abstraction that he defined, feared, and condemned marred his own work. His work read in its entirety is not only sibylline, it is ambiguous. What did Nietzsche want actually? Certainly not what the naïvely cynical interpretation of his so-called political disciples, fascists and communists, indicated. He wanted something delicate, subtle, pure.

In spite of his psychology of cruelty, of his knowledge of the law of violence, he knew very well that the attempts at returning to primitive health could have only brought into relief the modern inability to reproduce the native *élan* of the youthful (?) Antiquity, of the youthful (?) Renaissance (p. 146).

Actually what Nietzsche wanted was not so different from what Jesus wanted and the realization of this similarity made him insane. Nietzscheans and Christians cannot differ greatly even if they are enemies: they are of the same blood; they are both "modern." Constant should not therefore be surprised that he is derisory as a Nietzschean. Nietzsche is derisory if judged in his own terms: "Through being a Nietzschean, Constant ended by not recognizing the personal greatness of Nietzsche" (p. 148). After a life of action it is normal that Constant should progressively detach himself from the world and want to transcend it.

The meaning of his instinctive sympathy for Cormont becomes clear to him:

Strangely enough, he had pursued the theme of Judas as a parallel with his observations on the Cormont case. This parallel was suddenly becoming a convergence. They are all against Cormont. All those Frenchmen who claim they are still attached only to France. This has a singular similarity with the coalition which existed against Jesus: Pharisees and Sadducees, Jews and Romans (p. 108).

Cormont, like Constant or Judas in their youth, has remained passionately attached to the narrowly national conception of the salvation of his people by a King-Messiah even though his country is occupied and conquered. Bardy, Préault, Salis, representatives of the various Internationals, are leagued against him and want to sacrifice him. Constant, who has been thinking for some time that the time has come for him to die, decides to die an exemplary death and to act at the same time as Judas to this young Jesus: "For a few years, I have been telling myself that I must end my life, but also that I must realize an exemplary act in dying. Now, what is the exemplary act? Sacrifice. The center of human destiny is sacrifice" (p. 211). He carries out his plans as in a dream, with a diabolical cleverness, by taking Cormont and Susini to the vault where the ammunition and weapons are hidden. Before throwing a hand grenade which will destroy them all, he explains to his victims the meaning of the impending sacrifice. The Promethean theme is brought out and emphasized again: a death of one's choice is the supreme revolt against man's fate; it is the only way to affirm man's independence in an absurd world.

All man can do is to recognize that he is created to die; the best for him, is to take death in hand. To make of himself the executor. To be himself the executioner. To take away the sacrificing knife from God's hand (p. 227).

Symbolically, Constant is about to kill in Cormont the image of the young man he himself has been. By killing himself at the same time, he "realizes" both destinies. For a man tormented by a thirst for the absolute only death can transform the transient into the eternal. "... killing Cormont and Constant, I realize both of them, I give them the maximum of fulfillment and reality" (p. 228).

But in this absurd world, a man cannot even choose the hour of his death. In occupied France, a Frenchman can no longer be the master of his fate. By a whim of chance, a British bomb destroys the ammunition cache before Constant can explode his grenade. They are all blown up.

The ending is consistent with the philosophy of the rest of the novel; the sacrifice of the victims is truncated and loses its intended significance; all men are victims of a blind, apparently absurd, fate. The epigraph—borrowed from the Tao Tê Ching—sums up this view: "Heaven and earth are not human or benevolent in the manner of men; they consider all beings as if they were straw dogs [*chiens de paille*] which have been used in sacrifices."

The situation of a Frenchman is particularly hopeless: he cannot even be a man, that is to say try to impose by force his own values on the absurd chaos of the universe. He cannot even choose his own death. Constant had more ties than he realized with his country. As a Frenchman he was incapable of complete detachment because the outside pressure of his countrymen did not allow him to remain neutral, and because at the last moment an inner compulsion forced him to act in favor of his passionate preference. But as a Frenchman the realm of action is barred to him. He can only retire into the afterlife, that is to say, die. Drieu's last novel expresses his ineradicable nationalism: if he can no longer be a Frenchman, he can no longer be a man. Constant, the last fictional counterpart of Drieu, testifies to the "constancy" (and to the consistency) of the author of Drieu's novels, if not of Drieu himself.

eleven

**THE FICTION OF
TESTIMONY**

From *Etat-Civil* to *Les Chiens de paille*, Drieu's fiction offers a surprising variety of treatment in the exploitation of his basic subject—himself. When his novels and short stories are read chronologically they show the growth of an artist becoming more and more sure of himself and of his medium. They also produce a striking impression of unity for they really constitute a whole. As early as 1937, after *Rêveuse bourgeoisie*, Marcel Arland had noted this peculiar trait of Drieu's work: "Drieu La Rochelle undoubtedly is one of those writers in whose work one should not consider such or such successful book but the total sum in its inner relationship and rhythm."[1] The three novels which followed only serve to make the unity more striking.

Many critics have complained of the limited inventiveness of Drieu as a novelist; others simply condemn most of his novels because they fall under the "autobiographical" cate-

[1] Arland, "Chronique des romans," *NRF*, No. 283 (April, 1937), 605.

gory. Without starting a quarrel of language, the label "autobiographical" seems to me a contradiction in terms when applied to fiction. It is particularly inappropriate if used to describe Drieu's fiction as a whole. He himself has pointed out the classical and traditional aspect of this preoccupation with the self as a method of investigation.

Actually one may perhaps distinguish two sorts of egotists: those who take a complacent enjoyment in the petty charm and fascination of being prisoners and of loving in the universe only what they find in their prisons; and those who, inclined to observe everything, keep analyzing their ego only because they count on finding in it the most tanglible and the least deceptive human substance. Confident in their good faith, they believe that in this *tête-a-tête* with themselves, holding both ends, nothing will escape them. This is also an illusion, of course, and yet it is an entirely different viewpoint from that of Narcissus, a viewpoint which has certainly been that of the most objective novelists and the most classic thinkers.[2]

Who has complained—since Pascal—about the fact that Montaigne took himself as the subject of his book? In the same way that there are several Montaignes in the *Essais*, there are so many counterparts of Drieu in his fiction that the reproach of monotony is absurd.

It is true that he has not built a harmonious and impressive cathedral in the manner of Proust. But he belongs to the generation which at twenty saw the cathedrals fall under gunfire. He brought back from the war moral wounds much more difficult to heal than fleshly ones. He felt early that he was sick, that his country was sick and that nothing was more urgent than to expose the seriousness of the damage. Drieu, who is, with Apollinaire, the only poet of World War I, has also been the most reliable witness of the new *mal du siècle*. His testimony is indispensable to any historian of contemporary French sensibility.

The Drieu that emerges from a close analysis of the fiction is infinitely more complex than the human being who was sometimes so wrong and disappointing in actual life. Drieu's intimate thought is not to be found in his journalistic articles

---

[2] *Gilles*, preface, p. v.

nor always in his political essays. He confided in his fiction all the things that he could not express as a public figure. An artist can be much more truthful under the veil of fiction. He must paint man in all his humanity; he must see the two sides of any questions; and if he is a great artist he sees more than two sides. A man like Drieu felt all the freer to show the various aspects of a problem in a novel if he had first taken a firm position in an article.

What broadens—and limits—the scope of his testimony is that his greatest passion was for his country. This passion had all the traits of an illness: it often betrayed anxiety, spite, and even hatred. But the disposition toward passionate attachments, for unbreakable ties, underlies all of Drieu's works as well as his life. The fictional testimony of Drieu's novels often provides an explanation or a prefiguration of what happened in his life. This is true of the real-life climax of Drieu's relationship with his country. Drieu's last novel indicated that in 1943 he had already chosen to be the Judas of France since he could not be its Savior. Constant's tale, which is, in a way, Drieu's testimony on the German occupation of France, shows that the tragedy of the enigmatic villain is not necessarily sordid. For the role of Judas cannot be filled by anyone; one of the requirements is that he must have been first a disciple. Drieu's nationalism had been as passionate as de Gaulle's. His nationalism, however, was not that of a stubborn man of action but that of an indecisive, hypercritical intellectual. If his great sensitivity led him sometimes to penetrating insights into France's illness, it led him also to despair. He remained a Frenchman to the last in spite of his efforts to reach the detachment of Hindu philosophy. He makes Constant, his last hero, say: "If I had to start my life all over again and if I were not more interested in Tibetan philosophy than in anything else, I would become American or Russian, but I would not linger among the petty spasms of a second-rate nation."[3] When, however, the moment comes to make a choice and influence the events by decisive intervention, Constant is more

---

[3] *Les Chiens de paille*, p. 117.

the fiction of testimony

than ever aware of his Westernism: "One then remains always the same, he thought. The animal is just as nervous in my fifty-year old carcass as in my body when I was a callow young man. Actually, I was more sure of myself when I was a soldier. Now would be the time for me to do a yoga exercise, but—to Hell with it! What is Salis going to do to Cormont? Which one do I prefer?"[4] Constant must admit that he prefers Cormont, the idealistic, uncompromising French patriot with his "France, France alone" which sounds so much like de Gaulle.

In this last novel the admirer of Nietzsche also strips the intellectual hero of his legend and instead of mythifying him, in twentieth-century fashion, applies to him a clear-thinking analysis not very different, after all, from a Cartesian analysis and this despite the extensive irony Drieu had previously lavished on those who exploited the slogan: "France, the country of Descartes!"

In spite of the extreme positions he took in real life, in spite of his praise of French authors who showed some *démesure*, Drieu's fiction is a model of moderation, of "measure" both in form and content: "I said strictly what I saw ... but with a movement toward diatribe ... contained within strict limits, because, even though a great lover and defender of what is excessive, *démesuré*, in the history of French literature, I am a Norman, and like all Normans, scrupulously obedient to the disciplines of the Seine and the Loire."[5]

Like Montaigne, Drieu could have said of his work: "This is a book of good faith." His outstanding contribution to French contemporary literature has been the tone of authenticity which is unmistakably his and which pervades all his writings. He has been as sincere, as honest, as he could be within the limits of his own personality. In a generation haunted by the obsession of sincerity, he has outdone Gide. This preoccupation with sincerity and his attachment to the French reality has prevented Drieu from belonging to the "heroic" or "Corneillean" tradition as Malraux describes it,

[4] *Ibid.*, p. 173.
[5] *Gilles*, preface, p. ix.

and in which he places himself with Giono, Bernanos, and Montherlant.

It is difficult to place Drieu among his contemporaries. At first sight he would seem to be one of the literary heirs of Barrès along with Montherlant and Malraux, but a closer examination of his work reveals a subtle but striking kinship with Gide's works. Drieu has said that he puts himself somewhere among Céline and Montherlant and Malraux.[6]

Drieu decided early that the writer of his generation was plunged in a tragic period of total involvement. But the great experience of his life was World War I, not the Chinese revolution or the Spanish Civil War; and France and Europe remained the center of his preoccupations. He noted that, in order to escape French deficiency, Malraux had to choose Chinese and Spanish heroes or make his characters move in a China of war and revolutions.

He found it impossible to adopt the attitude of the detached *moraliste* like Montherlant. He was too involved in the drama of French decadence to look at it from the point of view of Uranus. The imprint of the *état-civil*, is indelible; Drieu is a French bourgeois, Montherlant an aristocrat.

In his short stories and in great parts of his novels, Drieu has written many cruel tales denouncing the horror of life in contemporary civilization. He has detected decadence in all human activity: religion, art, sex, war, government. He has had the vision of humanity rushing to destruction. In its most somber aspects, Drieu's fiction, like Céline's *Voyage au bout de la nuit*, is an exploration of the miseries of the "abandoned" modern man in an urban civilization. He has denounced this misery with the violence of one who takes life seriously and who makes his protest in the manner of a prophet. Like Céline, he depicts painstakingly the deficiency of his contemporaries in order to emphasize the lack of humanity in modern man. He has been restrained, however, by a classical sense of measure, a Gidean tendency to understatement and a naturally impeccable taste which differentiate him markedly

---

[6] *Ibid.*

the fiction of testimony

from the author of *Mort à crèdit*. His bent toward diatribe has very little in common with the truculence of a Céline who in Drieu's words, "spits, only spits, but puts at least the whole Niagara in this salivation."[7]

Drieu has depicted contemporary decadence from the inside. All the satirical part of his fiction could bear the title he intended for a book he never wrote: *Pamphlet contre moi et mes amis*. As I had occasion to point out in examining Drieu's individual novels, his fiction constitutes a damning document against fascism in exposing the secret recesses of what has been labeled in our times a "fascist personality." Conversely, his fiction also provides a lesson in tolerance: it shows that a fascist is not entirely inhuman.[8]

Drieu's style places him very high among his contemporaries. It partakes of the concision and restlessness of Malraux's without ever falling into obscurity. It is as elegant and lucid as Montherlant's but more consistently natural and rarely marred by rhetoric. It is popular, sometimes colloquial, faithful to the spoken language but it avoids the affectations and the vulgarity of Céline's. Drieu has written, along with Aragon, the best French of his generation.

Paradoxically, the development of Drieu's art as a novelist has brought the young rebel so opposed to all traditional literary forms to a typically French form of novel. Toward the end of his career, Drieu was reconciled to the fact; he pointed out himself how his fiction fits into the French tradition.

> The Russians and the English novels have been contrasted with the French novel, to the disadvantage of the latter.... But... the country which produced LaFayette, Marivaux, Voltaire, Stendhal, Constant, Balzac, Sand, Sue, Hugo, Flaubert, Zola, Maupassant, Barbey, les Goncourt, Villiers, Huysmans, Barrès, Proust has nothing to envy any other country.... In any case French techniques are as good as the English or Russian ones. They are, besides, very varied. What diversity between *Adolphe* and *Les Misérables*, Stendhal and Zola! The recent American novel seems to be a homage to French techniques more than to any other.

[7] *Ibid.*
[8] See above, Chapter Eight.

I say all this in self-defense. Because my novels are made according to the most typically French tradition: that of the unilinear narration, egocentric, rather narrowly humanist, to the point of seeming abstract.⁹

Although Drieu's novels have common traits which are rather accurately described in the passage just quoted, they offer a great variety of form. What difference, for instance, between the classic economy of *Le Feu follet* and the baroque profusion of *Gilles!* This variety stems mainly from the fact that Drieu was not imitating any preëxisting form but had to invent new forms to fit a new content. As Percy Lubbock pointed out: "The best form is that which makes the most of its subject—there is no other definition of the meaning of form in fiction."

Drieu's central "subject" is primarily metaphysical: it is the plight of the modern man for whom "God is dead," and his efforts to find purely humanistic values in a universe which is not human, in a society cowardly and insincerely clinging to an obsolete order. But, for Drieu, to repeat with Nietzsche that God is dead is not the calm statement of fact of a materialist. He has a Romantic nostalgia for the time when a mystique was possible and his analysis of decadence consists to a large degree in showing the vacuum left by the disappearance of a mystique. It is significant that Drieu saw in Baudelaire one of the first and certainly one of the most conscious exponents of the idea of decadence in French letters. His summing up of Baudelaire's message applies to his own work: "No mystique is possible in our time, but no man is possible without a mystique. Therefore there cannot be a man in our time, therefore our time goes to nothingness."[10]

In the same manner Drieu has summed up Nietzsche's philosophy in terms that apply to his own views while foreshadowing Camus' philosophy of the absurd and Sartre's existentialism: "Man is an accident in a world of accidents. The

⁹ *Gilles*, preface, p. xi.
[10] *Notes pour comprendre le siècle*, p. 112.

the fiction of testimony

world has no general meaning. The only meaning it has is the one we give it one moment, for the development of our passion, of our action."[11]

In such a perspective, politics assume a very important role in man's preoccupations since political anxiety replaces in concrete manner the problem of salvation and destiny. It is little wonder that political novels are so important in contemporary literature.

The novelty of his subjects made of Drieu more an innovator than a follower. We have seen in *Blèche* a case of conflict between form and content.[12] And yet this novel which is not completely successful marks a transition toward the renewal of the genre in contemporary French literature because the conventional novel of psychological analysis is assuming metaphysical dimensions. In this respect both *Blèche* (1928) and *Le Feu follet* (1931), which illustrate Drieu's skill at portraying emptiness and the negativism resulting from this emptiness, are significant forerunners of *La Nausée* (1938). Doubtless, a recent novel like *Les Mandarins* (1954) owes much to the form and the technique originated by Drieu in *Gilles*. At an opposite extreme, an allegorical symbolistic fable like *La Peste* (1947) offers great similarities of form to *L'Homme à cheval* (1943).

Drieu can be considered a forerunner in the introduction of politics in the contemporary French novel. His philosophy of history lends itself well to fiction because he sees history in terms of the most immediate and concrete reality which he transfigures and transposes. By considering human events from the point of view of history, he justifies the importance of his testimony. In that respect what Drieu says of a "noble" writer like Alfred de Vigny applies to himself who, without belonging to the nobility, had a highly developed sense of aristocratic values: "Necessarily the noble writer has the feeling that he derives personally from history, from its rhythm of

---

[11] *Socialisme fasciste*, p. 70. (See above, Chapters Three and Nine.)
[12] See above, Chapter Six.

growth and recession, of grandeur and decadence both his strength and his weakness; in other words, his main reason to testify."[13]

To see in Drieu the novelist only an author of transition, however, would be unfair. The elegant and cruelly ironic *Drôle de voyage* is a masterpiece of its kind and remains one of the best novels of the *entre-deux-guerres*. *Rêveuse bourgeoisie* alone would serve to establish a novelist's reputation. *La Comédie de Charleroi* can stand comparison with the best that has been written anywhere about war. *Les Chiens de paille* may well be a classic of the death agony of Europe.

Even though he always affected to despise the little world of men of letters, Drieu holds an important place in that world. Because of the intrinsic originality of the form of novel he developed, the novel of testimony, because of the opinions in the apparently autobiographical *Gilles*, critics have consistently been influenced by their opinion of the man in their literary judgment of the artist. They have forgotten the primary principle of all literary criticism: the work of art is turned toward us, not toward the author.

Drieu himself is partly responsible for the confusion. He has too often exaggerated his own failure. He has lamented his failure to fulfill the flamboyant dreams of his youth: he has not been a perfect ascetic nor lived the retired life of a contemplative monk; he has not been a man of great political power, nor a physical athlete of astounding performances, nor an unforgettable lover; he has been still less the great poet of his generation. But he has been an important writer of fiction—influential in his time, widely read and widely discussed. His claims as an artist remain. How great are they? One can do no better than to adopt his own conclusion after he had weighed his chances for passing to posterity. Will he survive as an artist? "Why not?" he decided with characteristic self-mockery.

One may decide that it is not even important whether Drieu

[13] *Le Français d'Europe*, p. 128.

the fiction of testimony

passes to posterity or not. He has experimented in form and content sufficiently to provide lessons to the generation that succeeded him—mostly unacknowledged—and he has left a body of work that testifies provocatively about certain aspects of life in our century in our Western World.

bibliography

abbreviations

LRH La Revue Hebdomadaire
LTM Les Temps Modernes
LTR La Table Ronde
NNRF Nouvelle Nouvelle Revue Française
NRF Nouvelle Revue Française
RE   Revue Européene
RN   La Révolution Nationale
RP   Revue de Paris

bibliography

note.—This listing is not complete. I have not been able to obtain copies of some of the periodicals in which Drieu's articles appeared, including the seven issues of *Les Derniers jours* published by Drieu during 1927 in collaboration with Emmanuel Berl. Place of publication is Paris, except as noted.

WORKS BY DRIEU: *chronologically arranged.*

1917
Interrogation. Gallimard, 1917.

1919
"Poèmes," *NRF*, No. 69 (June, 1919), 221–225.
"Le Dernier capitalistes," *NRF*, No. 73 (October, 1919), 715–725.
"Poème," *Grande Revue*, C (1919), 460–463.
"Secteur américain," *Ecrits Nouveaux*, III (1919), 18–19, 68–69.

1920
Fond de cantine. Gallimard, 1920.
"Nouvelle patrie," *NRF*, No. 79 (April, 1920), 531–536.
"Paul Adam," *NRF*, No. 79 (April, 1920), 577–579.
"Le Retour du soldat," *NRF*, No. 83 (August, 1920), 238–246.

1921
Etat-Civil. Gallimard, 1921.
" 'Anicet, ou le panorama,' par Louis Aragon," *NRF*, No. 94 (July, 1921), 97–99.

1922
Mesure de la France. Grasset, 1922.
"Abus de confiance," *Ecrits Nouveaux*, V (1922), 3–10.

1923
"L'Exemple," *NRF*, No. 112 (January, 1923), 231–234.
" 'Le Songe,' par Henry de Montherlant," *NRF*, No. 113 (February, 1923), 455–456.

bibliography

" 'Plutarque a menti,' par Jean de Pierrefeu," *NRF*, No. 119 (August, 1923), 220–223.
" 'Le Réveil des morts,' par Roland Dorgelès," *NRF*, No. 120 (September, 1923), 358–361.
" 'Vauban,' par Daniel Halévy," *NRF*, No. 121 (October, 1923), 484–486.
" 'La Vénus internationale,' par Pierre Mac Orlan," *NRF*, No. 121 (October, 1923), 496–498.
"Chronique des spectacles," *NRF*, No. 122 (November, 1923), 588–596.
"Chronique des spectacles," *NRF*, No. 123 (December, 1923), 729–735.

1924

Plainte contre inconnu. Gallimard, 1924.
"Chronique des spectacles," *NRF*, No. 124 (January, 1924), 96–99.
"Chronique des spectacles," *NRF*, No. 125 (February, 1924), 209–213.
" 'Choléra,' par Jean Delteil," *NRF*, No. 125 (February, 1924), 227–228.
"Chronique des spectacles," *NRF*, No. 126 (March, 1924), 342–346.

1925

L'Homme couvert de femmes. Gallimard, 1925.
"Expériences," *NRF*, No. 139 (April, 1925), 649–651.
" 'Le Puits de Jacob,' par Pierre Benoit," *NRF*, No. 141 (June, 1925), 1069–1070.
"La Véritable erreur des surrealistes," *NRF*, No. 143 (August, 1925), 166–171.
" 'Nouvel empire,' par Fritz von Unruh," *NRF*, No. 146 (November, 1925), 627–630.
" 'Meditation sur un amour défunt,' par Emmanuel Berl," *NRF*, No. 147 (December, 1925), 750–751.

1926

"Jugement de l'auteur sur lui-même"; "Une Ville d'Europe," in *Anthologie de la nouvelle prose française.* Le Sagittaire, 1926.
"La Fin de parti radical et de l'esprit petit-bourgeois," *LRH*, VII (1926), 5–10.
"Discours aux Français sur les étrangers," *LRH*, X (1926), 141–161.
"L'Automate," *RE*, XXXV (1926), 11–15.

1927

La Suite dans les idées. Au sans Pareil, 1927.
Le Jeune Européen. Gallimard, 1927.

"'Aux Fontaines du désir,' par Henry de Montherlant," *NRF*, No. 170 (November, 1927), 676–681.

1928
Blèche. Gallimard, 1928.
"Boucles," *Revue de France*, IV (1928), 577–613; V (1928), 37–76, 193–238, 433–461. ["Boucles" is the first title of the novel published in book form under the title *Blèche*.]
Genève ou Moscou. Gallimard, 1928.
"'Russie 1927,' par Alfred Fabre-Luce," *NRF*, No. 173 (February, 1928), 252–255.
"Lindbergh et ma vie," *NRF*, No. 176 (May, 1928), 608–613.
"L'Idée de décadence," *RE* (1928), 557–576.
"La Crise du capitalisme et le communisme de demain," *RE* (1928), 785–794.
"Une Femme et une déesse," *RE* (1928), 1026–1032.
"Les Bords de la Seine," *RE* (1928), 1237–1244.

1929
"Le Capitalisme, le communisme et l'esprit," in *Anthologie des essayistes français contemporains*. 1929. Pp. 356–364.
"A Propos d' 'A l'Ouest rien de nouveau,'" *NRF*, No. 194 (November, 1929), 725–730.

1930
Une Femme à sa fenêtre. Gallimard, 1930.
"A Propos d'un roman anglais," *NRF*, No. 206 (November, 1930), 721–731.
"L'Affaire Hanau," *Nouvelles Littéraires* (November 8, 1930).
"Malraux, l'Homme nouveau,'" *NRF*, No. 207 (December, 1930), 879–885.
"Le Mouvement dramatique," *RP*, I (1930), 926–936.

1931
L'Europe contre les patries. Gallimard, 1931.
Le Feu follet. Gallimard, 1931.
Preface to Marja Czapska, *La Vie de Mickiewicz*. Plon, 1931.
L'Eau fraîche. Les Cahiers de "Bravo," Supp. August, 1931.
"'Le Bourgeois et l'amour,' par Emmanuel Berl," *NRF*, No. 219 (December, 1931), 944–947.

1933
Drôle de voyage. Gallimard, 1933.
"'Chacun pour soi,' par Constance Colline," *NRF*, No. 232 (January, 1933), 186–187.
"Paris, ville d'exilés," *Nouvelles Littéraires* (January 28, 1933).

bibliography

1934

Journal d'un homme trompé. Gallimard, 1934.
La Comédie de Charleroi. Gallimard, 1934.
Socialisme fasciste. Gallimard, 1934.
Preface to D. H. Lawrence, *L'Homme qui était mort,* translated by Jacqueline Dalsace and Drieu La Rochelle. Gallimard, 1934.
" 'Le Messager' de Bernstein," *NRF,* No. 244 (January, 1934), 148.
" 'Petrus,' de Marcel Achard," *NRF,* No. 244 (January, 1934), 149.
"Une Semaine à Berlin," *NRF,* No. 245 (February, 1934), 393–394.
"Air de février 34," *NRF,* No. 246 (March, 1934), 568–569.
"Mesure de l'Allemagne," *NRF,* No. 246 (March, 1934), 450–461.
"Guerre et revolution," *NRF,* No. 248 (May, 1934), 887–888.
"Le Poème en prose," *Les Nouvelles Littéraires,* May 5, 1934.
" 'Essai sur la misère humaine,' par Brice Parain," *NRF,* No. 249 (June, 1934), 1019–1021.
" 'Demain la France,' par Robert Francis, Thierry-Maulnier, Jean-Pierre Maxence," *NRF,* No. 251 (August, 1934), 287–291.
"Le Monde pharisien," *NRF,* No. 251 (August, 1934), 309–310.
"Le Rajeunissement de la France," *Grande Revue,* CXLIV (1934), 14–17.

1935

"L'Homme mûr et le jeune homme," *NRF,* No. 257 (February, 1935), 190–210.
"Anniversaire," *NRF,* No. 257 (February, 1935), 319–320.
"L'Agent double," *NRF,* No. 262 (July, 1935), 26–37.
"Saint-Denis," *NRF,* No. 265 (October, 1935), 627–628.

1936

Beloukia. Gallimard, 1936.
Doriot, ou la vie d'un ouvrier français. Saint-Denis, Les Editions populaires françaises, 1936.
"La Fin des doctrines," *Nouvelles Littéraires* (February 22, 1936).
"Ce qui meurt en Espagne," *NRF,* No. 278 (November, 1936), 920–922.

1937

Rêveuse bourgeoisie. Gallimard, 1937.
Avec Doriot. Gallimard, 1937.
"L'Intelligence et l'espace," *NRF,* No. 282 (March, 1937), 471–472.

1938

"A Propos d'un certain A. V.," *NRF,* No. 292 (January, 1938), 117–123.
"La Duchesse de Friedland," *NRF,* No. 298 (July, 1938), 55–68.

1939
Gilles. Gallimard, first edition, with censored parts deleted, 1939. Definitive edition, with preface by the author, 1942.
"L'Actualité du XX° siècle," *NRF*, No. 314 (November, 1939), 782–789.
"A Propos des cent cinquante ans de la révolution française," *RP*, III (1939), 577–589.

1940
"Maurras ou Genève," *NRF*, No. 317 (February, 1940), 243–246.

1941
Ecrits de jeunesse. Gallimard, 1941.
Ne plus attendre. Grasset, 1941.
Notes pour comprendre le siècle. Gallimard, 1941.

1943
Chronique politique. Gallimard, 1943.
L'Homme à cheval. Gallimard, 1943.
"Le Siècle des maréchaux," *RN* (December 18, 1943).

1944
Charlotte Corday, pièce en trois actes; Le Chef, pièce en quatre actes. Gallimard, 1944.
Le Français d'Europe. Editions Balzac, 1944.
"Journal d'un délicat," *Chronique de Paris* (January, 1944), 44–60; (February, 1944), 36–52; (March, 1944), 39–56.
"L'Europe aux extra-Européens," *RN* (January 15, 1944).
"Confidences," *RN* (January 29, 1944).
"L'Ecrasement des Latins," *RN* (February, 12, 1944).
"Ephémérides," *RN* (February 19, 1944).
"L'URSS et les Anglo-Américains," *RN* (March, 1944).
"Perspectives socialistes," *RN* (March 11, 1944).
"En marge," *RN*, (March 25, 1944).
"En Afrique," *RN* (April 8, 1944).
"Pauvre Europe," *RN* (April 19, 1944).
"La Trahison en Afrique du Nord vue par un Américain, I," *RN* (April 22, 1944).
"La Trahison en Afrique du Nord vue par un Américain, II," *RN* (April 29, 1944).
"Thèses," *RN* (May 6, 1944).
"La Nuit du 4 Août," *RN* (May 21, 1944).
"Socialisme a l'épreuve," *RN* (June 3, 1944).
"Testament de Pierre Le Grand," *RN* (June 10, 1944).
"Propos parmi les ruines," *RN* (June 25, 1944).

bibliography

"En marge II," *RN* (July 15, 1944).
"Lettre à un ami Gaulliste," *RN* (August 12, 1944).
Les Chiens de paille. Printed in 1944. Unpublished.

1950

"Bilan fasciste," *84* (December, 1950). [This and the following works are posthumous publications.]

1951

"Cherbourg, port Américain," *Rivarol* (March 22, 1951).
Récit secret. Chez A. M. G., 1951. Limited to 500 copies.

1953

"Récit secret," *NNRF*, No. 9 (December, 1953), 391–419.

1956

"Signification sociale," *La Parisienne* (May, 1956), 33–37 [an article on Mauriac previously published in *La Revue du Siècle* (July–August, 1933)].

WORKS ABOUT DRIEU: *alphabetically arranged*

Alberès, R.-M. *Portrait de notre héros*. Le Portulan, 1945.
Andreu, Pierre. *Drieu, témoin et visionnaire*. Grasset, 1952.
———. "Socialisme fasciste avec Drieu," *La Parisienne*, No. 32 (October, 1955), 999–1002.
Anon. "Drieu La Rochelle ou la haine de soi," *Les Lettres Françaises*, No. 6 (April, 1943).
Anon. "Entretien avec Jean Bernier," *La Parisienne*, No. 32 (October, 1955), 1003–1007.
Anon. "Entretien avec Lucien Combelle," *La Parisienne*, No. 32 (October, 1955), 1010–1014.
Anon. "Le Suicide de Drieu La Rochelle," *La Parisienne*, No. 32 (October, 1955), 1047–1051.
Arland, Marcel. " 'Etat-Civil,' par Pierre Drieu La Rochelle," *NRF*, No. 103 (April, 1922), 491–495.
———. "Sur un nouveau mal du siècle," *NRF*, No. 125 (February, 1924), 156.
———. " 'Drôle de voyage,' par Drieu La Rochelle," *NRF*, No. 237 (June, 1933).
———. *Essais et nouveaux essais critiques*. Gallimard, 1952.
———. "Drieu La Rochelle I: Les Interrogations," *NNRF*, No. 12 (December, 1953), 1072–1080.
———. "Drieu La Rochelle II: Les Réponses," *NNRF*, No. 13 (January, 1954), 105–114.

———. "A Literary Letter from Paris," *New York Times Book Review*, January 1, 1956, p. 18.

———. "Drieu la Rochelle III: L'Epreuve," *NNRF*, No. 14 (February, 1956), 279–288.

Beaunier, André, *Au Service de la déesse*. Flammarion, 1923. Pp. 229–245.

Benda, Julien. "'Socialisme fasciste,' par Drieu La Rochelle," *NRF*, No. 256 (January, 1936), 295.

Berl, Emmanuel. *Mort de la pensée bourgeoise*. Grasset, 1929.

———. *La Culture en péril*. La Table Ronde, 1948.

———. *Sylvia*. Gallimard, 1952.

———. *Présence des morts*. Gallimard, 1956.

Billy, André. *La Littérature française contemporaine*. A. Colin, 1927. P. 196.

Bouvier, Emile. *Initiation à la littérature d'aujourd'hui*. Renaissance du Livre, 1928.

Brasillach, Robert. *Les Quatre jeudis, images d'avant-guerre*. Les Sept Couleurs, 1951.

Brissaud, André. "Une Vie ratée mais une mort réussie," *LTR*, No. 58 (October, 1952), 141–145.

Carré, Jean-Marie. *Les Ecrivains français et le mirage allemand*. Boivin, 1947.

de Catalogne, Gérard. "Un Témoin de la génération sacrifiée: Drieu La Rochelle," *Revue du Siècle* (March 1, 1926).

———. *Une Génération*. Edition Le Rouge et le Noir, 1930.

———. *Les Compagnons du spirituel*. Montreal, Editions de l'Arbre, 1945.

Chardonne, Jacques. "Un Silencieux: Drieu La Rochelle," *La Parisienne*, No. 32 (October, 1955), 1008–1009.

Chaumeix, André. "Les Nouveaux enfants du siècle: Drieu La Rochelle, 'L'Homme couvert de femmes,'" *Revue des Deux Mondes* (December, 1926).

Chauveau, Paul. *Caractères*. Cahiers Libres, 1933.

Clouard, Henri. *La Poésie française moderne*. Gauthier-Villars, 1924.

———. *Histoire de la littérature française*. Albin Michel, 1949. Pp. 309–311.

Corrigan, Beatrice. "Drieu La Rochelle: Study of a Collaborator," *University of Toronto Quarterly*, XIV (January, 1945), 199–205.

Cremieux, Benjamin. "'Fond de cantine,'" *NRF*, No. 76 (December, 1920), 948–951.

———. *XX° siècle* (Première série). Gallimard, 1924. Pp. 222–232.

bibliography

———. " 'La Suite dans les idées:' 'Le Jeune Européen'; 'Les Derniers jours,' par P. Drieu La Rochelle," *NRF*, No. 170 (November, 1927), 671–676.

———. *Inquiétude et reconstruction*. Corrêa, 1931.

Dominique, Pierre. *Quatre hommes entre vingt: Montherlant, Morand, Cocteau, Drieu*. Le Divan, 1924.

Ehrhard, Jean E. *Le Roman français depuis Marcel Proust*. Nouvelle Revue Critique, 1932.

Etiemble, R. "Drieu La Rochelle: Ecrits de jeunesse (1917–1927)," *Lettres françaises* [Buenos Aires], No. 3 (January, 1942), 79–80.

———. "Politique de Drieu ou la suite dans une idée," *LTM*, No. 84–85 (October–November, 1952), 802–810.

Fabre-Luce, Alfred. *Journal de la France: Mars, 1929–Juillet, 1940*. Imprimerie S. E. R., 1940.

———. *Journal: 1951*. Amiot-Dumont, 1951.

Fernandez, Ramon. " 'Plainte contre inconnu,' par Drieu La Rochelle," *NRF*, No. 136 (January, 1925), 104–106.

———. " 'L'Homme couvert de femmes,' par Drieu La Rochelle," *NRF*, No. 150 (March, 1926), 356–357.

———. " 'Blèche,' par Drieu La Rochelle," *NRF*, No. 183 (December, 1928), 867–869.

———. " 'Une Femme à sa fenêtre,' par Drieu La Rochelle," *NRF*, No. 200 (May, 1930), 767–769.

———. "Est-ce une trahison?" *NRF*, No. 284 (May, 1937).

Giron, Roger, and Robert de Saint-Jean. *La Jeunesse littéraire devant la politique*. Les Cahiers Libres, 1928.

Jaloux, Edmond. " 'La Valise vide,' par Drieu La Rochelle," *Les Nouvelles Littéraires* (December 5, 1924).

Lagarde, Pierre. *La Faillite du cœur*. L'Œuvre Latine, 1931.

Lalou, René. *Histoire de la littérature française contemporaine*. Crès, 1924. Pp. 460–462.

Lefêbvre, Louis. *Rectifications*. A. Messein, 1932.

Lefêvre, Frédéric. "Une Heure avec Drieu La Rochelle, poète, essayiste, romancier," *Les Nouvelles Littéraires*, January 2, 1926.

———. *Une Heure avec ...* (4° série). Gallimard, 1927. Pp. 69–95.

———. "Une Heure avec Drieu La Rochelle," *Les Nouvelles Littéraires*, March, 15, 1930.

Martin du Gard, Maurice. *Feux tournants*. Bloch, 1925.

———. "Interrogation," *La Parisienne*, No. 32 (October, 1955), 1015–1018.

———. *Les Memorables* (1918–1923). Flammarion, 1957.
Massis, Henri. *Maurras et notre temps*. La Palatine, 1951.
Maulnier, Thierry. "La Vie des idées, M. Drieu La Rochelle ou l'Exilé," *Revue Universelle* (February 16, 1933), 293–297.
Mauriac, François. "Drieu," *LTR*, No. 18 (June, 1949), 912–917.
Maynial, Edouard. *Précis de littérature française moderne et contemporaine*. Delagrave, 1926.
M. E. [Mounier, Emmanuel]. "Drieu La Rochelle: 'Gilles,' " *Esprit*, No. 91 (April, 1940), 87–90.
Morand, Paul. "Ascension de Drieu," *La Parisienne*, No. 32 (October, 1955), 1019–1022.
Mourre, Michel. "Devant l'Allemagne," *La Parisienne*, No. 32 (October, 1955), 1026–1034.
Nourrissier, François. "Une Mort utile," *La Parisienne*, No. 32 (October, 1955), 1035–1037.
Ocampo, Victoria. "El Caso de Drieu La Rochelle," *Sur*, Buenos Aires, No. 180 (October, 1949), 7–27.
———. *Lawrence de Arabia y otros ensayos*. Madrid, Aguilar, 1951.
Paulhan, Jean. *De la paille et du grain*. Gallimard, 1948.
Picon, Gaëtan. *Panorama de la nouvelle littérature française*. Gallimard, 1949.
Poulet, Robert. *Partis pris*. Brussels and Paris, Les Ecrits, 1943.
Ribadeau-Dumas, F. *Carrefour de visages*. Nouvelle Société d'Edition, 1929.
Rousseaux, André. *Ames et visages du XX*e* siècle*. Grasset, 1932. Pp. 269–276.
———. "La Plume et le pinceau," *Figaro*, February 24, 1932.
———. " 'La Valise vide' de Drieu La Rochelle," *Figaro*, March 13, 1932.
———. "Le Désespoir de Drieu La Rochelle," *Le Figaro Littéraire*, May 24, 1952.
Sartre, Jean-Paul. Preface to *Portrait de l'aventurier*, by Roger Stéphane. Editions du Saggitaire, 1950.
———. *Situations II*. Gallimard, 1948. P. 227.
Simon, Pierre-Henri. *Procès du héros: Montherlant, Drieu La Rochelle, Jean Prévost*. Edition du Seuil, 1950.
de Spens, Willy. "Drieu romancier," *La Parisienne*, No. 32 (October, 1955), 1038–1046.
Stansbury, Milton H. *French Novelists of Today*. Philadelphia, University of Pennsylvania Press, 1935. Pp. 165–187.

bibliography

Talvart, Hector, and Joseph Place. *Bibliographie des auteurs modernes de langue française. 1801–1927.* Chronique des lettres françaises, Aux Horizons de la France, 1933. Vol. IV, 327–331.
Thibaudet, Albert. "La Jeune Europe," *Les Nouvelles Littéraires,* August 15, 1931.
Thiébaut, Marcel. "Drieu La Rochelle," *RP,* No. 59 (August, 1952), 148–158.
Vandal, Jean. " 'Beloukia,' par Drieu La Rochelle," *NRF,* No. 276 (September, 1936), 543–544.
Vanderem, Fernand. *Le Miroir des lettres (1ère série).* Flammarion, 1919.
———. *Le Miroir des lettres (6e série).* Flammarion, 1925.
———. "L'Homosexualité en littérature, enquête: Réponse de Drieu La Rochelle," *Marges* (April, 1926), 242–244.
Varillon, Pierre, and Henry Rambaud. *Enquête sur les maîtres de la jeune littérature.* Bloud et Gay, 1923.

index

Action, cult of, 5, 9, 53, 59, 161, 215–228, 239, 254
　and literature, 4–5, 12–15, 207
　man of, 5, 76, 154, 158, 160–161, 215–228
　See also Nietzsche; Themes in Drieu's fiction
Adam, Paul, 6
Alain, 49
Andreu, Pierre, 32 n., 46, 51, 211
　Drieu, témoin et visionnaire, 32 n.
d'Annunzio, Gabriele, 6
Anouilh, Jean, 79
Antisemitism, 117, 196–198, 211
Apollinaire, Guillaume, 248
Aragon, Louis, 9, 10, 24–25, 44, 50, 132, 165, 206, 252
Arland, Marcel, 95, 101–102, 114, 132, 164, 207–208, 247
Art, theories of, 18, 20, 21, 30, 117, 131, 227, 230, 240. See also Literature; Themes in Drieu's fiction
Audiberti, 49, 50, 51
Authenticity. See Literature; Themes in Drieu's fiction
Autobiography, in Drieu's works, 14, 17, 28, 32–42, 52, 159–160, 232–233, 247–249, 255
　in fiction, 61, 248

Balzac, Honoré de, 105, 168, 170–174, 191, 223, 252

Barbey d'Aurevilly, Jules, 105, 252
Barrès, Maurice, 6, 8, 9, 11, 48, 99, 105–106, 125, 135, 150–151, 168, 174, 252
Baudelaire, Charles, 82, 83, 89, 94, 174, 218, 253
Beauvoir, Simone de, 254
Beethoven, Ludwig von, 227-228
Beloukia, analysis of, 154–161
　form, 135, 154
　publication of, 133, 154
　themes, 154
　　death (solitude), 158–161
　　sincerity, 160–161
　　the traitor, 156–160
　　women and love, 154–158
Benda, Julien, 7
Bergery, Gaston, 148, 206
Bergson, Henri, 7
Berl, Emmanuel, 45, 148
Bernanos, Georges, 48, 57, 211, 251
Bernier, Jean, 51, 148
Bernstein, Henry, 181
"Bilan," 48–49
Biographical data, 31–32, 43–54
Blèche, analysis of, 135–140
　form, 135, 139–140, 254
　themes, 17, 110, 132
　　authenticity (sincerity), 135–140
　　religion, 136–138
　　suicide (death), 138–139
Bonald, Louis de, 105
Bourget, Paul, 8, 105, 140

index

Boussenard, 37
Breton, André, 9, 44, 109, 207

Camus, Albert, 13, 25, 253, 254
Céline, Louis-Ferdinand (Destouches), 48, 50, 211, 251, 252
Chardonne, Jacques, 50
Charleroi, experience of, 54, 74, 112, 215
Chateaubriand, François-René de, 11
Châteaubriant, Alphonse de, 49
Le Chef, 55–56, 131
  analysis of, 77–80
  themes, 77
Les Chiens de paille, analysis of, 231–246
  Constant Trubert, 54, 232
  form, 135, 229, 232
  publication of, 32 n.
  style, 229, 231
  themes, 29–30, 48, 107–108, 247
    decadence, 234, 237, 241–242, 254
    politics, 229, 232
    religious inquietude, 238–246
    sacrifice, 245–246
    suicide (death), 53, 240, 245–246
Claudel, Paul, 62
Collaborationism, 26–30, 32, 47–54
La Comédie de Charleroi, analysis of, 61–73
  form, 61–62, 163, 254
  genesis of, 55–56
  point of view, 54–65
  characters, 60–73
  style, 62, 64–65, 114, 210
  themes, decadence, 63–72
    the leader (hero), 63–64, 69
    suicide (death), 72, 226
Communism, and Europe, 16
  Drieu's attitude, 10, 22, 45, 110
  in Drieu's fiction, 110, 130, 185
  See also Politics
Conrad, Joseph, 11
Constant, Benjamin, 11, 12, 29, 252
Contemporaries, relation to, 9–13, 24–25, 178–179, 250–255
  See also Literary influences
Crémieux, Benjamin, 60–61
Crevel, René, 84

Dada, 9, 84, 179, 207
Daudet, Leon, 50
Death, cult of, 7, 53, 59, 95, 139, 226. *See also* Themes in Drieu's fiction: death, solitude, suicide
Decadence, idea of, 1, 82, 103–104, 253
  key words, 98
  Nietzsche's influence, 107–112
  personal, 28, 33, 85, 170–175, 211, 248
  sexual, 17, 87–88, 97–100, 111
  See also France; Nietzschean philosophy; Religion; Themes in Drieu's fiction
Delteil, Joseph, 9
Les Derniers Jours, 15, 17, 45
Descartes, René, 206, 250
Diderot, Denis, 12, 14–15
Don Juanism, 99–100, 133, 134, 143–145, 179, 200. *See also* Decadence; Themes in Drieu's fiction
Doriot, Jacques, 25, 46, 75, 154, 163, 201, 219
Doriot, ou la vie d'un ouvrier français, 162
Dos Passos, John, 81
Dostoievsky, Feodor, 8, 111, 239
Drôle de voyage, analysis of, 114–132
  dedication, 45
  form, 115, 163, 255
  style, 113–114, 132, 210
  themes, 100, 111–112, 113
    decadence, 114, 115, 116–120, 129–131
    don Juanism, 133
    jeune fille, 97
    marriage, 120
    money and marriage, 120, 123
    sincerity, 124–128
    solitude, 123
    voyage, 124–125
    women and love, 114–132
Duhamel, Georges, 48

Les Ecrits Nouveaux, 4
Eluard, Paul, 9, 44
Emancipation Nationale, 26, 46, 162, 219

Engagement, cult of, 14, 24, 28, 189–190
  political, 1, 27–28, 76
Esprit, 47
Etat-Civil, analysis of, 33–42
  characters, le petit Cogle, 34–40, 97, 191
  publication of, 4
  themes, 17, 71, 96–97, 107, 165, 247
    death, 34, 53
    decadence, 33–42
    family relations, 33, 35, 36, 39–40, 164
    nationalism, 40–42
L'Europe contre les patries, 16
European unity, 16, 48–49, 194
Existentialism, 140, 154, 253

Fabre-Luce, Alfred, 50, 188 n.
Fascism, in Drieu's works, 22, 63, 73, 130, 188–190, 193–202, 214, 252
  Drieu's attitude, 22–25, 42, 45–46, 48–49, 214, 223
  and Europe, 22–23, 194
  See also Politics; Themes in Drieu's fiction
Faure-Biguet, J. N., 163
February riots, 77, 154, 188, 206
Une Femme à sa fenêtre, analysis of, 141–154
  dedication, 148
  style, 141–142
  themes, 17, 110, 132–133
    decadence, 151–154, 235
    communism, 143–154
    sincerity, 154, 160
    women and love, 141–161
Fernandez, Ramon, 49, 104, 163, 210
Le Feu follet, analysis of, 89–95
  inspiration of, 89
  style, 253
  themes, 17, 82, 89, 112, 254
    death, 89
Fieschi, 50
Figaro, 47
Fitzgerald, L. Scott, 81–82
Flaubert, 11, 88, 170, 180, 208–209
Floriot, Zenaïde, 37
Follain, 50
Fond de cantine, 4, 56, 58, 84

Form, in Drieu's fiction, 61–62, 135, 139–140, 163–167, 202, 212, 213–214, 229, 232, 250, 252–253, 256
  in literature, 13, 139–140, 165, 166–167, 212
Le Français d'Europe, 32 n., 221
France, decadence of, 15–16, 39, 67, 69, 185, 206, 208, 234–246
  defeat of 26, 39, 47–52
  love of, 28–29, 58, 236–248, 249
  occupation of, 39, 48–52, 219, 230–246, 249
  See also Nationalism; Themes in Drieu's fiction
France, Anatole, 8, 9, 20, 48
Freud, Sigmund, 171
Frohock, W. M., 5

Genève ou Moscou, 103, 108
Gide, André, 11, 20, 105, 106, 124–128, 131–132, 134, 135, 154, 174, 175, 176, 250, 251
Gille(s) characters, 85, 96–103, 113, 119, 164, 179, 190–191
Gilles, analysis of, 179–190, 208–212
  characters, 202–207
  form, 163, 164, 202, 212, 254
  preface, 89
  publication of, 178–179
  style, 209–210, 253, 255
  themes, 29, 190–212
    authenticity (sincerity), 181
    death, 181–190, 199
    decadence, 183–190, 196–202, 206, 208
    marriage and money, 191–192
    politics, 185, 187–190, 193–202
    war, 180, 181, 188–190, 192
    women, 180, 190, 191–193, 198–202
Giono, Jean, 48, 251
Giraudoux, Jean, 48
Goethe, 228
les Goncourt, 252
La Grande Revue, 4
Grenier, Jean, 49–50
Guillevic, 50

Halévy, Daniel, 26, 44
Hegelianism, 50, 185
Hemingway, Ernest, 8

index

Hero, in literature, 68, 227–228. See also Leader; Themes in Drieu's fiction
Herriot, Edouard, 46
L'Homme à cheval, analysis of, 214–228
  characters, 214–217
  form, 135, 213–214, 254
  publication of, 213
  style, 222, 229
  themes, 29
    action versus contemplation, 215–217
    the leader (hero), 227–228
    politics, 214, 218, 223
    sacrifice, 225–228
    women, 217–219
L'Homme couvert de femmes, analysis of, 95–103
  dedication, 44
  themes, 17, 82, 85
    decadence, 97–100, 111, 113
    God, 101
    women, 96, 100, 154
Homosexuality. See Decadence; Sex; Themes in Drieu's fiction
Hugo, Victor, 252
Huysmans, Joris Karl, 252
Huxley, Aldous, 97, 166–167

Intellectuals, anti-intellectualism, 182–183
  and art, 3, 5, 18, 20, 162–163, 207
Interrogation, 4, 43, 44, 61, 78
  themes, 56–60, 78
d'Ivoi, Paul, 37

Je Suis Partout, 47
Le Jeune Européen, 11, 17, 96, 103, 109, 221
  dedication, 109
Journal d'un homme trompé, themes, 111–112
Jouhandeau, Marcel, 49, 211

Kipling, Rudyard, 6

LaFayette, Mme. de, 252
Lamartine, Alphonse de, 100
La Rochefoucauld, 11, 145
Lawrence, D. H., 111, 131
Lawrence, T. E., 8, 148 n.
Leader, cult of, 64, 68–72, 227–228
Leautaud, Paul, 51

Lefebvre, Raymond, 148
Lenin, V. I., 9, 23, 49, 73, 149
Literary influences, 6–7. See also Balzac; Barrès; Contemporaries, relation to; Flaubert; Gide; Lawrence, D. H.; Huxley; Malraux; Montherlant; Nietzsche
Literature, and authenticity, 5, 12, 19, 27, 212, 250
  characters in, 233
  conception of, 1–30, 202, 212, 223
  Drieu's place in, 2, 250, 255–256
  fiction, role of, 212, 223, 255
  humanism in, 11–15, 253
  the novel, 30
    attitude toward, 1–30, 34, 92, 95–96, 230
    American, 81–82, 252
    definition, 167, 176
    English, 167, 252
    French, 167, 252
    Russian, 167, 252
    political factors, 15–30, 254
    sociological factors, 167
Literature, theories of, 5, 30, 166–167, 255. See also Form; Style; Themes in Drieu's fiction
Love. See Sex; Themes in Drieu's fiction: decadence, women

Maistre, Joseph de, 105
Malraux, André, 5, 8, 10–15, 24, 29, 48, 105, 132, 138, 141, 148, 149, 162, 208, 211, 250, 251, 252
Malraux, l'homme nouveau, 10–14 See also Contemporaries, relation to
Marianne, 163
Marivaux, Pierre de, 252
Marriage, Drieu's, 32, 44
  in Drieu's fiction, 44, 120, 123, 164, 166, 168, 171–173
Martin du Gard, Roger, 165
Marxism, 9, 25, 73, 185, 195
Massis, Henri, 105
Matisse, Henri, 117
Maupassant, Guy de, 252
Mauriac, François, 2, 25, 26, 48, 50, 105, 201, 202
Maurras, Charles, 6, 48, 105

Mesure de la France, 4, 15, 106, 132
Mohrt, Michel, 81 n.
Money. *See* Themes in Drieu's fiction
Montaigne, Michel de, 11, 248, 250
Montherlant, Henry de, 44 n., 50, 57, 61, 105, 144, 211, 251, 252
Morand, Paul, 49
Mysticism, 42, 54, 57, 65, 240, 243

Napoleon, 35, 228
Nationalism, 15–17, 23, 40–42, 62, 194, 234, 236–246, 249
"New" French literature, 1, 211
Nietzsche, Friedrich Wilhelm, 6–9, 73–74, 105, 127, 174, 239, 250. *See also* Nietzschean philosophy
Nietzsche contre Marx, 9, 73
Nietzschean philosophy, 7–9, 14, 23–24, 29, 73–74, 107–112, 131, 185, 223, 239–245, 253–254 *See also* Literary influences; Nietzsche
La Nouvelle Revue Française
  after World War II, 26, 47, 49–51, 77
  before World War II, 4, 10, 27, 44, 60, 83, 162, 178

Ocampo, Victoria, 45

Pareto, Vilfredo, 6, 9, 74
Pascal, Blaise, 6, 248
Paulhan, Jean, 51
Péguy, Charles, 48, 50
Petitjean, Armand, 48, 50
Picasso, Pablo, 117, 131
Picon, Gaëtan, 1, 29, 211
Plainte contre inconnu, publication of, 4
  themes, 17, 82, 90, 102, 111–112
Plato, 182
Poincaré, Henri, 9
Politics, and the artist, 15–30, 162–163
  cult of, 18, 187, 236, 249
  Drieu's engagement in, 3, 15, 18, 19–30, 162–163, 177, 249–251
  in Drieu's fiction. *See* Themes in Drieu's fiction
Proust, Marcel, 170, 248, 252

Racine, Jean, 11, 160
Ramsey, Warren, 230
Rationalism, 56
  and antirationalism, 6, 7, 21, 56, 68
"Récit secret," analysis of, 51–54
  publication of, 32 n.
Religion, Drieu's attitude toward, 53, 76, 249
  in Drieu's fiction, 99, 136–145, 226, 228, 233–248
  Ideas of God, 41–42, 101
  Judaism, 67, 242–243
  Oriental religions, 186–187, 233, 243, 245, 249
  Roman Catholicism, 17, 67, 136–145, 194–195
Remarque, Erich Maria, 60
Renéville, Rolland de, 50
Rêveuse bourgeoisie, analysis of, 165–177
  form, 163–167
  publication of, 162
  style, 165–167, 210
  themes
    death, 175
    decadence, 164–165, 175–177
    marriage and money, 168–169, 174, 191
    Paris and the provinces, 167–169
Revolution, cult of, 21, 77
  and war, 55–80
  See also Fascism; Politics; Themes in Drieu's fiction; War
Révolution Nationale, 51
Rigaut, Jacques, 84, 89, 95,
Rimbaud, Arthur, 6
Robin, Armand, 50
Romains, Jules, 165
Romanticism, 21, 39, 42, 97, 212, 214, 253
Rougemont, Denis de, 126
Rousseau, Jean-Jacques, 11, 14, 35, 111, 191

Saint, and the hero (soldier), 84, 108–109, 239
Saint-Simon, Louis de Rouvroy, duc de, 11
Sand, George, 252

index

Sartre, Jean-Paul, 13, 25, 44 n., 78, 80, 138, 140, 148 n., 160–161, 179, 211, 253, 254
Segur, Countess of, 37
Sex, 59, 87, 97–100, 111–112, 129, 137, 144–147, 152, 157–159, 171–172, 199–202. *See also* Decadence; Themes in Drieu's fiction
Simon, Pierre Henri, 222–223
Socialisme fasciste, 55, 73–76, 131
Solitude. *See* Themes in Drieu's fiction
Sorel, Georges, 6–7, 9, 48, 74
Soupault, Philippe, 9
Spengler, Oswald, 223
Stendhal (Henri Beyle), 11, 12, 42, 62, 153, 174, 182, 205, 252
Style, in Drieu's fiction, 62, 64–65, 113–114, 141–142, 165, 166, 209–210, 222–223, 229, 231, 252–253, 255
Sue, Eugène, 252
Suicide, Drieu's, 27, 32 n., 45, 51–54, 82, 222. *See also* Themes in Drieu's fiction: solitude; death; suicide
La Suite dans les idées, 17, 44, 110
Surrealism, 1, 8, 9–10, 44, 84, 110, 179, 207
Symbolism, 21, 229

Themes in Drieu's fiction
action versus contemplation, 4–5, 56, 76–80, 182–190, 196
the adventurer, 134–161
authenticity, 135–140, 154, 177, 181
death, 33, 53–54, 56, 89, 95, 138–139, 158–161, 175, 181–190, 199, 222, 226, 240, 245–246
decadence, 33, 82, 112, 164–165, 175–177, 251–252
the *délicat*, 94, 121, 132, 137, 159, 191–192
don Juanism, 99–100, 133, 134, 143–145, 179, 200
sex, 17, 87–88, 97–100, 111–112, 129, 137, 144–145, 201 *See also* Sex

social, political, and religious, 33–42, 63, 151–154, 183–190, 196–202, 206, 208, 218–220, 234, 237, 241–242
emptiness, 83–112, 200, 254
European unity, 200–222
family relationships, 33, 35, 36, 39–40, 164–177
the father, 36–37, 39, 170–175, 203
the hero, 36, 69, 227–228
interrelationship of, 59, 62, 122, 135, 239
love. *See* decadence, sex, women
man's fate, 94, 229
marriage and money, 120, 123, 168–169, 174, 191–192
misogyny, 56, 144, 146, 157–159, 171, 198–202
nationalism, 40–42, 62, 194, 217–218, 221, 234, 246
Paris and the provinces, 167–169
politics, 17, 29–30, 72–73, 141–154, 163, 173, 185, 187–190, 193–202, 229, 232, 249–256
the prophet, 186–187, 230–246
religious inquietude, 136–145, 238–246. *See also* Religion
sacrifice, 190, 225–228, 245–246
sincerity, 95, 102, 124–128, 135–140, 154, 160–161, 176–177, 189–190, 250
solitude, 93, 123, 137–138, 160–161, 185–186, 199, 234
suicide, 53–54, 90, 95, 138–139, 184, 190, 240, 245–246
the traitor, 156–160, 160 n., 229–246
the voyage, 113–133, 146
war, 55–80. *See also* War, cult of
women, *femmes du monde*, 217–218
jeunes filles, 97, 120, 199
and love, 96–103, 135, 141–161, 171–173, 190, 198–201
and money, 168–169, 174, 191–193, 198
prostitutes, 96, 199, 217, 219
Thibaudet, Albert, 163
Thomas, Henri, 50

Tolstoy, Leo, 61
Tragedy, sense of, 6, 7, 24, 83, 223

La Valise vide, analysis of, 83–88
  dedication, 44
  publication of, 83
  style, 86
  themes, emptiness, 83, 86, 88, 112
Van Gogh, Vincent, 239
Vigny, Alfred de, 203, 254
Villiers de l'Isle-Adam, Auguste, 252
Voltaire (François-Marie Arouet), 14, 135, 252

War, cult of, 5, 55–80, 175, 192
  Spanish Civil War, 18, 164, 180, 188, 190, 193, 196, 198, 235, 251
  World War I, 5–6, 21, 42, 43–44, 166, 237
    works inspired by, 56, 60–61, 178–212
  World War II, 47–52, 178
  See also Themes in Drieu's fiction

Zola, Emile, 165, 252

www.ingramcontent.com/pod-product-compliance
Lightning Source LLC
Chambersburg PA
CBHW021656230426
43668CB00008B/637